Studies in
Comparative Economics **12**

Studies in Comparative Economics

THE THREE
WORLDS OF
ECONOMICS

by Lloyd G. Reynolds

New Haven and London

Yale University Press

1971

Set in Baskerville type,
and printed in the United States of America by
The Carl Purington Rollins Printing-Office
of the Yale University Press.

Distributed in Great Britain, Europe, and Africa by
Yale University Press, Ltd., London; in Canada by
McGill-Queen's University Press, Montreal; in Mexico
by Centro Interamericano de Libros Académicos,
Mexico City; in Central and South America by Kaiman
& Polon, Inc., New York City; in Australasia by
Australia and New Zealand Book Co., Pty., Ltd.,
Artarmon, New South Wales; in India by UBS Publishers'
Distributors Pvt., Ltd., Delhi; in Japan by John
Weatherhill, Inc., Tokyo.

CONTENTS

PART TWO: ECONOMIC POLICY

PART THREE: ECONOMIC THEORY

PART FOUR: PERSPECTIVES

FOREWORD

Modern economics has been bred chiefly in Western Europe and the United States, and despite its aspiration toward generality it bears the stamp of institutions and issues characteristic of these areas.

But the economic world no longer revolves about London and New York. Dozens of new nations are struggling toward economic independence and industrial growth under institutional arrangements quite unlike those of the West. Economies of a novel type also extend eastward from central Europe to the Bering Strait and have been busily developing their own principles as a by-product of administrative experience. It is asserted that "Western economics" has only limited analytical value in these other countries.

The problem of the content and relevance of economics thus arises inescapably. Are the economic principles taught in the West really susceptible of general application? Or are they culture-bound and relevant mainly to industrial capitalist countries? Is it possible to create a general economics which would be as useful in Poland or India as in Canada or France? Or must we be content with several species of economics which will remain distinct in intellectual content and applicability?

"Comparative economics" has been regarded as a separate area of the economics curriculum, consisting of a botanical classification of national economics into a few loosely labeled boxes. But surely any course in economics is potentially comparative. A concern with comparative experience can profitably be infused into any of the standard branches of economic study. This series is inspired by the hope that a rethinking of particular branches of economics in world perspective, combined with a bibliography of available material from many countries, may help teachers to give their courses a broader and more comparative orientation.

In pursuing this objective, we deliberately chose autonomy over standardization. Each author was left free to determine his own approach and method of treatment. The essays thus differ considerably in length, analytical as against descriptive emphasis, geographical coverage, and other respects. How far the original intent of the series has been accomplished is for the profession to judge.

We are grateful to the authors who have struggled with possibly insoluble problems, to the Ford Foundation for its support of the enterprise, and to the staff of the Yale University Press for their helpful cooperation.

The Inter-University Committee on Comparative Economics: Abram Bergson, Arthur R. Burns, Kermit Gordon, Richard Musgrave, William Nicholls, Lloyd Reynolds (Chairman)

PREFACE

This book stems from several related convictions: that Western economic analysis cannot be transferred to either socialist or less developed economies without substantial rethinking; that economics, viewed in world perspective, is a larger subject than Lionel Robbins's famous definition suggests; and that exciting new directions are emerging for comparative economic study.

Economics is an empirical and policy science. So we begin by examining the structural characteristics and policy priorities of capitalist, socialist, and less developed economies. My interest lies, not in institutional comparison per se, but in what this may reveal about the usefulness of different branches of economic theory in different institutional settings.

This leads to a reexamination of the scope and content of economics. The conventional definition, which focuses on resource allocation, is too narrow even in the Western setting, and much too narrow on a world scale. We explore the main directions in which our conception of economics needs to be enlarged—indeed, is already in course of being enlarged.

A third purpose is to explore fruitful directions for comparative economic analysis. I suggest as possibilities: development of a general model of economic organization into which concrete economies can be fitted as special cases; development of a richer menu of "ideal types" of economy to supplement those now current in the literature; cross-country analysis of specific aspects of economic behavior, with "systems" classification entering as only one of several explanatory variables; comparative evaluation of overall economic performance; and exploration of the "convergence hypothesis."

My view of what economics is and might be differs from that implicit in some recent theoretical writings. I do not regard economics as form without content, as a branch of applied logic. Consistency and elegance are necessary but not sufficient. The ultimate test of good work is explanatory and predictive power and potential relevance to important policy issues. This view is thoroughly traditional and would be accepted almost universally in principle, but it is often disregarded by the kind of theorist who admires, and trades on, sheer manipulative ability. So it needs occasionally to be reasserted.

To deal with such broad issues in reasonable space compels a brevity of statement that may at times appear dogmatic. This is not at all my intention. My judgments are advanced tentatively, in a spirit of inquiry, with a view to stimulating discussion of questions that seem important for the future of economics.

I owe many debts for assistance and advice. The first draft of the essay was written during a period of residence at the Rockefeller Foundation's Villa Serbelloni in 1967. The final revisions were made during a visit to the Research School of Social Sciences, Australian National University, in 1970. I am grateful to these institutions for their provision of tranquil surroundings for uninterrupted work.

I am grateful to several colleagues who read part or all of an earlier draft: Heinz Arndt, Bela Balassa, Abram Bergson, David Bensusan-Butt, Noel Butlin, Sir John Hicks, János Kornai, Sir Arthur Lewis, John M. Montias, Alec Nove, Frederic Pryor, and Gustav Ranis. Many improvements have resulted from their comments, but they should not be associated with remaining imperfections or with my own judgments. I appreciate, as always, the skillful assistance of Mrs. Olive Higgins in typing and manuscript preparation.

In this concluding volume of Studies in Comparative Economics, it is appropriate to express my personal thanks to the Ford Foundation for its patient support of this lengthy enterprise, and my gratitude to the colleagues who served with me as members of the directing committee. Their advice and support helped to turn a duty into a pleasure.

Yale University   L.G.R.
March 1971

1 SOME UNSETTLED QUESTIONS IN ECONOMICS

"Economics is the science which studies human behavior as a relationship between ends and scarce means which have alternative uses."[1] Thus spoke Robbins in 1932; and thus, since economics is a very tradition-bound subject, we continue to repeat a doctrine which few of us entirely believe.

Was Robbins right? Or, if largely right at the time, is he equally correct forty years later?

Viewed against the background of its time, Robbins's brilliant essay made signal contributions. He demolished several vulgar misconceptions of economic theory. He emphasized that economics relates to an *aspect* of conduct rather than a *domain* of conduct. He distinguished between the role of the economist as analyst and as policy adviser in terms which would be broadly acceptable today.

Granted all this, the essay did not chart a path to the future. Rather, it crystallized a stage in the evolution of economics. It marked the end of an era which was dying even as Robbins wrote. It was pre-Keynesian. More serious, it came just before the recognition of centrally planned economies and "underdeveloped" economies as permanent features of the economic landscape.

1. Lionel Robbins, *An Essay on the Nature and Significance of Economic Science,* 2d ed. (London: Macmillan, 1935), p. 16.

Robbins thought that "Crusoe economics" and, by extension, the subsistence production of self-contained family units
presented no interesting problems. Nor did he consider
economics useful to the managers of a socialized economy.[2]
He viewed economics as limited to a decentralized exchange
economy with private ownership. In such an economy, the
interaction of individual units produces results which are not
intuitively obvious, and the task of the economist is to explore these interactions.[3]

In 1930 the exchange economies of the Western nations
were indeed predominant; and an economics based on them
might well lay claim to universality. The Soviet economy
had not yet taken definite form, and it stood alone as a possibly temporary economic variant. Most of Asia and Africa
were in colonial status, the domain of the administrator and
the anthropologist rather than the economist. The conditions of the 1970s are obviously very different.

When one enters the Lenin Library in Moscow and asks to
be directed to the economics reading room, the reply is
"Which economics reading room?" There is one room for the
doctrinal literature labeled "political economy," another for
what we would term "managerial economics," still another

2. "From the point of view of the members of the executive, the
generalizations of Economics would be uninteresting. Their position
would be analogous to Crusoe's. For them the economic problem would
be merely whether to apply productive power to this or to that. . . .
given central ownership and control of the means of production, the
registering of individual pulls and resistances by a mechanism of prices
and costs is excluded by definition. . . . the decisions of the executive
must necessarily be 'arbitrary.' That is to say, they must be based on its
valuations—not on the valuations of consumers and producers" (Robbins, *Essay*, p. 17).

3. "The utmost effort of abstract thought is required to devise generalizations which enable us to grasp them. For this reason economic
analysis has most utility in the exchange economy. It is unnecessary in
the isolated economy. It is debarred from any but the simplest generalizations, by the very raison d'être of a strictly communist society.
But where independent initiative in social relations is permitted to the
individual, there economic analysis comes into its own" (Robbins, *Essay*,
p. 19).

for "public economy," that is, for research studies of the economy and its policy problems. These correspond to the differing roles of Soviet economists in the universities, in research institutes, and in public administration.

What functions do economists perform in the Eastern countries, and what tools do they use? How much have they borrowed from the West, how much have they invented for themselves? Are they likely to make greater use of Western tools in the future?

Similar questions arise in the less developed countries. Most economists in these countries are engaged in administration rather than in teaching or research. They face a distinctive set of policy problems. They are eager for analytical concepts, but at the same time fearful of "intellectual colonialism." Many of them believe that their economies are so different from the advanced industrial nations that the Western tool-kit has only limited usefulness.

But is this equally true of all our tools? Are some of the things taught in American graduate schools more relevant than others to the less developed economies? To the extent that "Western economics" is irrelevant, what are the implications? The fact that such questions now appear important suggests that Robbins did not say the last word.

LIVE AND DEAD HORSES IN ECONOMIC METHODOLOGY

Nineteenth-century economists spent much time debating the foundations of their incipient science. Every eminent economist felt obliged at some point to deliver his pronouncement on scope and method.[4] The modern view, however, is that methodology is a bore. R. F. Harrod, before launching on another "scope and method" address, felt obliged to excuse himself as follows: "In my choice of subject

---

4. See, for example, the selection of presidential addresses to Section F of the British Association for the Advancement of Science, 1860–1913, collected in R. L. Smyth, ed., *Essays in Economic Method* (London: Gerald Duckworth, 1962).

today, I fear that I have exposed myself to two serious charges: that of tedium and that of presumption. Speculations upon methodology are famous for platitude and prolixity. . . . Exposed as a bore, the methodologist cannot take refuge behind a cloak of modesty. On the contrary, he stands ready by his own claim to give advice to all and sundry."[5]

The decline of interest in methodology doubtless reflects the growing maturity and self-confidence of economics as a discipline. Economists no longer feel compelled to explain what they are doing, to the public or to each other. They go ahead and do it. As Paul Samuelson once remarked, "Soft sciences spend time in talking about method because Satan finds tasks for idle hands to do. Nature does abhor a vacuum, and hot air fills up more space than cold."[6]

Who can disagree? The reader can relax in the assurance that he will be spared a lengthy disquisition on induction versus deduction, or on the relation between theoretical and historical work in economics, or on the uses and limitations of mathematical techniques. It is doubtful that anything useful can be added to the millions of words which have been written on these subjects.[7]

But while some methodological issues have been explored to the margin of profitability, this is not true of every issue. Important questions are still open, and the fact that they are rarely discussed does not mean that economists are agreed on the answers. The subjects on which they think it worthwhile

5. R. F. Harrod, "Scope and Method of Economics," *Economic Journal*, Sept. 1938, p. 383.

6. Paul A. Samuelson, "Problems of Methodology: Discussion," *American Economic Association Proceedings*, May 1963, p. 231.

7. Notable contributions, in addition to Robbins' *Essay*, include John Nevile Keynes, *The Scope and Method of Political Economy* (London: Macmillan, 1891); T. W. Hutchison, *Significance and Basic Postulates of Economic Theory* (London: Macmillan, 1938); Tjalling C. Koopmans, *Three Essays on the State of Economic Science* (New York: McGraw-Hill, 1957); a symposium on the uses of mathematics in economics in the *Review of Economics and Statistics*, November 1954; and a symposium volume edited by Sherman C. Krupp, *The Structure of Economic Science* (Englewood Cliffs, N. J.: Prentice-Hall, 1966).

to spend time reveal quite different conceptions of what economics is about. At this point one might fall back on the economist's traditional respect for individual preference: anything that a member of the guild chooses to do is economics, ex definitione. But perhaps something more can be said.

Among these unsettled questions are: (1) What are the appropriate boundaries of economic study, and what is the nature of our collaboration with other social sciences? (2) When we inquire into the "relevance" of a particular theoretical tool-set, whether to Western economies or to others, what precisely do we mean? (3) How far should economic theorizing be empirically oriented; how far does theory necessarily lead "a life of its own"? Do assumptions matter, or need one look only at predictions? (4) What is the relation of positive economics to policy? What is the status of value judgments in economics? (5) Is there (or can there be) a worldwide discipline of economics, or should one anticipate several species of economics flourishing in different institutional settings?

These questions take on a special interest against a backdrop of world experience. To debate them in a purely Western setting might well seem tedious. But when one broadens one's horizons, issues which may have seemed settled in the narrower framework are not necessarily so on a world scale.

THE BOUNDARIES OF ECONOMICS

The economist never tries to explain *everything* about a concrete situation. Some things are taken as exogenous, and only the remaining variables are determined within the analysis. The "breadth" of a particular analysis depends on the relative size of the exogenous and endogenous groups.

This varies, of course, with the purpose in hand. For analysis of a single firm or household, almost everything is taken as given. But as the canvas unfolds to reveal the industry, the sector, the economy, more and more of the givens become variables. The question here is: what do economists generally regard as exogenous even for economy-wide problems? What is the cut-off point between the things they try to explain and the things they relegate to other disciplines?

Over the past century there has been a clear tendency for the boundaries of the discipline to narrow, and this by deliberate choice. The ever-modest economist has become even more modest. Marshall conceived of economics as "a study of mankind in the ordinary business of life." This sounded as though the subject dealt with a concrete set of institutions and a certain domain of behavior. But with the spread of Max Weber's conceptual system via Lionel Robbins, Talcott Parsons, and others, it came to be accepted that economics deals only with an *aspect* of man's behavior in exchange relations —the economizing, or optimizing aspect. A particular individual, in his buying and selling activities, functions not only as economizer but as family head, patriot, churchman, and so on. Exploration of these roles, and the way in which they influence behavior in the economic arena, is not the economist's business. To hold otherwise is to be guilty of intellectual imperialism or, more technically, of "the fallacy of misplaced concreteness."

Consider next the treatment of factor supplies and techniques of production. Nineteenth-century economists thought that they could say something useful about population, about the increase of skill and productivity in the labor force, about the contribution of different social classes to capital accumulation, about the sources of invention and business entrepreneurship. This was associated with a profound interest in economic growth—or "progress," as a nineteenth-century Englishman was bound to say—an interest which continued from Smith through Marshall. But gradually the center of gravity of economics shifted toward the allocation of *given* resources among alternative uses, culminating in Robbin's dictum that this is *the* economic problem. Resources, tastes, techniques of production are taken as given, and the economist starts from there. The partly politico-social, often unquantifiable, determinants of resource supplies and techniques were gradually extruded from the proper domain of economics.

The same tendency is observable as regards institutional structure. Earlier economists tried to explain and project trends in size of firm, industrial concentration, financial organization, trade union development. Today we *assume* various market forms and explore their consequences; but we give little attention to the historical emergence and changing relative importance of these forms. These are relegated to the economic historian or to other social science disciplines.

This growing specialization of economics is usually justified on grounds of scientific division of labor. The economist, it is said, can be most productive on that narrow terrain to which his tools are best suited. There is obviously much to this. The variables with which economists work today are more quantifiable, the theorems more elegant, the research findings more precise than was true a generation or two ago. This gain in precision is purchased at the cost of narrower scope and less "roundness" in the analysis. But here it is argued that the problems which the economist has cast into outer darkness will be picked up by the sociologist, the social psychologist, the political scientist. Then in the fullness of time, interdisciplinary teams, well funded by foundations or government, will descend on the economy to give a full explanation of its operation.

But results thus far have been disappointing. Thomas Schelling's "parable of the fictitious colleague" does not seem to have been reduced to writing, but is certainly part of the oral tradition. The economist says solemnly, "Beyond this point I cannot go as an economist, and I hereby turn the problem over to my colleague the political scientist." But this is purely ritualistic behavior. The other chap isn't there. Or, if there, he is interested in building his own models rather than improving ours. So the social disciplines do not in fact intersect appreciably, and problems get lost in the shuffle. The cases of successful multidisciplinary activity

which come to mind are usually cases in which an imagina-
tive individual undertook the arduous task of acquiring a
second discipline.

Our object is not to point a moral but to pose a problem.
What is the economist to do? Should he make independent
forays outside the conventional boundaries of economics?
Should he work harder to enlist the effective aid of other
social scientists? Or what?

There is some evidence that the scope of economic studies
is already tending to widen. Population is creeping back into
economics through the work of quantitative economists such
as Kuznets, Easterlin, Ruggles, and Orcutt, and through the
studies of Leibenstein, Coale, and others on population
growth in the less developed countries. There has been a
similar creeping back of subjects such as the determinants of
labor force participation, the effect of education and job
training on productivity, the sources of invention and technical progress, the mechanism of collective decision making.
This reflects a renewed interest in long-term growth as against
short-term fluctuations, and in the economics of the public
sector. These developments are gradually altering the shape
of Western economics in ways which we shall want to examine.

THEORY AND REALITY

While propositions in economic theory have a formal
character, they are not purely formal as are statements in
logic and mathematics. Economic theory has substance in
the sense that some of the terms in the argument have real-
world counterparts. But the nature of this relation has led to
considerable controversy.

The meaning of truth in logic or mathematics differs from
its meaning in a "real science," such as biology or economics.
In the former case, the requirement is that the initial assumptions be complete and internally consistent, and that

reasoning from these postulates obey the canons of logic. Truth is tautological. It means simply freedom from internal contradictions.

In a real science, on the other hand, consistency of assumptions and logical reasoning are necessary but not sufficient conditions. The ultimate test of an acceptable theory is correspondence of its predictions with a reality. Unless the theorems deduced from the model can be tested by observation, unless they serve to interpret some aspect of real-world behavior, the supposed "theory" is not a theory in the real-science sense. Almost every economist would subscribe to this formulation in principle; but it is by no means invariably observed in practice.

We must distinguish here between positive and normative propositions in economics. The terms themselves are not free from ambiguity. "Normative" is often used broadly to include any application of positive economic knowledge in reaching policy decisions. When an economist proceeds beyond positive research and, by adding a welfare criterion, concludes that such-and-such *should* be done, his work is of a normative character.

We prefer here to use the term in a more restricted sense. By a normative model we understand one designed to solve an optimizing problem. This may be a maximizing problem, as in linear or nonlinear programming. Or it may be one of attaining a preferred combination of several policy targets, as in macro policy models. The essential feature of such a model is that all its economic characteristics are givens. There is a given initial situation, given possibilities of choice each of which has a given outcome, and a given decision criterion by which the choice is to be made. From this point on, as Kornai observes, solution of the problem is a purely logico-mathematical exercise.[8] It need observe only the first criterion

8. "Decision theory . . . is concerned exclusively with the determination of the rational decision once all this is given. This is exclusively a logical-mathematical problem. It is not necessary to observe empirically,

of "truth" stated above. In this sense, it is not an *economic* exercise at all.

It may or may not be a useful exercise. This depends on whether there is a real-world problem which corresponds in some measure to the hypothetical decision problem, and whether there is a decision maker with authority to apply the conclusions to an actual situation. Unless these conditions exist, the results have no economic significance.

The issue has been confused by the fact that, in constructing positive economic theory, we usually assume that households, business firms, and other decision units do optimize. But defining the rules for optimizing is quite different from assuming that optimizing actually occurs. Whether the latter assumption is useful depends on observations of behavior and, more fundamentally, on whether predictions derived from this assumption stand up well to inductive tests.

Our main concern here is with positive economic models. It has long been accepted in principle that positive economics progresses through an interaction of theorizing and observation.[9] The theorist exercises ingenuity in extracting essential elements of reality, which are used as assumptions in constructing simplified working models. From these are derived, by purely logical processes, predictions which can be subjected to empirical tests. To the extent that the predictions fail to correspond with reality, one goes back to reformulate, complicate, improve the model so as to obtain a better "fit" on the next round.

---

how many of a hundred clever men would actually choose the solution termed rational by theory. . . . The rationality of the solution is verified not empirically but in a purely logical way" (Janos Kornai, *Anti-Equilibrium* [Amsterdam: North-Holland, 1971], chap. 2).

9. As early as J. N. Keynes's study in 1891 one finds the comment: "If pure induction is inadequate, pure deduction is equally inadequate. It is a mistake . . . to set up these methods in mutual opposition . . . It is, on the contrary, by their unprejudiced combination alone that any complete development of economic science is possible. For . . . all induction is blind, so long as the deduction of casual connexions is left out of account; and all deduction is barren, so long as it does not start from observation" (*Scope and Method,* pp. 164–65).

The verification procedure may be more or less elaborate. In some cases rather generally known economic facts may be sufficient. More commonly, it will be necessary to assemble and analyze a large number of quantitative observations. In some cases it is useful to run simulation experiments until a pattern emerges which resembles that of actual data series. With the growth of quantitative economic information, principles of statistical inference, and availability of computer facilities, the process of hypothesis testing has grown steadily more complex. But it does not differ in principle from what economists were doing by simpler methods in earlier times.

The *results* of a positive economic theory, then, must be tested against observed behavior. Must its *assumptions* pass a similar test? The conventional wisdom is that realism in assumptionss, if not logically necessary, is at any rate highly desirable. British economists, up to and including Robbins, held that the most basic postulates of economics were facts of daily experience, most of which could be derived through introspection. Indeed, this possibility of knowing directly what goes on inside the "human atom" was considered a distinct advantage of economics. Additional postulates for reasoning, it was thought, could be derived from observation of economic processes, and such observation was in fact essential. This was strongly asserted by J. N. Keynes,[10] and from then on was taken as virtually a truism.

More recently, however, this view has been challenged both directly and by implication. Milton Friedman has argued that the only essential test of a theory is its predictive

10. "In the first place, observation guides the economist in his original choice of premises . . . these must not be taken at random or arbitrarily . . . the necessity for a somewhat intimate acquaintance with concrete economic phenomena arises at the very commencement of our inquiries. . . . In the second place, observation enables the economist to determine how nearly his assumptions approximate to the actual facts under given conditions. He thus learns how far his premises require to be modified" (Keynes, *Scope and Method*, pp. 215–17).

power.[11] To require an additional test of the assumptions is redundant and a waste of effort. The only relevant question about a set of assumptions is "whether they are sufficiently good approximations for the purpose in hand. And this question can be answered only by seeing whether the theory works, which means whether it yields sufficiently accurate predictions. The two supposedly independent tests thus reduce to one test."[12]

Friedman argues further that simpler assumptions are in general to be preferred to more complex ones, on grounds of greater generality of the conclusions. "Truly important and significant hypotheses will be found to have 'assumptions' that are wildly inaccurate descriptive representations of reality, and, in general, the more significant the theory, the more unrealistic the assumptions (in this sense)."[13] From this he proceeds to a defense of the assumptions of profit maximization and purely competitive markets. Assumptions of imperfect or monopolistic competition, Friedman believes, simply complicate price theory without adding to its predictive ability.

The subsequent professional discussion, on the whole, has run contrary to the Friedman view; but one cannot say that the issue is resolved. It is important for our purpose in that it bears on the "relevance" of Western economic theory in non-Western economies. When we ask about the relevance of Western microetonomics, do we mean the theory of maximizing behavior under purely competitive conditions, as Friedman would wish us to mean? Or should we include other theories of the firm, plus theories of imperfect competition in product and factor markets?

The notion that assumptions matter is also challenged

11. Milton Friedman, *Essays in Positive Economics* (Chicago: University of Chicago Press, 1953), pp. 1–43. For subsequent discussion of this view, see comments by Samuelson and others in "Methodology," and Koopmans, *Three Essays*, pp. 138–40.

12. Friedman, *Essays*, p. 15.

13. Friedman, *Essays*, p. 14.

implicitly in a good deal of recent theoretical writing. It has become common practice, for example in work on general equilibrium and on growth theory, to start with a set of extremely unrealistic assumptions. It is usually not contended that the conclusions have any predictive value. Rather, the exercise is justified on the ground that "one must start somewhere," and that more realistic models will follow in due course. But these models are usually to be constructed by somebody else, and this kind of "fictitious colleague," like the one mentioned earlier, is always vanishing around the next corner.

Beneath nominal adherence to the same ground rules, then one finds marked differences in "style" among economic theorists. As Weberian ideal types, one can contrast the "tool-oriented" theorist and the "empirically oriented" theorist. The tool-oriented theorist is more concerned with the internal structure of his models than with their external reference. He sometimes comes close to asserting that economics *is* a logical edifice—a deducing of all possible consequences of economizing behavior. The progress of economics consists in adding pieces to this structure. The test of the structure is its rigor, completeness, and "elegance." He is heavily influenced in his choice of subjects by the mathematical apparatus which he happens to possess. He often seems to be saying, "Here is a nice tool—what can I do with it?" rather than "Here is an important economic phenomenon—how can I explain it?" Cournot and Walras tended in this direction. Indeed, Cournot began his major work with an explanation that he had excluded all problems to which mathematics could not be applied.

The empirically oriented theorist operates closer to the earth. He is in close touch with empirical research and has often participated in such research. His choice of subjects is heavily influenced by judgments about the substantive importance of economic phenomena. He prefers "realistic" assumptions and short chains of reasoning. Even where he builds an elaborate theoretical structure, his main concern is not with the beauty of the model but with the testability of the propositions derived from it. This is the main tradition of British economics, as exemplified notably by Alfred Marshall. Such key Marshallian constructs as "the representative firm," increasing and decreasing costs, or short-run and long-run price determination, have an almost self-evident correspondence with economic phenomena. And while he normally used mathematical methods to work through a theoretical problem, he was also able "to establish by his shining example a highly effective style of writing, in which the technical aspects of reasoning are somewhat concealed between the lines, or relegated to appendixes."[14]

Robbins, who in some respects—denial of cardinal utility, espousal of Pareto optimality, emphasis on allocation problems, narrowing of the boundaries of eocnomics—might be regarded as closer to the Continental tradition, was in this respect a true British economist. He argues that "it is a complete mistake to regard the economist, whatever his degree of 'purity,' as concerned merely with pure deduction. It is quite true that much of his work is in the nature of elaborate processes of inference. But it is quite untrue to suppose that it is only, or even mainly, thus. The concern of the economist is the interpretation of reality."[15]

These differing theoretical postures raise important questions. What are the advantages (and dangers) of the two polar positions? In which direction does the "mix" of Western economic theorizing seem to be moving? Does this make our analytical work more or less relevant to the socialist economies and the less developed economies? We return to these issues in chapter 11.

POSITIVE ECONOMICS AND POLICY

Nineteenth-century economists drew little distinction between their analysis of the economy and what they con-

14. Koopmans, *Three Essays*, p. 131.
15. Robbins, *Essay*, p. 105.

ceived to be the policy implications of this analysis. J. N. Keynes felt it necessary to demonstrate that there could be a separate, value-free science of "positive economics." He argued successfully, however, and since his time it has been conventional that the contribution of economics to policy is indirect and instrumental. As the younger Keynes remarked, "The theory of economics does not furnish a body of conclusions immediately applicable to policy. It is a method rather than a doctrine, an apparatus of the mind, a technique of thinking."

In his scientific role, the economist may try to *predict* the consequences of a proposed policy action. He may be able to show that a specified target can be achieved by several alternative alternative routes, that is, by different kinds of *policy mix*. But he may not himself choose among targets, or make statements in the imperative mood.

These strictures were reinforced by the widespread adoption of Paretian welfare economics from the 1930s onward. A pillar of this system is the noncomparability of individual utilities and the consequent impossibility of any scientific statements about income distribution. Almost any conceivable policy action, however, will have differential income effects. If the economist can say nothing about the desirability of the new income distribution, it would seem to follow that he can—as economist—say nothing at all.

How seriously is one to take the ban on distributional judgments? Is it actually observed in the work of Western economists? Is it observed equally by economists in other parts of the world? Can one avoid distributional judgments by such devices as the compensation principle, or by positing a social welfare function?

The conventional view of the relation between economics and policy grew up in the "liberal" market economies of Britain, Western Europe, and the United States. Such economies operate through the interaction of a multitude of firms and households. The economist is a bystander whose first task is to analyze these interactions. On the basis of his understanding of this decentralized mechanism, he can advise government in those limited areas where government action is required. In a strongly market-oriented economy, this would be mainly provision of economic infrastructure, production and financing of public goods, management of international economic relations, and institutional engineering to repair gaps in the market mechanism. It is no accident that these are among the oldest preoccupations of Western economics.

But how applicable is this outlook to the centrally planned economies? Why is it necessary to *predict* when one can *control?* As Marx said, "the philosophers have only interpreted the world. . . . the point, however, is to change it."[16] Is the role of the observer any longer appropriate? Is there any place for an economics divorced from policy?

In the less developed countries, too, most economists are directly involved in public administration. They customarily assert the validity of certain policy targets, or often simply take these for granted. Should they not be doing this? Or should we say that, in doing it, they are playing a dual role —part scientific economist, part political decision maker? Do they (should they) keep these roles separate in their own minds?

We have already noted the existence of normative as well as positive economics. Instead of the cautious, "*if* you do that, these consequences will follow," some economists now use the imperative mood: "*do* that, if you wish to economize." These tools range in scope from the very micro tools of operations research to economy-wide models of optimal investment allocation or optimal growth over time.

What is the logical status of these tools? Do they somehow escape the ban on value judgments which the positive econ-

16. Or see the similar statement by the early Soviet economist Strumlin: "Our task is not to study economics, but to change it. We are bound by no laws. There are no fortresses the Bolsheviks cannot storm. The question of tempo is subject to decision by human beings." (Both citations are from Peter J. D. Wiles, *The Political Economy of Communism* [Cambridge: Harvard University Press, 1962], pp. 47–48).

omist is expected to observe? If so, how is this ingenious trick accomplished?

We shall be concerned in Part Three with the usefulness of Western economic analysis—on its home ground and in other parts of the world. This raises the question of what one means by "usefulness," and whether there are objective tests which can be applied.

It has long been conventional to say that "economics is what economists do." But economists do many different things. They try to minimize costs for General Motors or the Department of Defense. They study competitive behavior in the aluminum industry. They prepare input-output tables for the economy of Pakistan in 1970. They construct short-run macro models of the American economy. They theorize about optimal growth in a two-commodity world.

While one might be able to show that these inquiries are ultimately related, they are also quite specialized and different. Thus it makes most sense to view Western economic analysis, not as an integrated structure of thought, but as an array of specialized tools. In chapter 8 we outline the present content of this tool-kit.

This view permits a desirable flexibility in two directions. First, there is no need to assert that all the tools are equally useful (or useless) under all circumstances. We can give higher marks to some than to others, and the grading can differ for different types of economy. Second, we can ask whether useful new tools, rather different from anything in the Western tool-kit, have been devised in the Eastern countries or the less developed countries. And we can do this without being forced to assume that there is a coherent body of "socialist economics" or "less-developed-country economics" which can be contrasted with Western theory in toto.

We propose to apply two tests of usefulness: that of "realism," and that of "relevance." The former involves explanatory and predictive power while the latter involves relation to high-priority policy issues.

The explanatory value of a particular tool-set depends on the organization of the economy in question. Thus, an aggregative theory of economic fluctuations would have little value in an economy of isolated peasant households. Nor would a theory of optimal administrative organization for a centrally planned economy have much bearing on the operation of a market economy under private ownership. These are extreme examples. The more common situation is one in which the structure of the economy has some resemblance, but far from complete correspondence, to the structure of the conceptual model. In such cases, the "realism" of the model becomes a matter of judgment. We shall make many such judgments in later chapters, and the reader should look at these with a critical eye.

Relevance we define as the extent to which a set of concepts contributes, directly or indirectly, to policy decisions which are "important" in the sense defined below. It is quite possible for a particular tool to have realism but little relevance. Thus one may think that neoclassical growth theory is helpful in analyzing actual growth processes in the Western countries. But if these economies are growing at a satisfactory rate, or if government action to influence the growth rate is viewed as inappropriate, the policy relevance of the theory is low. It is difficult to think of converse cases, of relevance without realism. Unless a conceptual structure has explanatory power, it can scarcely be used for prescriptive purposes.

To make judgments about relevance, then, we must first ask, "What are the high-priority issues of economic policy in this kind of economy?" Here it may seem that we are on slippery ground. Who is to say whether one policy issue is "more important" than another? Can any priority list be more than the subjective estimate of an individual?

There are at least two directions in which one can seek an objective frame of reference. First, one can sometimes estimate the number of people liable to injury from a particular

economic defect—for example, the number affected by recession unemployment, or the number injured by rapid inflation. Or one can try to estimate the magnitude of the gains
achievable through remedial action—for example, the potential increase in national product from removal of barriers
to international trade. To the extent that this is possible,
quantitative standards can be applied: the priority problems
are those which involve the greatest potential gain for the
largest number of people.

Second, we can refer to the explicit or implicit judgments
of those responsible for economic policy. We can look at the
issues to which legislators and administrators devote time.
This might be taken as an indication of "revealed priorities,"
analogous to revealed consumer preference. An experiment
in this direction for several of the Western countries will be
described in chapter 5. One could also poll a representative
group of economic officials, say in Washington, plus some
"outside" economists with Washington experience. Their
priority lists would differ in detail, but would probably show
substantial consensus. Similar priority lists could be com-
piled by inquiries in Paris, Moscow, or Bangkok.

These approaches are clearly not free of difficulty. We
mention them only to suggest that priority ranking of policy
problems is not a meaningless exercise; it is admittedly a
difficult and partially subjective exercise.

A SINGLE SCIENCE OF ECONOMICS?

There are certainly different kinds of *economy,* though
we defer the question of just what is meant by this statement. Does this mean that there are also different species of
economics? Or is economics, in some sense or at some level
of abstraction, a universal science whose generalizations are
applicable at all times and places?

Economists in the West have usually answered this last
question in the affirmative. Robbins was quite clear that
economics is one and indivisible: "It has sometimes been as-

serted that the generalizations of Economics are essentially historico-relative in character, that their validity is limited to certain historical conditions, and that outside these they have no relevance. . . . This view is a dangerous misapprehension. . . . No one will really question the universal applicability of such assumptions as the existence of scales of relative valuation, or of different factors of production, or of different degrees of uncertainty regarding the future. . . . It is only failure to realize this, and a too exclusive preoccupation with the subsidiary assumptions, which can lend any countenance to the view that the laws of Economics are limited to certain conditions of time and space."[17]

Lange, on the other hand, asserts that "economic laws are not universally valid covering all stages of social development but are historical laws dealing with definite stages." Thus, there is "the political economy of the primitive community . . . the political economy of feudalism, the political economy of capitalism, and the political economy of socialism. Each of these 'political economies' deals with the economic laws specific to its social formation, the mode of operation of that formation and its 'economic laws of movement' thereby providing an explanation of the process of emergence, development and decay of each social formation concerned."[18]

Differences on this issue are related to the question of boundaries. Lange's (or Marx's) "political economy" is clearly a much broader subject than Robbins's "economics," the former including such things as property ownership, income distribution, and the political structure. Lange argues also that, under capitalism, economic laws operate "spontaneous-

17. Robbins, *Essay*, pp. 80–81.
18. Oskar Lange, *Political Economy*, vol. 1 (London: Pergamon Press, 1963), pp. 63, 94. This is, to be sure, the latter-day Lange functioning in his capacity as a Polish planning official. In his earlier period of American residence, his views on methodology appeared more similar to standard Western doctrine. In addition to his famous essay on market socialism, see his "The Scope and Method of Economics," *Review of Economic Studies* 13 (1945–46): 19–32.

ly," while under socialism they operate in a way "intended by man." The difference between a spontaneously coordinated market economy and a centrally guided economy strikes him as fundamental.

Reading between the lines of other writings by East European economists one judges that their position would be broadly similar to Lange's. In these countries, the use of economic instruments for control purposes is in the center of the stage. The economist is actor rather than observer. While Western concepts of cost and price may have some relevance, their use for control purposes raises novel problems which can be resolved only in the laboratory of experience. Out of this experience there may emerge an operational "socialist economics'" which is different from anything in the traditional literature. So many Eastern economists would probably say.

There has been debate also over the applicability of Western economics to the less developed countries, with one tool after another being rejected as inapplicable. Thus it has been argued forcefully that the Keynesian analysis of underemployment does not fit the LDCs, though much underemployment is obviously present. If this is correct, it follows that the standard Keynesian policy measures are also inappropriate. Some Latin American economists have argued that inflation in these economies arises from structural features not found in more developed countries, and that standard antiinflation measures will merely stop growth without checking inflation. International trade theory teaches that, if two countries trade at all, there will normally be an output gain in which both will share. Further, under simple assumptions, factor prices in the trading countries will move closer together, which for the LDCs would mean a rise in the price of labor and a decline in that capital. But Prebisch and others deny the applicability of such propositions, and maintain that the present trade patterns of the LDCs bring them little gain or possibly a loss.

While the attack on Western concepts has been forceful, it

is not clear that an alternative body of thought has emerged. Do we have a satisfactory explanation of Indian underemployment, or Brazilian inflation, or Colombia's gains and losses from international trade? It would be difficult to get a consensus on this in any international economic gathering.

The question whether the "universalist" or the "relativist" position is more nearly valid thus turns out to be complicated. It comprises such issues as: whether the boundaries of the subject are conceived in the same way in different types of economy; the usefulness of Western analytical concepts in these other economies; the extent to which new analytical concepts have been devised in the socialist economies and the LDC's; whether these concepts are mergeable with traditional Western economics in some higher synthesis; and whether one can resolve the problem via a hierarchy of theoretical models, some of broader and others of more limited application. This last approach is traditional in Western writings on methodology. Can it be stretched to cover the non-Western economies as well?

THE MEANING OF COMPARATIVE ECONOMICS

The tradition of Western economics is parochial. American textbooks and courses have dealt mainly with the American economy, with illustrative references to other Western countries. British economists, too, have usually taken the British economy as a starting point, though with rather more attention to international trade than in this country. But international trade courses did not bring "foreign" economies into the curriculum in a serious way. Trade theory remained highly abstract. To the extent that the trading nations were given any realistic attributes, they looked like neighboring Western countries. The colonial areas remained the domain of the anthropologist, who reported on the odd economic behavior of primitive peoples.

The first serious intrusion of the outside world occurred in the 1920s and 1930s because of the intellectual shock waves set up by the Russian Revolution. Books began to appear on the Soviet economy, comparative economic systems, capitalism versus socialism, plan versus no-plan. The "comparative systems" courses added to the curriculum at this time were rather descriptive and unanalytical, somewhat burdened with political ideology, and preoccupied with the question whether one "type" of economy was demonstrably superior to another. Because of the heavy weight of academic tradition and the long tenure of university professors, patterns of thought and course organization established at this time still carry weight today.

Developments after 1945 put a firmer floor under "comparative systems" courses, since there were now a dozen socialist economies to serve as objects of research. The logic of such courses, however, is rather unclear. They often start from the concept of a "type" of economy: "capitalism," "socialism," "communism," and (until recently) "fascism." Each type is first outlined in abstract terms, and then a particular economy is described as representative of the species. The United States and the USSR are usually chosen to represent capitalism and communism. Britain or Sweden is fitted with some awkwardness into the socialist category. Fascism used to be exemplified by Italy or Germany.

This approach has several defects. First, the categories used are not very satisfactory. It is doubtful that fascism ever constituted a distinct and coherent form of *economic* organization. Communism, too, describes a political doctrine and a political party. Its only *economic* meaning is the Marxian apocalyptic vision of an eventual age of affluence, in which the economy will be so productive that goods can be distributed freely to every citizen "according to his need." The criteria by which Sweden, say, is considered "socialist" while other Western economies remain "capitalist" are not clear; and it may be doubted that there is any general model of socialism in this sense.

Second, the identification of a national economy with an ideal type commits the fallacy of misplaced concreteness.

Pure types occur only in our minds. No actual economy constitutes a "system" in the sense of conforming to a single principle of organization or control. It is a historical product, a hodge-podge of differing control principles, the mix of which is changing over time. This misidentification contains also some danger. If one finds the image of a competitive market economy attractive, as many economists do, there is an almost irresistible temptation to impute its virtues to actual capitalist economies. There is a similar tendency to impute the difficulties which would confront a fully centralized "command economy" to the actual economies of the USSR and Eastern Europe. This has encouraged the "capitalism versus socialism" kind of controversy, in which image and reality become hopelessly entangled, with no constructive result.

Third, a botanical classification of economies implies that those in each box closely resemble each other and tends to reduce one's interest in exploring significant differences. The general label "Soviet-type economies" or "centrally planned economies" blurs the lines of institutional innovation now underway in Eastern Europe, not to mention Yugoslavia, Cuba, or China. There is a similar divergence among the Western economies. It is not clear which of them can claim to stand as the archetypal representative of capitalism; nor is it useful to fudge over the differences by drawing a blurred portrait of a "typical" capitalist economy.

Anyone who doubts the heterogeneity of actual economies can try the following experiment: feed the measurable characteristics of fifty national economies into a computer, carefully removing all "systems" labels. Then develop regression equations to explain operating characteristics in which one might be interested: gross capital formation as a percentage of GNP, output of educational services as a percentage of GNP, average scale of plants and firms in manufacturing, or whatever. A good statistical explanation can often be obtained without reference to "systems" categories. Per capita income, a rough proxy for level of development, is often the most important independent variable. One can hypothesize, indeed, that a country's economic structure and performance is related more closely to its per capita income level than to property ownership and other institutional features.[19]

Fourth, the traditional approach is quite static. It implies that an economy can be labeled once for all. But economies are always undergoing institutional change, and the question of typical direction of change is an intriguing one. Students of economic systems have not been unaware of dynamic problems, as witness recent discussions of "the convergence hypothesis." But these problems have not yet received the emphasis they deserve.

Finally, the traditional approach reflects the pre-1945 era in which the economic world could be regarded as consisting largely of Europe and North America. It makes no place for the Asian, African, and Latin American economies which include most of the world's land area and population. It may be said that these economies are taken care of elsewhere in the curriculum by courses on economic development. But this is a somewhat artificial separation. All countries are underdeveloped relative to their economic potential, and most of them are developing or trying to develop in one fashion or another. The growth problems of China and Cuba are not entirely unlike those of India or Jamaica. It would seem that a course in comparative economies should somehow take account of the full range of the world's economies.

If one believes that intereconomy comparisons are useful, but that the conventional "comparative systems" course is defective, what morals can be drawn? What new content might be given to the term "comparative economics"? We shall return to this question in chapter 10. Meanwhile, as an

19. The idea that level of development may often be more significant than "systems" differences runs through the work of Frederic Pryor, which will be discussed in later chapters. It has also been emphasized by Bela Balassa, for example, in his "Growth Strategies in Semi-Industrial Countries," *Quarterly Journal of Economics,* Feb. 1970, pp. 24–47.

appetite-whetter, some of the possibilities may be listed without comment:

1. Development of a generalized conceptual scheme for
   describing a national economy, into which any concrete
   economy can be fitted
2. Comparison of ideal types of economy, including new
   types not included in our present repertoire
3. Comparison of concrete national economies, recognizing
   that this is a quite different enterprise from no. 2 above,
   and including efforts to evaluate performance
4. Cross-country analysis of specific aspects of economic
   structure and performance, without reference to "system" categories
5. Cross-country analysis of major themes, such as:
   a) Varieties of "economic planning"
   b) Differing blends of "market control" and "adminis-
      trative control" in actual economies
   c) The hypothesis that capitalist and socialist econ-
      omies are becoming in some respects more nearly
      similar over time

A Look Forward

The inquiry on which we now embark has a threefold
purpose: First, we are interested in exploring the central features of economic organization and economic policy in different groups of countries. This is a substantive venture in economic comparison. Second, we are interested in exploring the
questions raised above about the scope and method of economics, in the light of world experience rather than purely
Western experience. Third, we are interested in possible new
directions for comparative economic studies.

These three strands of the inquiry, we believe, are complementary and mutually reinforcing. But since one cannot discuss everything at once, we shall proceed as follows:

Part One is concerned with *economic organization*. At the
end of that Part we consider what can be said in general
about the operating characteristics of capitalist economies,
socialist economies, and less developed economies.

Part Two endeavors to sort out the high-priority issues of *economic policy* in each group of countries. A summary comparison at the end of that Part suggests that the three lists differ substantially. The most pressing problems in one group of countries are, in general, not the most pressing problems in the other two groups.

In the light of the foregoing, we proceed in Part Three to examine the usefulness of the main tools of Western *economic theory* in socialist countries and in less developed countries.

In Part Four, we return to the issues raised in this chapter. Chapter 10 explores possible new directions for comparative economic studies. Chapter 11 examines the "scope and method" issues set forth above. The views expressed in Part Four are necessarily somewhat subjective, speculative, and controversial. The object is not to win the reader to a particular point of view. Rather, it is to stimulate thought and discussion on issues sometimes taken as settled, but which are not really so, and which are important for the future of economics as a world discipline.

PART ONE
ECONOMIC ORGANIZATION

2 CAPITALIST ECONOMIES

Our first task is to classify the world's economies for comparative purposes. We are not concerned here with ideal types—the competitive market economy, the command economy, market socialism, and so on—though we shall consider the usefulness of such constructs in chapter 10. We want rather an empirical classification of actual economies.

The classification which we propose is familiar, even obvious. It divides economies into three groups: the modified capitalist economies of the West, the socialist economies of the East, and the less developed economies of Asia, Africa, and Latin America. More specifically, these categories comprise:

1. *Modified or "mixed" capitalist economies.* The hallmarks of this group are: a pluralistic society with multiparty government; a relatively high level of industrial development and per capita output; built-in capacity for continued growth; substantial but not dominant public sectors; elaborate development of private markets and "modern" economic institutions. Geographically, the group includes the countries of North America, Australasia, Japan, South Africa, and the noncommunist countries of Europe (though Greece, Spain, and Portugal might be considered only semideveloped or fringe members).

2. *Socialist economies.* The hallmarks of this group are: a

31

monolithic governmental system dominated by a single
party; state operation of nonagricultural industries, and in
some countries of agriculture as well; centralized direction of
the economy, but with experiments in decentralization; semiindustrialized production structures, with agriculture still
important; per capita output levels more variable from country to country than in the West, and with a lower group
median; strong commitment to economic growth and demonstrated growth capacity. Geographically, this group includes
the USSR, the East European countries, China, the small
Asian economies of Outer Mongolia, North Korea, and North
Vietnam, and Cuba.

3. *Less developed economies* or countries, for which we
shall often use the common abbreviation LDCs. The hallmarks of this group are: prevalence of one-party governments or military governments, often unstable and with
limited capacity for public administration; small public sectors; fragmentation of the economy along geographic and
modern-versus-traditional lines; imperfection of markets and
limited development of "modern" economic institutions;
limited industrial development and continued predominance
of agriculture; per capita output lower, and more variable
among countries, than in the other two groups; small "economic size" and marked dependence on foreign economic
relations; demonstrated growth capacity usually lacking.
Geographically, this group includes all of Central and South
America; all of Africa except South Africa; all of Asia except Japan and the socialist countries; and many small island
economies (Jamaica, Trinidad, Mauritius, Fiji, etc.) scattered throughout the world.

This organization seems superior to any other empirical
classification which might be devised. At the same time, it
presents several obvious difficulties: the countries within each
category are quite heterogeneous; it is not always clear to
which group a particular country should be assigned; and
the appropriateness of our proposed labels might be questioned.

The countries within a particular category differ in many important dimensions. This is true particularly of the less developed countries. One might well wonder whether it is meaningful to group Iran, Uganda, and Argentina together. Most students of development economics agree that it would be desirable to work out a subclassification of LDCs to achieve greater homogeneity within each subgroup. We propose to cope with this difficulty in two ways: first, we shall focus on *median behavior* within each group, rather than on the characteristics of particular countries. Second, where there is wide variation in a particular dimension, we shall try to indicate the range of variation.

While most economies fall clearly in a particular category, this is not always true. For example, Yugoslavia, which we include in the socialist group, is a distinctly maverick member of that group. Indeed, in East-West statistical comparisons, it is sometimes classified as a "Western" economy. Israel, judged by per capita output, should now be considered a developed rather than a less developed country. Yet it has institutional characteristics rather different from those of the Western industrial nations.

We have already mentioned the socialist countries which are starting from a predominantly agricultural base and a low level of per capita income: China, the other socialist countries of Asia, and Cuba. One could argue that they should be assigned instead to the less developed category. Our classification reflects a judgment that, by virtue of their socialist organization, they are likely to follow a significantly different growth path from the other LDCs. But other scholars may well disagree, either with the judgment itself, or with using it as a prime basis of classification.

The line between "more developed" and "less developed" countries, usually defined in terms of per capita income, is purely conventional. There are a number of medium-income countries which could plausibly be assigned to either group, or which might be regarded as constituting a separate class of "semideveloped" economies. Further, as per capita incomes rise, countries "graduate" out of the LDC category. Recent examples are Greece and Israel. Mexico, Iran, Taiwan, and others may follow within the foreseeable future.

Finally, there is the problem of labels. All the familiar labels have political overtones. At one stage of the work, we considered using neutral terms borrowed from geography— "West," "East," and "South." But on further reflection this seemed rather precious and, even from a geographic standpoint, not quite correct. We concluded finally that the terms used herein, if not very good, are at least less bad than others which might have been chosen.

"Capitalist economies" clearly does not mean either the hypothetical free market economy of economics textbooks or the relatively laissez-faire systems of the nineteenth century. All the Western countries now have a substantial public sector and many types of government intervention in economic affairs. This is recognized in such terms as "mixed economies," "modified" or "regulated" capitalist economies, and so on. While for brevity we shall usually omit these qualifying phrases, the reader should remember that this is what we actually mean.

Writings on comparative economic systems sometimes imply that certain of the Western economies are sufficiently different from the rest that they should be classified as "socialist" rather than "capitalist." Sweden and the United Kingdom are usually selected for this purpose. We disagree with this judgment, for reasons which will be explained. We conclude rather that capitalist elements still predominate in all the Western countries, though some are doubtless more "purely" capitalist than others.

Economists in the USSR and other Eastern countries usually refer to their economies as "socialist." This is objectionable to many Western socialists, who feel that the politico-economic structure of the Eastern countries is quite different from that to which they themselves aspire, and that those countries should not be allowed to appropriate a term which has a long and differing tradition in the West. Partly on this account, many Western scholars prefer to term these economies "planned," or "centrally planned," or "communist." But these terms are also open to serious objection. "Planning" is a highly ambiguous term. In varying senses, and in varying degrees, it exists in almost every economy. The planning system of the Eastern countries themselves differ substantially. The term "communist" has a variety of possible meanings: the name of the dominant political party; the political philosophy asserted by this party; the anticipated golden age in which productive capacity will have risen sufficiently that it will be possible to distribute goods freely to each citizen "according to his needs." It does not, however, describe any concrete, presently existing system of economic organization.

For these reasons we have decided to conform to Eastern practice and use the "socialist" label. The reader who does not agree with the label will at any rate be clear about which group of economies we are describing.

The poor countries of the world have been subjected to a great variety of terminology. Labels such as "the Third World" or "countries of the South" seem a bit exotic. "Primary producing economies" is more descriptive of some countries than of others. "Underdeveloped countries" was used for a time, but turned out on reflection to be virtually meaningless. "Developing countries" is inaccurate, since many of these countries are not in fact developing. Thus "less developed countries" can be defended as a least-bad choice, and seems now to be coming into general usage.

Having defined and labeled our categories, what do we do next? In Part One we ask, with respect to each category: what kind of economies are these? how are they organized? how do they operate? It may seem foolhardy to touch briefly on matters on which there is already a vast descriptive literature. But each observer will view the economic scene somewhat differently, and perhaps something new can be said. Clearly, we shall have to make a judicious selection of major features of the economic landscape, while lesser features and fine shadings of detail are deliberately ignored. We shall aim to focus on characteristics which are in some sense *analytically significant*—to go for the jugular.

It may seem particularly different to say anything new about the Western economies. Most of us have grown up in one or other of these economies and have an intuitive feel for their operation. We shall try in this chapter to say just enough to remind the reader of what, in essentials, he already knows.

MEDIUM-SIZED PUBLIC SECTORS

While these are often termed "private enterprise" economies, output of public and quasi-public goods is large and growing in relative importance. In most countries, too, the public sector includes a considerable array of nationalized industries, notably rail transport, electric power production, and other "natural monopolies."

How can one measure the importance of government in the Western economies? The measure most commonly used —tax revenue as a percentage of national income—is not very satisfactory. It shows financial flows rather than productive activity, typically including a large volume of transfer payments. Three other indicators, shown in table 2.1 are more significant: (1) Government consumption expenditure as a percentage of total consumption expenditure indicates the relative importance of private and public goods in household consumption pattern; (2) the capital formation columns provide two indicators of government's importance in gross domestic capital formation; (3) the final column shows how much of household income comes from transfer payments rather than from sale of productive services in the market. This is a rough indicator of government's income-redistribution function.

For the group as a whole, government consumption expenditure forms about 20 percent of total consumption expenditure, this being divided into 15 percent for civilian

TABLE 2.1

Indicators of the Scope of the Public Sector, Selected Countries, 1960–66

Country	Government consumption expenditure as percentage of total consumption expenditure			Government fixed capital formation as percentage of total fixed capital formation		Government transfers to households as percentage of household income
	Civil	Military	Total	Gen'l gov't	Public sector	
	(1)	(2)	(3)	(4)	(5)	(6)
Australia	10.3	3.8	14.1[a]	—[b]	35.4	7.4
Belgium	12.1	3.8	15.9	12.3	—	12.4
Canada	13.7	5.0	18.7	18.0	29.5	11.4
Denmark	15.1	3.4	18.5	11.9	22.8	9.3
Finland	17.0	2.3	19.3	20.0	37.4	8.5
France	11.2	6.1	17.3	12.9	37.1	17.6
Germany (West)	15.4	5.3	20.7	16.2	—	15.3
Italy	14.4	3.3	17.7	13.6	—	13.6
Japan	—	—	14.3	—	29.5	5.3
Netherlands	15.3	5.4	20.7	18.8	35.0	14.0
New Zealand	14.8	2.6	17.4	—	38.7	8.5
Norway	16.9	4.6	21.5	13.5	28.8	—
South Africa	—	—	15.2	17.8	41.7	3.0
Sweden	18.7	5.8	24.5	16.0	41.2	11.1
United Kingdom	13.1	7.3	20.4	12.3	43.3	8.7
United States	12.3	10.8	22.8	15.7	18.2	6.5
Median, all countries	14.6	4.8	18.6	15.7	35.4	9.3

a. Excludes road repairs, which are counted as capital formation.

b. Dash indicates data were not available.

Sources and Methods: Data are from the U.N. Yearbook of National Accounts Statistics. They are averages for the calendar years 1960–66 inclusive. All figures except those in column 5 relate to general government only, excluding public enterprises and public corporations. Column 6 shows transfer payments as a percentage of total personal income before income taxes.

services and 5 percent for military services. There is moderate variation in the ratios for individual countries. Thus output of government civilian services is relatively low in Belgium, France, and the United States, and relatively high in the Scandinavian countries and West Germany. There is wider variation in military expenditures, as might be expected in view of differences in countries' size, geographic location, and foreign policy objectives. The military expenditure ratio for the United States is much above that for any other Western country, while Finland, New Zealand, and Japan have unusually low ratios.

These figures relate to *general government* only. It would be convenient to have information also on the *public sector,* including public corporations and other semiautonomous enterprises. This information is not readily available, since the U.N. system of national accounts classifies output by type of product rather than form of ownership. Thus a separate calculation would have to be made for each country from primary sources.

The substantial difference between the two concepts is shown by the capital formation columns (4) and (5). General government's share of fixed capital formation averages about 16 percent for the Western economies as a whole. This rises to 35 percent, however, if public corporations are included. This is partly because capital-output ratios in transport and power are unusually high. But it would not be surprising to find that, on the average for all capitalist countries, public sector *output* is in the neighborhood of 30 percent of total output.[1]

1. Kuznets' estimates show that, for a sample of ten Western economies, output of transportation, communication, electric power, gas, and water forms about 10 percent of GNP. In most countries, these are predominantly public sector industries. (Simon Kuznets, *Modern Economic Growth: Rate, Structure, and Spread* [New Haven: Yale University Press, 1966], p. 128.) One would not, however, expect the public sector share of consumption output to be as high as the public sector share of capital formation. This is because of the high capital intensity of such activities as power production, rail transport, river development, and construction of public buildings.

There has been much attention to government's role in redistributing personal income. Redistribution tends to mean equalization as well, since social insurance and welfare payments go predominantly to those near the bottom of the income scale. The importance of such payments as a component of personal income varies considerably among the capitalist countries, depending partly on how long a social insurance system has been in existence. In general, the longer the lifetime of the system, the greater the relative importance of transfers under it.

The percentage of household income which comes from government transfer payments is shown in column 6. The median for all capitalist countries is a bit under 10 percent. The United States, Japan, South Africa, Australia, and New Zealand are at the bottom of the range, while Belgium, Holland, Italy, France, and West Germany are at the top. The high ratios in the latter countries arise partly from more generous family allowance systems.

Table 2.1 bears on the question whether, in some Western economies, the importance of government is so great as to warrant their being classified as "socialist," while the remainder continue to be regarded as "capitalist." It is clear that different indicators yield different results. In terms of public goods output, Norway, Sweden, and the United Kingdom would appear as relatively "socialist," but so would the United States, whose ratio is the second highest on the list. Australia, South Africa, and Japan would be most "capitalist" by this test. The capital formation ratios, however, would indicate a different ranking, which the reader can work out for himself. The income redistribution column, finally, would indicate France, Italy, and West Germany as having the strongest "welfare state" characteristics, while the United States, Japan, Australia, and South Africa have lowest ratios. The only countries which have above-average government activity rates across the board are West Germany and Sweden.

We conclude that there is no clear basis for any subdivision within the Western group. They are all "mixed economies," with the bulk of production in private hands, but with a substantial infusion of government activity.[2]

COORDINATION THROUGH MARKETS

In the Western economies, most products and most factor supplies are traded on private markets at prices not set by government. These markets register the effects of changes in such basic data as consumer and worker preferences, factor supplies, products, and production techniques. The existence of monopoly power and market imperfections typically does not prevent price-quantity adjustments from being in the "right" direction over the long run, though it does influence their size and timing. In this sense the market network coordinates the economy and ensures appropriate adjustments to economic change.

Recognition of the existence of a "workable" market mechanism, however, can easily slip over into identifying it with the perfectly competitive model of economic theory. Any such identification is unwarranted. The hypothetical advantages of all-round competition cannot be imputed to actual market economies. The question how far a particular national economy at a particular time resembles the competitive model is a question of fact, requiring careful investigation on many fronts.

Free consumer *choice* is not the same thing as consumer *sovereignty;* nor does it necessarily lead to a unique position of maximum welfare. Product innovations, as Galbraith and others have emphasized, originate with producers; and while

2. Professor Frederic Pryor has tried to assess the importance of public sector activities in a number of countries on the basis of *employment* in those activities as a percentage of total employment, since data on government's share of the capital stock are less readily available. Pryor's "nationalization ratios" for selected Western countries, as of about 1960, were as follows: West Germany, 9 percent; Japan, 10 percent; United States, 15 percent; France, 17 percent; Sweden, 20 percent; United Kingdom, 25 percent; Austria, 31 percent; Finland, 34 percent ("The Pattern of Public Ownership in Developed Economics," *Weltwirtschaftliches Archiv,* forthcoming, table 3–1.)

Capitalist Economies

41

consumers have a certain veto power, they have little power of initiative. The origin of consumer preferences is obscure—indeed, economists usually refuse to inquire into it. But fashion, competitive emulation, and the persistent pressures of mass advertising are clearly important. It requires a large leap of faith to assert that consumers get what they "really want," or that they achieve the maximum satisfaction permitted by available resource supplies. A more modest claim is that free choice—"the right to be wrong"—has some value independent of its consequences.

Discussion of the reality of competition has focused heavily, perhaps unduly, on the degree of seller concentration in product markets. This obviously varies by country and by industrial sector. Heavy manufacturing, with its large optimum scale of plant relative to market size, is the natural province of oligopoly. In the retailing and service industries, on the other hand, optimum scale is lower and seller concentration less prevalent.

What of differences among countries? In an earlier volume in this series,[3] Bain undertook to compare plant size, plant concentration, and firm concentration in numerous branches of manufacturing in eight countries: United States, Canada, United Kingdom, France, Italy, Sweden, Japan, and India. The comparison is clouded by the fact that in Japan and India, and even to a limited extent in the European countries, there is a "dual" structure of industry, with many workshops too small to be captured by censuses of manufacturing. The Bain comparisons are essentially for the "modern" sector, excluding cottage industries and other very small establishments.

It is perhaps not surprising that, for most industries, the absolute size of plants is much larger in the United States than in other countries. Only the United Kingdom approaches the average scale of American plants. In most of the

3. Joe S. Bain, *International Differences in Industrial Structure* (New Haven: Yale University Press, 1966).

other countries studied, plants were only one-quarter to one-third as large as in the United States. But when one looks instead at plant *concentration*—the percentage of industry output coming from a given number of largest plants—the findings are reversed. Plant concentration in the other countries is significantly higher than in the United States, and for the smaller economies (Canada, Sweden, India) substantially higher. The picture is broadly the same for *company* concentration. The United States and the United Kingdom have the lowest firm concentration ratios, and the Japanese ratio is almost as low. The other countries, in order of ascending concentration ratios, rank as follows: France, Italy, Canada, India, and Sweden.

These results pose interesting questions. If one assumes that similar technology is available to all the Western countries, why should there be such wide intercountry differences in plant sizes? Possible contributing factors include: (1) long-run average total cost curves may typically be saucer-shaped rather than cup-shaped, permitting wide variation in scale with little effect on unit costs; (2) factor price-ratios may differ sufficiently among countries to produce substantial differences in optimum scale even with a common technology; (3) new technology may be disseminated from more inventive to less inventive economies with a substantial lag; (4) "embodied" technology may differ because of differences in capital accumulation rates, and hence in the average age of the capital stock; (5) differences in national policy may have some effect. The United States, Canada, and the United Kingdom have emphasized preservation of competition, while most of the European countries have looked favorably on cartelization. In the latter group, cartel arrangements may have tended to shelter relatively small and inefficient enterprises. But as Bain emphasizes, further research is needed to arrive at a satisfactory explanation.[4]

4. Professor Frederic Pryor presently has underway an ambitious study in this area, some preliminary results of which have been communicated to the writer. The study covers some thirty countries, in-

It is interesting also to inquire whether seller concentration is increasing or decreasing over time in a particular country. The outcome will depend on: (1) trends within each economic sector—for example, the much-investigated manufacturing sector of the American economy; (2) weight shifting among sectors in the course of economic growth; and (3) trends in the exposure of domestic producers to international competition, which since 1945 has been once more in the ascendant. The lowering of trade barriers among countries of the European Economic Community has brought a marked intensification of competition in the manufacturing sector of those countries; and important industries in the United States have felt the impact of growing international competition.

Present knowledge warrants only an agnostic conclusion. Prophecies of "the decline of competition," which have been current in the United States since at least 1900, appear to be premature. Much more information, including information on important dimensions of market structure other than seller concentration, would be needed for an adequate test of this hypothesis.

A further question: if we knew what was happening to economic structure in the Western countries, how should we evaluate what is happening? Should the growth of monopoly power in product markets (if it exists) be greeted with approval (Schumpeter), or complacency (Galbraith), or resolute opposition (Stigler and Friedman)? Debate over this issue on resource-allocation grounds has ended in a cul-de-sac. Virtual-

---

cluding several East European countries and the USSR. Pryor finds that, for a particular industry, prevailing size of firm varies directly with the size of the national economy. Large economies have large steel and textile firms, while small economies have smaller ones. Interestingly enough, this pattern appears to hold in the socialist as well as the capitalist economies. Czechoslovakia and Hungary, however, are off the scale on the high side, having firms considerably larger than would be indicated by the size of their economies. In socialist countries, of course, firm size is a direct expression of policy, since firms are founded, enlarged, or merged by administrative decisions.

ly everything that can be said at a static level has been said, and it is doubtful that monopolistic distortion of resource allocation is quantitatively important.

In the last two decades, therefore, attention has shifted to the issue posed originally by Schumpeter: is monopolistic organization more favorable than competitive organization to research and innovation, and thus to a secular decline of costs and prices? Results to date provide no clear support for either Schumpeterians or anti-Schumpeterians. But this line of research is still in its infancy, and will undoubtedly intensify in the years ahead.

Preoccupation with product markets tends to obscure the equal importance of factor markets, and particularly of markets for labor.[5] In the early stages of industrialization, labor markets are usually very imperfect. Barriers to education, and thus to movement among occupational strata, are high. Workers' information and market sophistication are low. Employers have to some extent a vested interest in market imperfection, and do not work actively to remove it. So market improvement requires government action, which has been evident in Western countries since the 1920s, and particularly since 1945. This usually begins with creation of public employment exchanges, and goes on to educational subsidies, occupational forecasting, vocational training and counseling in the schools, retraining schemes for adult workers, and aids to geographic mobility, culminating in a comprehensive "labor market policy" on the Swedish pattern.

A second major trend is the rising percentage of manual workers, and to a lesser extent of white-collar workers, who are organized in trade unions. Wage rates are determined in-

5. "The marginal disutility felt by workers is from every point of view as important as the marginal utility felt by consumers. . . . Consumer's sovereignty unopposed by workers' sovereignty would be a curious form of tyranny, over man in one of his aspects by himself in another of his aspects. The freedom to 'sack the boss' and, perhaps, to strike is not only a basic political freedom, it is also . . . an integral but normally neglected part of welfare economics" (Wiles, *Political Economy of Communism*, p. 97).

creasingly by negotiation rather than by unilateral employer action. How far this alters the detailed structure of wages is difficult to determine. In the United States, at least, there is considerable consensus that the alterations, while significant, are not as large as might have been expected a priori—for example, on the assumption that each union attempts to maximize its wage bill. Union officials seem to operate as satisficers rather than maximizers, and one can find plausible reasons for this behavior. As regards labor mobility among industries and occupations, the direct effects of unionism do not seem very strong, though the indirect effect of bargained wages in altering the distribution of employment opportunities may be substantial. Altogether, it is easy to exaggerate the influence of unionism relative to that of worker preferences, employer preferences, and government-sponsored labor market institutions. The most important function of unionism—defense of the individual worker against arbitrary treatment by supervisory officials—has little effect on the structure of labor markets.

The familiar thesis that the capitalist countries have moved over the past century from a "competitive" to an "organized" economy, that there has been a marked increase in the power of quasi-monopolistic private groups, should thus be viewed with considerable reserve. There is probably *something* to the argument, but it is easy to overstate and oversimplify it.

URBAN-ORIENTED PRODUCTION STRUCTURES

After one to two centuries of sustained growth, the capitalist economies have now reached a relatively high level of per capita income. Increasing affluence, as Kuznets has documented, is accompanied by systematic changes in the structure of production.[6] The share of agriculture in national output declines continuously, the manufacturing share rises but eventually levels off, government services expand continu-

6. Kuznets, *Modern Economic Growth,* chap. 4.

ously, private service activities show differing trends. In terms of income produced, a typical pattern for the Western economies at present would be: agriculture 10 percent; "industry," including manufacturing, construction, and public utilities 50 percent, of which manufacturing constitutes about two-thirds; government services somewhat below 20 percent; private trade and service activities somewhat above 20 percent. But there is considerable inter-country variation. For example, agriculture provides about 15 percent of GNP in Canada and Denmark, but only about 5 percent in Britain and the United States.

As a country advances toward high income levels, it would seem that these shifts must decrease in magnitude and the sectoral composition of output become more stable. Agricultural output can scarcely fall to zero. Domestic service can fall to zero, but only once. The sectors which might be visualized as expanding indefinitely are professional and other personal services, and government services. But where is the necessary labor to come from, once agriculture and domestic service have been milked dry? Mainly, from continued automation and declining employment in manufacturing, from a similar automation of routine clerical labor, and from an increase in the average size of retailing and service establishments, with consequent economies in labor requirements.

The relatively slow expansion of agricultural output, accompanied by a continuing rise of agricultural productivity, leads eventually to an absolute decline in the agricultural labor force. The villages and small towns which serve as market centers for the rural population tend to wither, and larger towns which are now accessible by motor transport take over the retailing and servicing functions. A growing proportion of the population is concentrated in metropolitan areas. Since city residents consume more public services per capita than village and rural residents, growing urbanization is partly responsible for the rapid increase in output of public goods. Growing congestion of population produces well-known diseconomies: air and water pollution, noise, transportation difficulties, housing congestion, loss of privacy and of access to outdoor recreation, concentrated pockets of poverty and crime. Kuznets has argued convincingly that part of the apparent growth of output in a highly urbanized economy consists in efforts to offset these diseconomies, and that welware thus rises more slowly than the GNP figures suggest. Efforts to civilize the cities have been more successful in some countries than in others, but are everywhere complex and expensive.

BUILT-IN GROWTH CAPACITY

In all the Western economies, per capita output has been rising for a long time and can be expected to continue rising in the future. Economic growth has become routine. Per capita output is high today precisely *because* it has been rising for a long time in the past. The growth rates are not startling. Kuznets has calculated that, over the century 1860–1960, GNP rose in most of the Western countries at between 3 and 4 percent per year, with GNP per capita rising at about 2 percent. Since 1945, however, the median has been higher—better than 5 percent per year for GNP, about 4 percent for GNP per capita. This is partly because the pre-1945 "business cycle" has been tamed by policy measures.

There are substantial differences among countries. Britain and the United States have had relatively low growth rates. On the other hand, Japan since 1950 has raised per capita output at a rate of more than 8 percent per year. More generally, the countries with lowest per capita income have tended to grow more rapidly than those with highest income. Thus within the capitalist group, intercountry differences in per capita income are diminishing.

The sources of growth are well known, though their quantitative importance is harder to determine. They include: (1) continued upgrading of the labor force through general education, specialized vocational training, and improved health and nutrition; (2) continued improvement in the coordinating mechanisms of the economy—in the management of particular enterprises, and in interenterprise coordination through markets; (3) a high rate of innovation in products and production methods, which permits rapid capital accumulation without depressing the marginal yield of capital; (4) high rates of saving, increasingly institutionalized and thus in a sense "painless," so that finance is not a serious constraint on desired investment. Investment rates, like output growth rates, vary substantially among countries. In Britain and the United States, gross investment has averaged a bit less than 20 percent of GNP during the postwar period. Japan, on the other hand, has maintained an average of more than 30 percent. (5) There have probably also been increasing returns to scale for the economy as a whole.

While these elements can be separated statistically, in reality they are highly interdependent. Desired levels of (full-employment) saving could not be realized without adequate investment demand, investment could not remain vigorous without technical progress, more elaborate equipment could not be operated without improvements in the skill of managers, engineers, and workers. The statistical decomposition does violence to what is analogous to a biological process.

Economic progress includes, not simply increased per capita output, but also release of time for education and leisure activities. The work week, 70 or 80 hours in the early decades of the Industrial Revolution, has now fallen to 40–45 hours in most Western countries. Hours worked per year have been further reduced by the spread of paid holidays and vacations, extending in the United States to the point of lengthy "sabbatical leaves" for steelworkers and some other groups. In the United States, at least, the labor force participation rate has not declined overall, but there has been an interesting redistribution of effort among age and sex groups. Young people now spend much more time in education than was true fifty years ago, and begin work considerably later. Older people retire from employment considerably earlier. These reductions have been offset by a large increase in labor force participation by women from 35 to 65, who are past the peak of child care responsibilities. The new pattern of labor force participation surely comes closer to satisfying individual preferences than did that of 1900. In this sense, too, welfare has increased.

STRONG INTERACTION THROUGH TRADE

Most Western nations export a substantial proportion of their national output. The ratio of exports to GNP ranges from around 15 percent for France, Germany, and Italy to about 20 percent for the Scandinavian countries and more than 30 percent for Belgium and the Netherlands. The United States ratio is less than 5 percent but, because of the vast size of the American economy, it is the world's largest trading nation.

These trade relations, moreover, are becoming stronger rather than weaker. For most Western countries, the ratio of trade to GNP is higher today than it was a century ago. The reverse is true for the United Kingdom and the United States, but these seem to be exceptional cases rather than proof of any general "principle of declining trade."

The exports of the capitalist economies form more than two-thirds of world exports; and about 70 percent of the trade of these countries is with each other. This central current of intra-Western trade has been rising considerably faster since 1945 than has world trade in general. In an important sense, then, the Western nations are the center of gravity of the world economy.

In this they differ markedly from the socialist and the less developed countries. Historically, those countries have been peripheral, and this has left a strong imprint on their economies. Russia was a "latecomer" to the development parade, considerably behind France, Germany, and Sweden, and even farther behind Britain and the United States. Most of today's East European countries did not exist as independent nations before 1919, and even in 1945 some of them were at an early stage of development. A key issue for these countries is how to strengthen and rationalize their trade relations, both with each other and with the Western countries.

A similar issue confronts the LDCs. They have traditionally supplied raw materials to, and imported manufactures from, the Western countries to which they were economically attached and often politically subordinate. Some have argued that this politico-economic attachment, far from hastening their development, was an important factor in retarding it. With the virtual disappearance of political colonialism, accompanied by rising nationalism in the newly independent countries, the issue of "trade and growth" has been sharply posed. Should trade with the ex-colonial powers be curtailed? Can it be turned into new channels more advantageous to the LDCs?

These issues will be explored at a later point. We mention them here only because their very existence stems from the dominance of the Western nations in the world economy.

NEW INSTABILITIES FOR OLD

Older economists can remember the days when the "business cycle" was an important concept and a troublesome reality. Minor downturns were annoying, major downturns disastrous. Unemployment could be portrayed as the fatal defect which outweighed all possible virtues of capitalism. So strong was this tradition that, during the 'forties and 'fifties, most economists hesitated to proclaim the demise of the business cycle. After all, this had been proclaimed by noted authorities in the late 1920s. Once bitten, twice timid.

Today it does not seem venturesome to assert that the "old" business cycle is dead, or at least that it has been replaced by a "new" business cycle. Slowdowns still occur. But they usually take the form of *decelerations in a positive growth* rate, rather than an actual decline of production. These "periods of hesitation" are typically brief and mild, partly because of structural changes in the Western economies, partly because macroeconomic policy has become more fashionable and more effective. Policy makers have become quite skillful in applying monetary-fiscal stimuli as needed to avert threatened recessions.

But this gain has costs in other directions. As one steers farther away from the shoals of unemployment, one comes closer to the rocks of inflation. In the postwar period, the capitalist economies have experienced persistent upward pressure on the price level. The 1950–67 increase in the consumer price index ranged from 29 percent in the United States to 86 percent in Japan, with a median of 65 percent for the entire group. The rate of price increase has been relatively low in Britain and the United States; but so has the rate of output expansion. In the most rapidly growing economies—France, Germany, Italy, Japan—prices have climbed rapidly. It may not be true that price *instability* has increased, since the "old business cycle" produced substantial price fluctuations. But the expectation that these fluctuations would cancel out over a period of years has been replaced by an expectation of secular inflation.

National rates of inflation are coordinated somewhat by relatively free trade plus currency convertibility among the Western countries. If Italy inflates faster than France, its trade balance suffers while at the same time its "export" of inflation tends to push up the French price level. Within the Common Market, these interactions are so strong that coordination of national monetary-fiscal policies seems a logical future development. But export competition and nationalist sentiment are powerful forces. A country which succeeds in outmaneuvering its neighbors—say, by lagging an inflationary movement—strengthens its competitive position. So national autonomy in monetary-fiscal matters, combined with relative openness to trade and capital movements, will continue to pose balance-of-payments problems for the capitalist countries.

On the other hand, the difficulties arising from "export of unemployment" from one country to another are much less severe than before 1945. Fluctuations in aggregate demand *within* each country are smaller than they used to be, and these fluctuations are not fully synchronized among countries. France and Germany may be expanding while the United States is stagnating, or vice versa, so that world demand fluctuates less than national demand.

THE EGALITARIAN DRIFT

Inequality of incomes is a long-standing fact of life, and a long-standing source of criticism, in the capitalist countries. But measured by such yardsticks as the Gini coefficient,[7] or the percentage of personal income received by the top 5 or 10 percent of households, the distribution of household incomes has been growing gradually more equal over time. This is true even of pretax incomes, and is even more true of income after taxes and transfer payments.

Reasons for the decline of inequality include: (1) shrinkage of the agricultural sector, where incomes are typically below those in urban activities; (2) a decline in the property share of national income, which is much less equally distributed than the wage-salary share; (3) a decrease in wage rates for the higher occupational grades relative to lower grades, arising partly from continued enlargement of educational opportunities; (4) low unemployment levels since 1940, and consequent reduction of the number of low incomes arising from unemployment.

These factors have tended to equalize pretax incomes. The influence of governmental fiscal operations is felt in two additional ways: (5) all the Western countries rely in some measure on personal income taxes with progressive rate structures, though this is less true of the EEC countries than of Britain, the United States, and Canada. Thus posttax in-

7. The Gini coefficient is a measure of income equality which is related to the area under a curve which graphs the percent of total income received by the lowest x percent of the population. If everyone has the same income, the Gini coefficient is equal to one. If all income is received by just one person, it is equal to zero.

comes are more equal—in Britain and the United States, substantially more equal—than pretax incomes. (6) Western governments make substantial transfer payments averaging, as
we saw earlier, close to 10 percent of all household income.
These transfers take such forms as old age pensions, unemployment compensation, family allowances, subsidized housing and health care, and direct cash relief. They go predominantly to households near the bottom of the income structure,
raising them above where they would be on a market-income
basis.

There are still many rich people in the capitalist countries,
and a substantial percentage at the other end of the scale are
living in poverty. But this percentage is shrinking. In the
United States, the percentage classified as living in poverty
by conventional definitions has fallen from about 30 percent
in 1950 to less than half that percentage today. It is now
within the economic and fiscal capacity of most Western
countries to bring all households up to a modest minimum
income.

GOVERNMENT INTERVENTION, PLANNING, THE
WELFARE STATE

The term "mixed economy" connotes, not only a substantial output of public goods, but a variety of government
activities in the private economy. There are two main sources
of such intervention. First, organized private interests discover that they can use state power to increase their incomes.
Manufacturers seek tariff and quota restrictions on competitive imports. Farmers secure price supports, often buttressed
by output restrictions. Retailers sponsor resale price maintenance legislation. Truckers secure subsidies in the form of
publicly financed highway construction. The gains won by
such groups are at the expense of the consuming and tax-
paying public. But where a unified group with a direct and
powerful interest in government protection confronts a large,
diffuse group whose members have a smaller individual in-

terest in the matter, the democratic political machinery seems to yield an advantage to the group with a special interest.

A second source of government action is the growing electoral power of wage earners and other low-income groups, associated with widening of the franchise, rising educational levels, and strengthening of trade union organization. This leads to demands for protection against the vicissitudes of employment—accidents, disability, illness, unemployment, old age—which result in a variety of social security measures. The demand for regular employment, combined with growing knowledge of the sources of economic instability, has led all the capitalist countries to develop systematic full-employment policies. The demand for redistribution of income has led not only to transfers of generalized purchasing power but to subsidization of specific kinds of consumption by low-income groups: food, housing, education, health care. Thus government comes to have a strong influence on the organization and financing of these industries.

This ad hoc intervention to meet specific demands produces much inconsistency and confusion, and this leads to efforts to rationalize government policy within particular sectors—to programming or "planning," if you will. The initial patchwork of social security measures gets knit together into a comprehensive system of income support. Various types of aid to education become the basis of an overall educational policy. Instead of attending separately to the needs of the railroads, the local transport system, and the trucking industry, government begins to develop a transportation policy. Plans are drafted for development of whole regions which, for one reason or another, are economically depressed. These efforts usually tread on some toes and arouse political opposition, and so progress is slower than economists and planning technicians might wish. But the trend is clearly toward greater coordination and rationalization of policy.

Economy-wide planning in the capitalist countries dates from the adoption of full-employment policies in the 1930s and 1940s. This is quite different from planning in the other two groups of economies. It is primarily financial planning rather than "real" planning. Both targets and instruments are highly aggregated. But in some countries, notably France, there has been considerable effort at disaggregation through consultation with major branches of industry about their investment and output plans.

The inflationary pressure associated with sustained high employment has led most countries to experiment with "incomes policy." Ideally, and as approached to some extent in the Scandinavian countries, this would involve an agreed share-out of projected private income for the year ahead among business owners, wage earners, farmers, and others. The difficulties of such a program are enormous, and even its wisdom or necessity is still being debated. Success has thus far been quite limited. But since inflationary pressures show no sign of diminishing, and since few people now believe that they can be countered solely by monetary-fiscal instruments, experiments with incomes policy will doubtless continue.

These activities of government in the economy are often interpreted in doctrinaire ways which do not stand up under close examination. To some, the state is still the instrument of the property-owning class, serving to increase its power and income. Whatever validity this view may have had in the Britain of Marx's day, it is difficult to defend at present. There is active competition in the political market place. The reforms instituted by leftist political parties are usually consolidated rather than overturned when their conservative opponents return to power. The distribution of political power as well as income is substantially more equal today than it was a century ago.

To others, growing government activity is evidence of a "drift" or a "march" into socialism. This view is also difficult to sustain. The measures described above do not undercut the main premises of a market economy. Indeed, most of them may be regarded as conservative (or conserving) tendencies. By stabilizing the upward movement of the economy, and by yielding substantial benefits to low-income groups in the population, they attach those groups more firmly to the existing order. The most plausible prognosis for the capitalist economies is not revolutionary change but rather "more of the same"—continued economic growth, continued rationalization of government economic policy, continued redistribution of income and political power, increasing consensus on the desiderata of a modern industrial economy.

It should be reemphasized that we have been describing broad "family characteristics" shared by the capitalist economies. In each of these dimensions, there is considerable variation of individual countries around the group median. Some have larger public sectors than others. Some are growing faster than others. Some are more trade-dependent than others; and so on. These moderate differences in degree, however, do not warrant a conclusion that the economies are different in kind. They are all "mixed" or "modified-capitalist" economies. Nor is the United States necessarily the "most capitalist" member of the group, whatever such a term might mean. In modern times, Japan might well lay claim to that title.

One interesting difference may be noted in conclusion. Although these economies are organized in broadly the same way, although they have access to the same body of scientific and managerial knowledge, although they interact strongly and increasingly through trade flows, they operate at quite different levels of *total factor productivity*. The range, from top to bottom, is of the order of 3:1; nor is there clear evidence that it is diminishing over time. Why is this? Why are technology, managerial techniques, and other skills not diffused rapidly enough to bring the Western economies closer to a common productivity level? Differences in natural resource endowment might be thought to provide part of the answer. But with the diminishing importance of agriculture, and the growing importance of trade, resource endowments are less consequential than they were a century ago. What else can account for the observed productivity gap? This is an important and relatively unexplored area for future research.

3 SOCIALIST ECONOMIES

The heterogeneity of the economies in this group should be emphasized once more. To refer to them all as "Soviet-type economies" is if anything more misleading than to call all capitalist countries "American-type economies." It would be hard to imagine two economies more different than Cuba and Czechoslovakia. China's millennia of history as an intermittently unified country have left marks which make it distinctively different from others in the socialist group.

Even the Soviet Union and the East European countries, to which we shall largely confine our discussion, differ in many important respects: in size, income level, production structure, participation in foreign trade, and mechanisms of economic control. While they are often grouped as "planned economies," the content of this term varies from country to country. Yugoslavia, which we shall treat as an idiosyncratic member of the socialist group, has a decidedly different control structure. Moreover, in most countries, the system of economic administration has been in considerable flux over the past decade. In this chapter we emphasize the traditional pattern of Soviet economic organization. Efforts to modify this pattern in a number of countries will be examined in chapter 6.

Judgments about the key characteristics of socialist economic organization are bound to differ with the observer. In our view, the most important characteristics are: (1) the influence of Marxian thought; (2) predominance of public ownership; (3) pervasiveness of wage-salary incentives; (4) relatively centralized economic administration; (5) chronic excess demand; (6) medium levels of per capita output, and a characteristic composition of output; (7) convenient built-in mechanisms for capital accumulation; (8) built-in growth capacity; (9) limited trade participation; (10) multiple instruments of income distribution, leading (probably) to a more egalitarian distribution than in the West.

THE INTELLECTUAL BACKGROUND

Keynes pointed out that "practical men, who believe themselves to be quite exempt from any intellectual influences, are usually the slaves of some defunct economist." Westerners swim naturally in a sea of preconceptions about politico-economic organization which has developed over the past two centuries. Similarly, the thinking of Eastern economists and administrators is conditioned by their training in Marxian theory. Some familiarity with this intellectual climate is helpful in understanding the economic practices which appear "natural" in the socialist countries. Without attempting to redo Marx in three pages, we can emphasize a few salient points.[1]

Politics and economics inseparable. The notion of an economics which abstracts from ownership systems, class relations, and political power is to Marxians a contradiction in terms. As propounded in the West, it is simply a bourgeois evasion designed to veil the exploiting power of the owning class. There can be no "pure" economics. There is only political economy.

Particular interest attaches to property ownership, which is regarded as basic to the political superstructure. Private ownership and private profit are anathema because they are

---

1. For a perceptive discussion, see Wiles, *Political Economy of Communism,* chap. 3, "The Peculiarities of Marxist Economic Thought."

an integral part of an exploitative social system. State ownership is superior simply because it is a more advanced social
form, because it symbolizes and consolidates the political
triumph of the proletariat. Western doctrines of "the managerial revolution," "the unimportance of ownership," and
the like are regarded as either superficial or deliberately misleading.

Eastern economists, who may be quite flexible in discussing planning techniques, will not compromise this central
point. When they advocate greater attention to profit criteria
or greater enterprise autonomy, this has nothing to do with
private profit or *private* enterprise—a point not always clearly
understood in the West.

A dynamic, historical approach. Marxian economics, if
Ricardian in technique, is thoroughly German historical
school in spirit. It is a "stage theory" of politico-economic
development. The central problem is how different ways of
organizing production, with their associated ownership systems and political superstructure, succeed each other over
the course of time. The progression from slavery to feudalism to capitalism to socialism is regarded as historically inevitable. It is the duty of all good Marxians, however, to help
history along. This is no more inconsistent than the behavior
of Calvinists who believe in predestination but continue to
do good works.

Once socialism has been achieved, the central task is to
build a *communist* society, that is, a society in which the
productive apparatus has been so greatly enlarged that citizens can have all the goods they require without charge—"to
each according to his need." This vision of a communist
"affluent society" hovers always on the horizon of policy. And
it should be achieved *rapidly*, partly for its own sake, partly
to outstrip capitalism. Eastern political leaders are thus
"growthmen" par excellence. They worship rates of increase
in material production, and tend to worship capital accumulation as the main instrument of growth.

No scarcity concept. Marxian economics has remained pre-marginal. It has never been penetrated by the post-1870 doctrines of marginal choice, efficient resource allocation, and Pareto optimality. So when Robbins says that economics *is* the study of how scarce resources are allocated among competing uses, he is (to a Marxian) talking nonsense. It follows that there has been little interest in the economic as distinct from the accounting function of prices, and in the significance of relative prices as scarcity indicators. There is, indeed, no real Marxian microeconomics.

Egalitarianism. Marxians share with other branches of socialist thought a strong egalitarian tendency. Under communism, each will have what he needs, with an implication that needs will not vary greatly among households. During the transition stage of socialism, wage and salary differentials will be needed for incentive reasons. But this is a regrettable necessity, which should be tempered as much as possible by free or subsidized provision of basic goods and services.

Other features. Several more technical aspects of Marxian economics deserve mention. In Marx, as in Adam Smith, *production* means *material production.* Effort expended on services is unproductive. The national accounts of the Eastern countries count only material output in GNP. While such a conceptual system *need* not lead to a relative neglect of service outputs, it probably tends to do so in practice.

The *labor theory of value* bases value on cost of production; and cost includes only direct labor plus materials plus depreciation of capital goods (a using up of the labor congealed in their production). The rent and interest charges exacted by property owners under capitalism are not costs and should not be considered in socialist calculation. This view is changing, as we shall see in chapter 6; but changes have to make their way against a heavy weight of tradition.

There is also no concept of *diminishing returns to scale* of enterprise. Average cost remains constant as scale is increased. Marx may even have regarded average cost as decreasing indefinitely with scale. This is suggested by his argument that the larger capitalists would consistently outcompete and swallow up the smaller, leading to a steady increase in industrial concentration. The tendency toward "giantism" in both industrial and agricultural enterprises in the socialist countries may stem from this view.

PREDOMINANCE OF PUBLIC OWNERSHIP

Public ownership of the means of production is the hallmark of the socialist economies. Politically, there is no group of private owners whose property provides a power base independent of the state. Economically, imputation of income to property is a matter of accounting, and any income attributed to property becomes part of government revenue.

While public ownership predominates, there is some variation in the pattern among countries and among production sectors. In agriculture, there is usually coexistence of state farming, collective farming, and private farming, in proportions which vary from country to country. Under collective farming the land itself is state owned, but members of the collective have occupancy rights subject to various payments to government. They collectively own the tools, machinery, livestock, and other assets used in farm operations; and, in addition to receiving wages for work performed, they derive part of their income from the posttax profits of the farm. The "state farm" on the other hand, employs wage labor, and is organized more nearly like an industrial enterprise. It is considered a superior form in principle; but the collective farm is more congenial to peasant preferences, and so is allowed to continue as a matter of expediency. New agricultural development schemes, such as settlement of the "virgin lands" of Western Siberia, or the Chinese settlement schemes in the northwestern and northern extramural regions, are often organized as state farms. In the USSR state farms presently control about two-fifths of the sown acreage, and own about one-quarter of the livestock.

The peasants' first preference, of course, would be private farming; and in some countries, including Poland and Yugoslavia, this has been recognized by permitting most land to remain in private ownership for the time being. Moreover, even under collective farming, each farm family is usually allowed to cultivate a "private plot" of a half-acre to two acres in size. In Soviet practice, the farmer sells the produce of this plot on the local free market, and pays a modest income tax on the proceeds. Although the acreage involved is small, it produces a substantial output of fruits, vegetables, eggs, poultry, milk, and meat. Public policy has varied, at times encouraging the expansion of private plots, at other times seeking to curtail them. But in a food-scarce economy, their contribution is valuable enough so that they have been allowed to continue. In China there has been a similar ambivalence of policy and a similar persistence of private plots, which contribute importantly to the output of pigs, poultry, eggs, fruit, and vegetables.

Farm families have effective ownership of the houses which they occupy. As regards urban housing, about two-fifths of urban housing in the USSR, located mainly in the smaller towns and villages, is privately owned, and this proportion has not changed much over several decades.[2] The remaining urban families rent apartments, at heavily subsidized rates, from the enterprises for which they work, from cooperative associations, or from state agencies.

Outside agriculture, virtually one hundred percent public ownership prevails in the "commanding heights" of the economy: banking, public utilities, transportation and communication, heavy manufacturing. But in other sectors there is considerable variation. Some socialist countries have found it expedient to permit the continued existence of some private retail and service establishments, small-scale manufacturing, and even private professional practice. These serve consumers'

    2. Abram Bergson, *The Economics of Soviet Planning* (New Haven: Yale University Press, 1964), p. 24.

convenience while constituting no threat to the central apparatus of socialized production.

The study of Frederic Pryor mentioned in chapter 2, which
included five socialist countries, found that the USSR and
Bulgaria adhered most consistently to public ownership, with
"nationalization ratios" (based on employment) between 90
and 100 percent in almost all sectors. But practice in Poland,
East Germany, and Yugoslavia is more variable. Thus in services, public and private, the nationalization ratios were:
Poland 90 percent, Yugoslavia 86 percent, East Germany 84
percent; in construction, Yugoslavia 100 percent, Poland 90
percent, East Germany 67 percent; in manufacturing and
mining, East Germany 84 percent, Poland 83 percent, Yugoslavia 72 percent, with the ratio falling as low as 50 percent
in clothing, leather goods, and furniture manufacture; in
commerce and finance, Yugoslavia 79 percent, East Germany
55 percent, Poland 53 percent. These calculations, however,
do not count cooperative organizations as part of the public
sector. If they were so counted, the nationalization ratios
would be much closer to 100 percent.

EVERYONE A WAGE EARNER

Self-employment is predominant in the less developed
countries, and common in the capitalist countries; and in
both groups there is also a substantial body of employers. A
distinctive feature of socialist economic organization is that,
outside of agriculture, the great majority of people work for
a wage or salary. Executives of all socialized enterprises are
salaried people; and so are the government officials responsible for economic policy. (Strictly, everyone is in a sense a
public official, but some more so than others. In the USSR
people connected directly with producing enterprises seem to
regard themselves as "economic officials," or as we would say,
"in business." Those working in higher supervisory organizations, territorial or industrial, are "in government." Many
executives in the USSR seem to share the preference of many

American business men for an economic rather than a governmental role.)

Moreover, labor is recruited in a relatively free labor market. This constrains the primary distribution of income. The wage-salary structure must induce people to enter, and perform proficiently in, the range of occupations available at a particular time. This constraint, however, is not as binding in practice as it may appear in principle. First, there is a considerable conventional element in wage determination. Differentials which have persisted for a certain period of time tend to be regarded as "right." The labor market mechanism does not dictate that a Soviet enterprise manager must receive precisely five times as much as a factory laborer, rather than four times or six times as much. Second, over a period of years, increased supplies of labor can be channeled to shortage points through the educational system. Supply can be adapted to a fixed price rather than price being dictated by a spontaneously emerging supply.

A further consequence is that incentives to greater effort, to improvement of personal skills, to efficient management, to innovation and risk taking must take a wage form,[3] including in this bonuses, premiums, and various forms of

3. This assumes that, in Eastern as well as Western economies, productive effort is motivated primarily by income rather than by altruism and concern for the general welfare. As Professor Sir Arthur Lewis has remarked, "In a group where all the members have highly developed propensities to serve each other, men will work without comparing closely their shares in the group effort and in the group reward. But very few groups, other than the small family group itself, can rely exclusively or primarily on these ideals. . . . men put forth more effort if the fruit is to be enjoyed by themselves and by their intimate circle than if it has to be shared with a wider group." (*The Theory of Economic Growth* [Homewood, Ill.: Richard D. Irwin, 1955], p. 58.) Or see a similar comment by a leading Czech economist: "At the socialist stage of development labour is still relatively onerous (long hours) and intensive. There is a relative lack of variety, work is monotonous, and for most people, offers little creative scope. . . . Consequently, as a general rule people expend their labour for others primarily because labour is the condition for acquiring from others the use values needed by themselves" (Ota Sik in Charles H. Feinstein, ed., *Socialism, Capitalism and Economic Growth* [Cambridge University Press, 1967], p. 139).

profit sharing. Such systems are widely used in the socialist countries, both for management personnel and ordinary workers.

In agriculture, the employee of a state farm is strictly a wage earner. On collective farms, the income-sharing system may be regarded as analogous to group piecework. Each working member accumulates credit based on the amount and type of work performed, and shares in the net income of the collective in proportion to his credits.[4] The relation between effort and income is here twice diluted. First, the net income available for distribution depends on higher-level decisions about farm prices, contract deliveries to state agencies, income taxes, amounts to be set aside for reinvestment in the farm, and so on. An increase in farm output may or may not increase net income. Second, the worker's share in net income depends on quantity of work done rather than on effectiveness of this work. He has tilled so many acres of land or tended so many milk cows. But how effectively? The difficulties of supervision and quality control are akin to those of the capitalist farmer and his "hired hand." It is usually thought, with reason, that an hour of the hired hand's effort is less productive than an hour of the farmer's own time.

The Soviet collective farmer also has the option of allocating time to his private plot, where income is more directly related to output. These plots produce almost all the milk, meat, eggs, potatoes, fruits, and vegetables—that is, almost everything except cereals—consumed by the farm households. They also produce a marketable surplus, which according to a 1966 estimate accounted for 28 percent of collective farmers' cash income.[5] In China, too, peasants reportedly lavish labor, manure, and managerial attention on their private plots; and while these comprise less than 5 per-

4. This income is partly in cash and partly in kind, that is, farm produce retained for home consumption. The distribution of both kinds of income is based on labor day credits.

5. M. Makeenko, "The Economic Role of Personal Subsidiary Husbandry," *Problems of Economics,* May 1967, pp. 35–44.

cent of the arable acreage, they provide a substantially larger share of household consumption and cash income.

CENTRALIZED ECONOMIC ADMINISTRATION

The socialist economies are often termed "centrally planned economies." But centralization is a matter of degree. Planning practices differ from country to country and are evolving continuously. It is perhaps better to say that these are "guided economies," whose development is shaped in broad outline from a central point.

We begin with the traditional Soviet mechanism of economic control, which was taken over more or less intact by the East European countries in the late 1940s. This is the tradition against which "economic reformers" in the socialist countries have been reacting over the past decade or so. The main directions of reform will be considered in chapter 6. Here we stick to the "orthodox" model.

Its main features are, first, that the division of output between consumption and capital formation is centrally determined. Second, the allocation of capital among sectors and establishments is (except in Yugoslavia) *mainly* determined by the central authorities. Third, national production targets are established for a list of key commodities, usually running into several hundreds. These are firm targets for the year ahead, somewhat more tentative for years beyond that. Fourth, each producing enterprise is given a list of the outputs which it is expected to produce and the inputs which it is permitted to use. In principle, the national plan is an internally consistent aggregation of the enterprise plans. Finally, raw materials, intermediate goods, and capital goods are rationed among the using industries by administrative orders.

All this requires an elaborate administrative hierarchy, with several levels of authority between the prime minister and the plant manager. The problems of managing such a hierarchy, which exist on a smaller scale in General Motors or AT&T, are familiar: the dependence of higher levels on information filtered up from lower levels, with inevitable attenuation and distortion of the information flow: the need for some—but not too much—autonomy for lower-level officials to interpret and modify the instructions received from above; the need for an incentive structure which will induce desired behavior and deter undesirable behavior by the grassroots production managers; and so on. The hierarchy is usually constructed along product lines, under ministries in charge of specified branches of industry. In very large countries such as the USSR, however, the territorial principle competes for attention. Under Premier Khrushchev, increased responsibilities for production management were entrusted to the republic governments and to regional economic councils (sovhnarkozi) operating under them. This tendency was reversed and the ministerial structure reinstated under Premier Kosygin. But except for key products of all-Union importance, republic and local government officials retain considerable authority over goods produced and consumed within their own borders.

The position of the individual plant manager in such a control system is a large subject in itself. What is he expected to do, how much can he actually do, what incentives are offered for effective performance? Much of the recent discussion of economic reform has hinged on how far, and in what directions, to enlarge the plant manager's freedom of action. So we had best leave this subject to chapter 6, where reform proposals and actions will be discussed.

The fact that the economy is guided by administrative orders couched in physical terms implies that the role of *prices* is less important than in capitalist economies. In this connection one must distinguish several categories of price, which are regarded as having different functions:

1. *Industrial prices.* These have the accounting function of measuring the "socially necessary labor time" required to produce a unit of output. Traditionally (though practice is now changing) cost includes only direct labor, materials and

supplies, and depreciation on capital equipment. To this is added a profit margin, calculated as a percentage of variable cost rather than of capital. This serves mainly as a vehicle of capital accumulation, but can also be used via profit sharing for incentive purposes. At any rate, industrial or wholesale prices are "cost-plus" prices. In principle, demand has no influence upon them. Because of the administrative effort involved in calculating many thousands of interdependent prices, industrial price lists are usually not revised oftener than once every five years. Thus while prices may be aligned with costs at the time of each revision, they tend to diverge from them increasingly over the course of time.[6]

2. *Consumer goods prices at retail.* These prices, as is well known, contain a large excise tax element, the "turnover tax." The general level of this tax, and hence of the gap between producer and consumer prices, is a macroeconomic decision. From one standpoint, the yield of this and other taxes must be sufficient to finance planned capital accumulation plus output of public goods. From another standpoint, the price level serves to balance the money value of the planned output of consumer goods against the posttax income of wage and salary earners.

Variations in the turnover tax rate, and hence in the prices of specific consumer goods relative to cost, are designed in part to serve a *market-clearing* function. Given the demand schedule for a good, and given the quantity which the authorities have decided to produce, there is a price which will just move the available supply. If price is not set at this level, there will be either unsold "surpluses" on one hand, or "shortages" accompanied by queuing on the other. The price

6. This sketch necessarily glosses over such problems as: (1) cost differences among producers of the same product, which are particularly large in mining and other extractive industries (prevalent practice is apparently to align price with average industry cost and to subsidize high-cost producers); (2) treatment of transport costs, which are a substantial item in a large country (in the USSR uniform delivered prices throughout the country [that is, freight absorption] seems to be the general rule).

structure also serves an *income-distribution* function. Housing, most basic food and clothing items, and "merit goods" such as books and theatrical performances, are priced relatively low (though sugar, cloth, kerosene, and salt are exceptions). Luxury items usually carry higher tax rates. Moreover, within each category, the tax is often higher on the better-quality items—black bread carries a lower tax than white bread. The result is to make the distribution of real income more nearly equal than the distribution of money income. This is a more thoroughgoing application of a principle which is used also in capitalist economies, where luxury goods are sometimes subjected to special taxation.

3. *Farm procurement prices* determine the terms of trade between the farm and city populations. On the other side, prices are the main incentive for farm production. These two functions are somewhat in conflict—lower food costs for urban wage earners mean lower incomes and less incentive for farmers.

4. *Foreign trade prices* are set by trade agreements, and may be quite different from domestic prices for the same goods, the differences being absorbed by taxes or subsidies. A common practice is to use world market prices for goods which are sufficiently standardized and widely traded to make this feasible.

The Yugoslav economy is substantially less centralized than the other East European economies; and we may comment briefly on its distinctive characteristics.[7] Agriculture, as noted earlier, is predominantly in private hands. In addition, private ownership is permitted for firms with less than five employees. There were estimated in 1968 to be about 100,000 such handicrafts units, mainly in light industry. Larger industrial enterprises, some 2,500 in number, are public but "their property is not owned by the state but is held in trust

7. For a good brief description, see Joel Dirlam, "Problems of Market Power and Public Policy in Yugoslavia," in Morris Bornstein, ed., *Comparative Economic Systems: Models and Cases* (Homewood, Ill.: Richard D. Irwin, 1969).

by the firm for society." De facto control rests with workers in the enterprise, who elect a workers' council which in turn chooses a management committee. The choice of a director for the enterprise must be approved by the workers' council, and in effect by the local government of the area. New enterprises may be launched by existing enterprises, trade associations, the local, republic (= state), or federal governments, or by private citizens.

Once established, the enterprise is expected to be self-financing. It chooses its own outputs, sets prices, and markets its products (with some regulation by higher bodies where foreign trade is involved). Whatever income remains after production expenses and profit taxes may be divided between reinvestment and payments to workers in whatever proportion the enterprise decides. Investment funds may also be secured from local or republic governments or by borrowing from the state bank. Thus, while the federal budget is important in launching major infrastructure projects, it does not handle as large a percentage of investment funds as in the other Eastern countries.

Given this degree of enterprise autonomy, "economic planning" takes on a quite different content. There is no list of physical output targets enforced on the enterprises. Central guidance operates mainly through general fiscal and monetary measures, and through "indicative planning" not unlike that found in some Western countries. As a natural consequence, Yugoslavia has some of the problems encountered in Western economies. It has inflationary pressure. It has balance-of-payments difficulties. It has at times had substantial unemployment. But it has also maintained an unusually high growth rate over the past twenty years.

Industrial organization and planning procedures in China also depart substantially from the Soviet pattern.[8] No five-

8. See in this connection Audrey Donnithorne, *China's Economic System* (London: Allen and Unwin, 1967), chap. 6, 7, 17. See also Dwight H. Perkins, "Industrial Planning and Management," in Alexander Eckstein, Walter Galenson, and T. C. Liu, eds., *Economic Trends in Communist China* (Chicago: Aldine, 1968).

year plans have been issued since the beginning of the "Great Leap Forward" in 1958. It is not clear that even comprehensive annual plans exist at the present time. National output targets are announced, but only for two to three hundred products, compared with more than fifteen hundred products in the USSR. The linkage between these national targets and individual enterprise plans, and the degree of central control over distribution of materials and components, appear weaker than in the European socialist countries.

Throughout Chinese history, the central government has had a problem of maintaining control over regional leaders throughout the vast extent of the country; and most of the time regional autonomy has prevailed. The Communist victory of 1949 ushered in a period of tighter central control, and during the first five-year plan period (1952–57) most industrial enterprises operated under ministries in Peking. In 1957, however, about 80 percent of these enterprises, including virtually all of light industry, were transferred to provincial jurisdiction. Even the enterprises retained by central government are subject to some measure of provincial control under a system of "double-track" supervision; and they remit 20 percent of their profits plus depreciation allowances to the provincial authorities. Many industrial enterprises of smaller scale are operated by country governments or by communes. All in all, geographic decentralization has an importance which it never attained in the USSR even during the Khrushchev period.

Cost calculations in Chinese enterprises are strictly orthodox, omitting capital and rental charges. So, too, is the strong emphasis on physical output as the test of enterprise performance. Efforts to shift this emphasis to overall profitability, along the lines of Soviet and East European reform proposals, have been sternly rebuffed. Price and tax policies also differ substantially from Soviet practice. Instead of the rather low profit margin included in Soviet prices, Chinese profit margins are large—so large that they typically cover the costs of even the least efficient enterprises in an industry. Enterprises must turn over the great bulk of their profits, *plus depreciation allowances,* to the central or lower governments as the case may be. These remittances provide about two-thirds of the revenue of the central government, while sales or excise taxes provide only about one-quarter.

A small proportion of profits, and particularly of above-plan profits, may be retained by the enterprise; but this appears to be less than 10 percent of the total. Thus the great bulk of investment is financed from government allocations. Managers do not receive personal bonuses for plan fulfilment or overfulfilment, again in contrast to Soviet practice. Socialist enthusiasm plus Party supervision are counted on to provide adequate incentives for efficient performance.

EXCESS DEMAND AND PLANNING TENSION

Unlike capitalist economies, the socialist economies rarely suffer from a deficiency of aggregate demand. On the contrary, they are typically in a situation of excess demand and inflationary pressure. The effort to repress this through administered prices leads to "shortages" of almost everything in the economy. Kornai has aptly labeled this pervasive sellers' market a "suction economy." The opposite situation, which he believes usually prevails under capitalism, he terms a "pressure economy"—pressure of would-be sellers who are operating below capacity and hence compete actively for buyers.[9]

There appear to be several reasons for chronic excess demand. One contributing factor is wage pressure. Labor is scarce along with other inputs; and in a tight labor market, socialist managers compete for workers in familiar ways. They overclassify jobs, overrate workers' qualifications, and permit loose piece rates. If they exceed their planned wage budget, this is a minor offense in a system oriented toward maximum output. Under capitalism, the employer usually has *some*

9. Kornai, *Anti-Equilibrium,* chap. 19.

incentive to resist the advance of wages. In a socialist economy, this incentive is largely absent.

Consumer income thus tends to rise faster than the money
value of available consumer goods. Retail price increases are
unpopular, and in any event take time. The lag of prices behind incomes intensifies the problem of queuing, informal
rationing, and disappointment of consumers' buying plans.

A second factor is the tendency to set higher output targets
than can be attained with available plant capacity and input
supplies. This is often termed "planning tension," or a tendency toward "taut plans." Enterprises straining toward these
targets find themselves chronically short of basic materials
and intermediate products. This produces a sellers' market
for everything from raw materials through to finished goods.

A third factor is overambitious investment programs,
which exceed the capacity of construction enterprises and of
the machinery and building materials industries. This often
leads to stretching-out of construction projects beyond the
targeted completion date. The backlog of delayed work from
previous periods, when added to the new projects initiated
in the present period, intensifies pressure on the investment
goods industries.

These pressures interact in a complicated way. The effort
to relieve consumer goods shortages by new plant construction intensifies the pressure in the investment sector. The
fact that workers in the investment industries are earning
current income, while the increased outflow of consumer
products is long delayed, increases the pressure in consumer
markets.

The pervasiveness of sellers' markets throughout the economy has important side effects. In consumer markets, the fact
that buyers must court sellers rather than vice versa imposes
costs on consumers which, however, are not counted as costs
in national economic calculations. Consumers must spend
considerable time in search activity and in queuing. There is
often a long lag between a consumer's decision to buy an item
and his ability to do so. Beyond a certain point he will aban-

don his original intention and switch to some item more readily available, thus ending in a less preferred position.

The fact that consumers must buy what is available removes the incentive for producers to take an interest in quality, variety, and styling of consumer goods. It also leaves little incentive for major product innovations; and it is perhaps significant that few such innovations have originated in the socialist countries.

Some of the familiar inefficiencies of industrial operation, which are particularly well documented for the Soviet Union, should perhaps be attributed to excess demand rather than to centralized administration per se. Chronic shortage of inputs presents the danger that production may actually break down from time to time. It prevents the plant manager from selecting the least-cost combination of inputs, even if he had the knowledge and authority to do so. The effort to avert shortages leads to material hoarding, which ties up an undue amount of working capital in inventories. It also leads enterprises to strive for self-sufficiency by producing their own materials, tools, and production components whenever possible. This in turn means a failure to take full advantage of industrial specialization and potential economies of scale. The tendency toward enterprise self-sufficiency is reported to have gone especially far in China, partly because of the geographic decentralization already noted, and perhaps partly because the allocation of materials is not yet as well organized as in the European socialist countries.

THE LEVEL AND COMPOSITION OF OUTPUT

Comparison of per capita output in capitalist and socialist economies is a specialized art. The socialist countries count only "material production" as part of GNP, which excludes the labor service component of defense, education and health, passenger transportation, and other public and private services. These have to be estimated and added to secure a GNP total comparable with Western totals. There are also the usual difficulties associated with valuation: differing "market baskets," price-index biases, intercurrency conversions, and so on.

Despite these difficulties, one can conclude that: (1) There is marked variation of per capita income levels among the socialist economies. Per capita income in Czechoslovakia and East Germany is more than double that of Bulgaria and Romania. The spread is roughly the same as that between the United States and Italy. (2) The median income level of the socialist countries is substantially below that of the capitalist countries. It has been estimated that, in the early 1960s, Czechoslovakia and East Germany were considerably below the level of West Germany and even farther below the United States and Canada. The USSR was at about the level of Italy, while Bulgaria and Romania were comparable to Greece.[10] This income difference, of course, is not necessarily linked to the difference in economic system. More significant is the fact that the socialist countries are latecomers to modern economic growth, and have been industrializing for a relatively short period.

Except for China and other socialist LDCs, the socialist countries are middle-income countries. Kuznets and others have shown that the distribution of national output among productive sectors is related systematically to the level of per capita output. The socialist economies have some of the earmarks of middle-income countries, notably a continued prominence of agriculture. In these countries, except for Czechoslovakia and East Germany, agriculture contributes 20 to 30 percent of GNP, compared with 10 percent or so in the capitalist countries.

10. Frederic L. Pryor, *Public Expenditures in Communist and Capitalist Nations* (Homewood, Ill.: Richard D. Irwin, 1968), p. 401. See also Maurice Ernst, "Postwar Economic Growth in Eastern Europe," in George R. Feiwel, ed., *New Currents in Soviet-Type Economies:* A Reader (Scranton, Pa.: International Textbook, 1968), pp. 75–112. Ernst estimates that, on the basis of adjusted exchange rates, the East European countries (excluding the USSR) had an average per capita income in 1963 of 1,020 U.S. dollars compared with an average of 1,680 dollars for the West European countries (excluding the U.K.).

There are, however, substantial differences between Eastern output patterns and those of middle-income economies (contemporary or historical) in the West. This is true, first, as regards the distribution of manufacturing between "heavy" and "light" industry. As income levels have risen in the capitalist countries, heavy industry has expanded proportionately faster than light industry, and in the richest countries now dominates the manufacturing sector. But this is a relatively recent phenomenon. The socialist countries are "prematurely heavy-industry oriented"; that is, the relative weight of heavy industry in their manufacturing sectors is greater than one would expect from their income level. This stems from policies of forced industrialization and rapid capital formation, with heavy industry regarded as the essential foundation of the economy.

Second, trade and services (business services, repair services, personal services) have considerably less weight than is usual at medium-income levels. This reflects a policy judgment that service outputs are less important than material outputs, or at any rate less strategic at this stage of development. It may also reflect the fact that small-scale trade and service establishments are less amenable to centralized direction than are large industrial concerns.

Third, there is an unusually wide gap between the percentage of national output produced in agriculture and the (higher) percentage of labor force employed in agriculture. This amounts to saying that the productivity gap between agriculture and nonagriculture, which exists in almost all countries, is unusually wide in the socialist economies.

Fourth, the socialist economies produce a variety of public and quasi-public goods, including general administration, defense, policing, urban services, health care, education, and so on. This corresponds more or less to "public sector output" in the Western sense. (In the West, however, education and some other services are privately produced, in part, so that private and public output must be added to obtain East-West comparisons of service levels.)

How is this category of output affected by the politico-
economic regime? Do the socialist countries devote more or
less resources to producing public and quasi-public goods
than do capitalist countries *at the same income level?* Musgrave has investigated[11] this question on theoretical grounds,
concluding that not much can be said about it a priori. Pryor
has made a comparative statistical analysis of seven Eastern
and seven Western economies, trying to separate the effect of
differing regimes from that of per capita income and other
relevant variables. He concludes that the economic system
variable is significant for "education, research and development, nonmilitary external security, and possibly internal
security excluding traffic control."[12] The total amount of
education provided is roughly the same in the two systems,
for comparable levels of per capita income; but a larger share
is privately financed in the Western countries. For the other
services mentioned, the expenditure/GNP ratio is higher in
the East. On the other hand, the economic system variable is
not significant for expenditures on defense, welfare, and
health. Here the variation among countries with the same
economic system is much greater than the variation between
the two systems per se.

BUILT-IN CAPITAL ACCUMULATION

Any growing economy needs mechanisms for capital
accumulation. The alternatives are well known: discretionary
household saving; automatic or institutionalized household
saving via life insurance, annuity and pension systems, and
mortgage payments; reinvestment of business profits; and
savings effectuated through the government budget. A distinctive feature of the socialist economies is their heavy reliance on the last of these channels.

From one standpoint, the heart of the matter is that physi-

11. Richard A. Musgrave, *Fiscal Systems* (New Haven: Yale University
Press, 1969), chap. 1.
12. Pryor, *Public Expenditure*, pp. 284–85.

cal output is planned. The planned production of capital goods relative to other goods determines the real capital formation rate. But money flows are also important in an economy which uses monetary accounting and money income payments. On one side, the flow of money income to consumers, minus income taxes and personal savings, should equal the retail value of consumer goods and services. On the other side, the excess of government revenue over current expenditure, plus reinvestment by enterprises, should equal the money value of inventory accumulation plus fixed capital formation. To the extent that the planned or ex ante financial flows fail to anticipate the actual good flows over the planning period, financial maladjustments will arise en route to the ex post identities.

State revenues come partly from direct taxation—on enterprise profits, on the cash income of collective farms, and on personal incomes. The other main revenue-producer is the turnover tax, which closes the gap between the production cost of consumer goods and the higher level of retail prices. This is the financial counterpart of physical production plans which, by restricting the output of consumer goods, necessitate high retail prices to clear the market.

In this as in other respects, the Yugoslav system is decidedly different. Enterprises are permitted to earn substantial profits and to retain part of these for reinvestment. Enterprise self-financing plus state bank loans are much more important than in the other Eastern countries. And government allocations for investment come in large measure from the republic and local governments rather than from the federal government. In China, too, a large proportion of investment allocations come from provincial and the lower levels of government.

Granted the difficulties of national account comparisons, it appears that capital formation rates in the socialist economies are somewhat higher than in the West. In the USSR and five East European countries, over the years 1965–68, gross fixed capital formation as a percentage of GNP averaged about 28 percent, ranging from about 22 percent in East Germany to 32 percent in Bulgaria and Hungary.[13] For the capitalist economies, over the period 1955–65, the median capital formation ratio was about 23 percent.[14] Several capitalist countries, however, were operating in the "socialist range," including Japan (32.5 percent), Norway (30.2 percent), Australia (26.7 percent). West Germany (25.9 percent), and Holland (25.9 percent).

One should remember, however, that a country's capital formation rate normally varies positively with its per capita income. The middle-income socialist countries would on this account be expected to have a considerably lower capital formation rate than the capitalist countries. The fact that their rate is actually somewhat higher testifies both to the importance they attach to capital formation as a policy target and to the effectiveness of their mechanisms for achieving it.

A DISTINCTIVE GROWTH PATTERN

The socialist economies, like the capitalist economies, have built-in growth capacity. Whether, on the average, national growth rates are higher in the East than in the West is difficult to say. The difference in GNP concepts and measures has already been noted. Since service outputs have grown less rapidly than goods outputs in the socialist countries, the Western definition of GNP puts them in a less favorable light than their own definition would do. Moreover, the unusually rapid shifts in the *composition* of output in the socialist economies raise difficult problems of aggregation and valuation. In the Soviet case, it is well known that a weighting by 1928 prices, 1937 prices, or 1950 prices produces decidedly different growth rates; and the procedure of averaging two or more conflicting results is not very satisfactory.

13. U.N. Economic Commission for Europe, *Economic Survey of Europe in 1968* (New York: 1969), pp. 144–45. See also Ernst, "Postwar Economic Growth," p. 94.

14. Data calculated from U.N. Yearbook of National Accounts.

Finally, since growth rates vary over time, a period of several decades is needed for reliable conclusions. A 1950–60 comparison would show a higher median growth rate in the socialist countries. But growth in the USSR and most of the East European countries has been slower during the 1960s, and a 1960–70 comparison would show them in a less favorable light. At present one can say only that growth rates vary considerably among the Eastern economies, as they do in the West. It is possible, but not at all certain, that their median growth rate will turn out to be higher over a generation or more.[15]

Economic growth in the East has several interesting features. First, growth rates differ substantially among economic sectors. The sector rates diverge more widely than in Western economies, which makes the overall rate harder to interpret. If heavy industry output rises at 15 percent per year, light industry output at 8 percent, agricultural output at 4 percent, and output of nongovernmental services at 2 percent, a statement that total output is rising at 5 percent loses some of its meaning. The picture is one of an economy moving forward rapidly in some sectors but not in others. This results in large measure from policy decisions, notably the well-known preference for heavy industry. In the USSR and Eastern Europe, industry typically receives about half of the annual investment fund; and of this, 85 to 90 percent goes into heavy industry. These proportions have not changed very much in the past twenty years.[16]

Second, growth rates vary decidedly over time. Years of unusually rapid growth are sometimes followed by years of near-stagnation. Indeed, one analyst has concluded that the

15. Some estimates by Maurice Ernst for the years 1951–64 appear in his article cited above. The unweighted average of country growth rates in GNP over this period was 5.1 percent for the East European countries (excluding the USSR) and 5.0 percent for the West European countries (excluding the U.K.). Inclusion of the USSR on one hand and the U.K., U.S., Canada, Australia, and Japan on the other would make the comparison slightly more favorable to the Eastern countries.

16. UNECE, *Economic Bulletin for Europe* 18, no. 1 (1966): 40–45.

year-to-year variance of output is now wider in the socialist than in the capitalist countries.[17] The presumption that growth which is centrally directed will be more consistent over time is not necessarily warranted. A Czech economist, Josef Goldmann, has argued that output fluctuations are natural in a relatively small, industrially developed, socialist country such as Czechoslovakia. Manufacturing growth in excess of some optimum rate will encounter bottlenecks arising from an inadequate rate of increase in domestic raw material supplies, foodstuffs, and imported materials and components.

"The disproportions and acute economic difficulties, ensuing from an above-optimum rate of growth, can only be overcome by slowing down the pace of economic development. This breathing period will continue until new investment projects, initiated in the preceding period, predominantly in the basic industries, will successively mature and go into operation. As a result of both, the slow-down in growth and the contribution of new output facilities, the supply situation will gradually improve. Thus, conditions will be set up which . . . will permit such a quasi-cycle to restart again."[18]

Goldmann documents the existence of such cycles of faster and slower growth in Poland, Hungary, and Czechoslovakia during the years 1950–65. An actual decline of output from one year to the next is unusual, though it apparently occurred in Hungary in 1954–55 and 1961; and in Czechoslovakia in 1954 and 1962–63. In the capitalist countries, too, aggregate fluctuations now take mainly the form of variations in the growth rate, and an absolute decline of output is rare.

17. George J. Staller, "Fluctuations in Economic Activity: Planned and Free Market Economies, 1950–1960," *American Economic Review*, June 1964, pp. 385–95. The same impression of large year-to-year changes in national growth rates is obtained from "A Fifteen-Year Review of Investment and Output in Eastern Europe and the Soviet Union," UNECE, *Economic Bulletin for Europe* 18, no. 1, (1966): esp. 31–44.

18. Josef Goldmann, "Fluctuations and Trends in the Rate of Economic Growth in Some Socialist Countries," in Feiwel, p. 117.

The socialist economies do not collect information on unemployment, which is sometimes regarded as nonexistent by definition. Professor Emily Brown's study[19] suggests that labor markets in the USSR show many of the phenomena observed in the West: substantial labor turnover, despite the best efforts of personnel managers; substantial rural-urban and interregional migration; occasional displacement of labor by technological or locational changes; and a level of frictional unemployment perhaps comparable with that observed in capitalist countries.

The unorthodox Yugoslavs do collect and publish unemployment statistics. During the 1950s unemployment in nonagricultural activities varied between 3 and 5 percent.[20] When the pace of industrialization slowed in the early 1960s, however, unemployment rose to 5.9 percent in 1961 and 6.8 percent in 1963. Dirlam reports it as in the neighborhood of 8 percent in 1968. During these years, a continued influx from the countryside was swelling the labor force more rapidly than new industrial jobs were being created. In this respect, Yugoslavia might be classed with the less developed countries, many of which are experiencing a similar phenomenon.

Statistically, growth can be separated into rates of increase in factor supplies and "the residual," also termed the rate of increase in total factor productivity. Bergson has applied this technique to growth in the USSR since 1928; and a number of Soviet and East European economists have recently begun to make similar calculations.[21]

Growth of inputs has clearly been very important. The high

19. Emily C. Brown, *Soviet Trade Unions and Labor Relations* (Cambridge: Harvard University Press, 1966), chap. 2.
20. Robert G. Livingston, "Yugoslavian Unemployment Trends," *Monthly Labor Review*, July 1964, pp. 756–62.
21. See Abram Bergson, *The Real National Income of Soviet Russia Since 1928* (Cambridge: University Press, 1961; Abram Bergson and Simon Kuznets, eds., *Economic Trends in the Soviet Union* (Cambridge: Harvard University Press, 1963); F. G. Denton, "A Recent Study of Soviet Economic Growth, 1951–63," *Soviet Studies*, April 1968, pp. 501–09; and A. Miklos, and I. Zhukova, "Experiences in Economic Growth in Certain CMEA Countries," *Acta Oeconomica, 1968, 3.*

rate of physical capital formation has already been noted. The existence of a large agricultural population has made it possible to increase the industrial labor force very rapidly by transferring labor out of agriculture, though lagging agricultural productivity has acted as a constraint. There has also been heavy investment in education, with a strong vocational orientation, so that the quality of the urban labor force has risen rapidly.

The rate of increase in factor productivity has varied considerably. Bergson found that, in the USSR, factor productivity rose scarcely at all during the 1930s, an increase in the industrial sector being almost offset by a decline in agriculture. During the 1950s, on the other hand, it rose at some 3 percent per year, and accounted for about 40 percent of the output increase. During the 1960s, however, the rise of factor productivity has slowed down once more; and it is mainly this, rather than a reduced rate of increase in factor supplies, which has produced a retardation in the Soviet growth rate.

Balassa has compared the increase of output and total factor productivity in manufacturing only from 1953–65 in five East European economies (Bulgaria, Czechoslovakia, Hungary, Poland, and Romania) and four West European countries at a comparable level of development (Spain, Greece, Norway, and Ireland). While the rate of output increase was somewhat higher in the Eastern countries, this was due entirely to more rapid growth of factor inputs. The rate of increase in total factor productivity was almost identical for the two groups.[22]

22. Bela Balassa, "Growth Performance of East European Economies and Comparable West European Countries," *American Economic Review Proceedings*, May 1970, pp. 314–20. An interesting feature of the results is that the rate of increase of factor productivity turns out to be highly correlated with the rate of increase of inputs, and both are associated with level of per capita income. Thus the least developed countries in both groups (Bulgaria, Romania, Greece, and Spain) had the highest rates of increase in manufacturing output, manufacturing inputs, and factor productivity. This "level of development" effect seems clearly to overshadow any "economic systems" effect.

Such results, of course, do not really explain what has happened. Total factor productivity is a "black box." We can give names to some of the items in the box, and, for the Western economies, can begin to assess their relative importance. But for the Eastern economies this task lies mainly in the future.

TRADE LEVELS AND PATTERNS

In interpreting trade levels and patterns in the socialist economies, one cannot ascribe everything one observes to the existence of central planning. Two other considerations are important. First, very large economies tend to be relatively self-contained. Thus it is natural that China and USSR should have much lower trade ratios than Czechoslovakia and Romania. Second, most of the socialist countries are starting from a low level of industrial development, and are undergoing a process of forced-draft industrialization not unlike that being attempted in some of the less developed countries. They are making a strenuous effort at import substitution in heavy industry as well as consumer goods. This has some of the same effects observed in semiindustrialized countries outside the socialist group.[23]

There are aspects of the planning system, however, which affect both the level and pattern of trade. First, the fact that foreign demand is less predictable than domestic demand makes it difficult to fit into a planning system in which predictability and control are of the essence. The trade volume of the socialist countries appears to be considerably more unstable from year to year than that of the Western countries.[24] Montias has shown, for example, that the less industrialized countries of Eastern Europe have used machinery imports as "filler," to close the gap between investment requirements and the output of domestic machinery industries,

23. This point is emphasized by Bela Balassa in "Growth Strategies in Semi-Industrial Countries," pp. 24–47.
24. George J. Staller, "Patterns of Stability in Foreign Trade, OECD and COMECON," *American Economic Review*, Sept. 1967, pp. 897–88.

which has been growing rapidly as part of the industrialization drive. There are considerable fluctuations in investment from year to year, and this leads to even larger fluctuations in machinery imports.[25] The sudden loss of an export market does not have the repercussions on domestic income and employment which would result in a capitalist country under either the classical or Keynesian adjustment mechanisms. It is quite possible in principle to shift resources to other, though less preferable, uses. But this is still a nuisance from an administrative standpoint, and so risk avoidance may induce an antitrade bias in planning decisions.

Second, the East European currencies are not convertible, even with each other. If Poland ends up holding a surplus of Hungarian forints, it cannot be sure of being able to spend them even in Hungary, since any foreign purchase of goods requires state permission. This situation, which has been termed "commodity inconvertibility," intensifies the inconvertibility of currencies. It is risky for one country to extend credit to another, since it cannot be sure in what commodities or at what prices it may be able to get repayment.

Trade thus takes the form of bilateral negotiation among pairs of countries, with an effort to achieve balance on an annual basis. This is a quite cumbersome and bureaucratic procedure. It starts from an analysis of the imports needed to meet the production plan, and a similar analysis of physical export availabilities. As Wiles points out, quantities are decided before prices. Foreign trade prices are arbitrary in the sense that there is no need for them to correspond with domestic prices, since the subsidies (and profits) of the state trading organization act as a buffer. But the fact that domestic prices in the socialist countries do not accurately measure real resource costs makes it difficult for each country to judge

25. John M. Montias, "Socialist Industrialization and Trade in Machinery Products: An Analysis Based on the Experience of Bulgaria, Poland, and Rumania," in Alan A. Brown and Egan Neuberger, eds., *International Trade and Central Planning* (Berkeley and Los Angeles: University of California Press, 1968).

what it can advantageously export and import. Moreover, since price ratios among commodities differ from country to country, there is a problem of agreeing on equitable terms of exchange.

The common way around this problem has been to adopt world market prices as a reference point. But once it has been agreed that world prices of, say, 1967 will be taken as a benchmark, these prices are apt to be used for years at a time (as is true also of domestic price schedules). During this period the "official" 1967 prices may diverge substantially from current world market prices as well as from price relations in the trading countries. Moreover, the world price is only a starting point for further bargaining, so that the actual trade prices may be considerably different. Exporting countries are in a monopoly, or at least an oligopoly, position; and this raises a question whether any of the socialist countries has been able to gain a persistent advantage over the others. The Soviet Union, which might be expected to have greatest bargaining power, has in Wiles's judgment not gained any consistent advantage in prices, though it has sometimes insisted on larger deliveries than its trading partners might have preferred to make at the bargained price.[26] He hazards a further estimate that East Germany and Czechoslovakia (both major exporters of machinery and other manufactures) may have been exploited by the other members of the group, while Bulgaria may have enjoyed favored price treatment.

We have already noted that the socialist economies are marked by persistent excess demand, associated with "taut" plans and ambitious growth strategies. This creates strong pressure for imports, combined with a reluctance to export goods (say, foodstuffs) which could be used advantageously at home. In capitalist countries, exports tend to be regarded as desirable per se, while imports are a menace to home in-

26. Peter J. D. Wiles, *Communist International Economics* (New York: Praeger, 1968), chap. 9.

dustries. In the socialist countries this preference is reversed. Exports are a regrettable necessity whose only function is to pay for essential imports; and this may lead to a failure to push export production aggressively. Moreover, the individual producing enterprise in a socialist economy has no incentive to export, since it sells to the foreign trade organization at the domestic price, and in any event can usually market its full output at home.

In view of all this, it is not surprising that trade ratios (exports plus imports divided by GNP) in the East are somewhat lower than in Western countries of comparable size. The Soviet ratio of about 5 percent is well below the 8 percent figure for the United States. As regards the East European countries, Pryor has estimated that in 1928 their trade ratios did not differ significantly from those of comparable West European countries. But in the 1950s, after the change in regime, they were only 50 to 60 percent as high as those of Western countries of similar size and income level.[27] This situation seems to have continued at least through the early 1960s.

It is not clear that the socialist countries aim at reducing the trade ratio as an end in itself. But there are strong nationalist aspirations toward across-the-board industrialization as a basis of economic and military power, which are voiced in Eastern Europe in much the same terms as in the LDCs. Like many of the LDCs, the Eastern countries seem to prefer home production over imports, manufacturing over agriculture, heavy industry over light industry. Such a preference pattern, while it may increase trade in the early stages of import substitution, tends to reduce it eventually. The low trade ratios can thus be interpreted as ex post autarky, something which grows out of other features of the system, rather than as an ex ante policy objective.

27. Frederic L. Pryor, "Discussion," Brown and Neuberger, *International Trade and Central Planning* pp. 163–64. Compare, however, the contrasting opinion of Wiles (*Communist International Economics*, chap. 15.) that Eastern ratios were not out of line in the early 1960s.

Turning from the level to the structure of trade, about two-thirds of socialist trade is with other socialist countries, about one-quarter is East-West trade, and about 10 percent is trade with the less developed countries. The East-West proportion was substantially higher in the 1960s than in the 1950s, and may continue to increase gradually. There has been a particularly marked shift in Chinese trade since the Sino-Soviet split. About two-thirds of China's trade is now with nonsocialist countries.

East-West trade has been hampered by political attitudes: reluctance of the Eastern countries to become dependent on a capitalist world which might suddenly turn hostile, and on the other side the Western embargo on "strategic" exports to the East. But probably a more serious obstacle is lack in the socialist countries of attractive export products. Traditionally, the East European countries were the breadbasket of Europe; but most of the Western European countries now have burdensome surpluses of agricultural products. In most lines of manfacturing, Eastern quality standards would have to be raised considerably to make their products competitive in Western markets.

Within the socialist group, trade is dominated by exchange of foodstuffs and raw materials against machinery and to a lesser extent finished consumer goods. East Germany and Czechoslovakia, the most heavily industrialized countries of the group, are the major machinery exporters. The USSR functions mainly as a raw materials supplier, and imports both machinery and manufactured consumer goods from Eastern Europe. As all members of the group become increasingly industrialized, however, East Germany and Czechoslovakia face a serious problem of how to use their machine-building capacity, and this has already generated considerable intercountry tension. It would be convenient if these countries could continue large-scale exports of machinery to the other East European countries in exchange for food and raw materials, and they tend to advocate "socialist division of labor" along these lines. But Romania does not

want to remain a hewer of wood and drawer of water for
the Czechs and Germans, any more than Brazil wants to
occupy this position vis-à-vis the United States. The arguments of contemporary Romanian economists on this point
do not read very differently from those of Manoilescu, Rosen-
stein-Rodan, and others in presocialist days. Indeed, economic writings in the East European countries, while all
professing adherence to socialist fraternity and cooperation,
carry strong overtones of national interest.[28] Chinese leaders
have also complained frequently that the USSR desires a division of labor which would retard China's industrial development; and this must have been an important factor contributing to the breakdown of relations from 1960 onward.[29]

Such cleavages of interest have prevented the Committee
on Mutual Economic Assistance (COMECON) from developing into a supranational planning organization. It has remained a loose framework within which the members negotiate bilateral agreements on specific projects. It is much closer
to being a GATT than to being an EEC. A large number of
bilateral agreements have been concluded: mixed companies,
credits by country A for exploitation of natural resources in
country B which are then exported in part to country A,
cooperation in canal development and border-area water
systems, specialization and exchange of components in par-

28. For documentation of this point, with particular reference to
Czech and Romanian writings, see John Michael Montias, *Economic
Development in Communist Rumania*. (Cambridge: M.I.T. Press, 1967),
chap. 4.

29. "You constantly accuse us of 'going it alone' and claim that you
stand for extensive economic ties and divisions of labor among the socialist countries. But what is your actual record in this respect?

"You infringe the independence and sovereignty of fraternal countries
and oppose their efforts to develop their economy on an independent
basis in accordance with their own needs and potentialities.

"You bully those fraternal countries whose economies are less advanced
and oppose their policy of industrialization and try to force them to remain agricultural countries and serve as your sources of raw material
and as outlets for your goods."

(Letter from Communist Party of China to Communist Party of the
USSR, cited in Eckstein, Galenson, and Liu, *Economic Trends*, p. 554.)

ticular types of machine production.[30] But these are not in any realistic sense accomplishments of COMECON.

MULTIPLE INSTRUMENTS FOR INCOME DISTRIBUTION

In capitalist economies, the main instrument for altering the market-determined distribution of income is the personal income tax. In socialist economies, on the other hand, there are ways of controlling the pretax distribution directly, so that income taxation is less important. The USSR levies a flat percentage tax at a low level, mainly to achieve a macroeconomic balance rather than as a measure of distributive policy.

The main policies affecting income distribution are:

1. *Farm price policy* and related measures. Under collective farming, rural incomes are under close control. By varying the quantities of produce which must be delivered to state purchasing agencies, the prices paid for this produce, the charges for machinery, fertilizers, and other state-supplied inputs, and the rate of income taxation, average rural incomes can be varied relative to urban incomes. It is a plausible hypothesis that agricultural policy in the socialist countries has typically worked against the farmer, and has held his relative income below what it would have been in an unregulated market. (In capitalist countries farm prices are equally political, but price support systems are usually designed to *raise* farm incomes.) The economic reasons for taxing agriculture to finance industrial development are probably reinforced by ideological considerations. Agriculture is a "backward sector," in ownership terms as well as productivity terms, which is tolerated but not really approved. The urban workers, main pillar of the new socialist society, are favored by being supplied with low-cost foodstuffs.

2. *The wage-salary structure*. Wage and salary scales are

30. For illustrations, see Wiles, *Communist International Economics*, chap. 12.

centrally determined. Yet at the same time enterprises must bid for labor in a tight market. The "scarcity wages" which the market would tend to establish must thus be considered in drafting the centrally determined wage schedules. Moreover, competition for labor in an overscheduled economy leads to overpayment of official scales in ways quite familiar in the West, such as overclassification of jobs and loosening of piece rates.

The wage structure of the Soviet Union has been studied more thoroughly than those of the other socialist countries. Wage differentials among manual workers are in expected directions—substantial skill differentials, a premium for heavy industry over light industry, sizeable differentials for work in remote and unattractive regions of the country. Skill differentials were widened deliberately in the 1930s as a recruitment device, and this tendency continued until the midfifties. More recently, with the much-expanded educational and training system turning out larger supplies of skilled labor, there has been some tendency toward a narrowing of differentials. But they remain considerably wider than in most of the capitalist countries.

Salaries, on the other hand, are not as high relative to wages as in the West. Managerial salaries appear rather modest by Western standards. Professional salaries, including those of doctors and other medical workers, are not as much above the manual level as in capitalist countries. This is partly because of the vast educational effort which has been going on since about 1930; but it is also because of the fuller mobilization of women's work potential, and the unusually wide range of occupations open to women. In the capitalist countries, the percentage of all women aged 15 and over who are in the labor force is typically in the range of 30 to 40. In the socialist economies, the corresponding ratios are typically between 50 and 70 percent. The USSR in 1959 had an overall female labor force participation rate of 66.8 percent, with rates above 75 percent in the age groups 20–50. Moreover, women constitute a high proportion of the technical and professional workers. In 1964, out of all employed persons with university and secondary specialist training, women formed 31 percent of the engineers, 41 percent of the agricultural engineers and veterinarians, 63 percent of the economists, statisticians, and commodity experts, 68 percent of the teachers, librarians, and cultural officers, and 74 percent of the doctors (excluding dentists).[31]

This enlargement of the supply of talent available to the professions has doubtless tended to depress their relative earnings. Clerical salaries, too, are generally below the level of semiskilled factory labor. The supply of girls who prefer a "nice" job in the office to work on the factory floor is apparently large enough to permit this adverse differential.

Measures of earnings dispersion for the entire labor force are not readily available. Data assembled by the U.N. Economic Commission for Europe for a number of East European and West European countries, however, make possible a very rough comparison of the *distribution of wage-salary income among households*.[32] The percentage of all wage-salary income received by the top 5 percent of households was as follows: United Kingdom, 1963–64, 13.2 percent; West Germany, 1964, 13.6 percent; Netherlands, 1962, 18.8 percent; France, 1962, 19.0 percent; Sweden, 1963, 16.2 percent; Hungary, 1962, 10.4 percent; Czechoslovakia, 1958, 9.8 percent; East Germany, 9.0 percent; Poland, 1965, 12.1 percent. One must remember that these are pretax earnings and, since income taxation in the West is relatively high and progressive, a posttax comparison would show less difference between the two groups of countries. The "top 5 percent"

31. UNECE, *Economic Survey of Europe, 1968* (New York, 1969), chap. 3; and UNECE, *Incomes in Postwar Europe* (Geneva: 1967), chap. 8. It must be remembered, of course, that the demographic situation of the USSR is still strongly influenced by the unusually heavy losses of men during World War II. The relatively high proportion of the labor force engaged in agriculture in the East European countries tends also to raise the female labor force participation rate.

32. U.N. Economic Commission for Europe, *Incomes in Postwar Europe* (Geneva: 1967), chap. 6, p. 21, and chap. 9, pp. 23–26.

measure, too, may not be a good proxy for the overall concentration measures which we do not have. The data permit a surmise that income from labor is more equally distributed in the socialist economies; but it cannot presently be more than this.

3. *Free and subsidized consumption.* In assessing the distribution of real income among households, one must consider that much of it is distributed directly rather than via money payments. Consider an average family in Moscow or Kiev. Apartment rentals are heavily subsidized, and take no more than 3 to 5 percent of family income. Medical and hospital care are essentially free; and so is education at all levels. Transportation, while not free, is again heavily subsidized. (Moscow still has a "nickel fare" on its subways.) Vacation trips to the Black Sea or elsewhere are often paid for by the employer. So the family needs money income only for food, clothing, household equipment, and incidentals. (The car will take its bite in time, but this is only the beginning). Inequality among households, then, can only mean inequality in these areas of consumption; and even here the price structure, which favors basic items of food and clothing, tends to bring these items within the reach of everyone.

A logical extension of the system would be to provide a basic minimum of food, clothing, etc. free of charge. Money income would then become even less important. Movement in this direction is contemplated, as the growing productive power of the socialist economies makes possible an approach to full communism; but achievement of this goal is clearly quite remote.

Meanwhile, the opposite side of the subsidy coin is supply shortages. The most notable example is housing, where there are long queues of customers waiting for low-rent apartments. This introduces a special kind of inequality into the system—between those who have gotten an apartment and those who have not, and between those at the head of the queue and those five years farther back. Housing shortages, incidentally, are the most serious practical restriction on labor mobility. A man who has living space, perhaps in enterprise-owned housing, is reluctant to throw up his job because, while finding another job may be easy, finding another apartment is sure to be difficult.

It is usually thought that extensive provision of nonpublic goods on a below-cost basis violates the canons of welfare economics. Housing and other consumption goods, it is argued, should be priced at cost. Income should be distributed in money form, with whatever degree of equalization is judged desirable and feasible; and consumers should then make their own selection in the market. There are counterarguments, however, which will be examined in chapter 6, where we consider the main policy issues in the socialist economies.

Value judgments apart, the problem of comparing household income distributions in the socialist and capitalist countries is clearly very complicated. It is not sufficient to compare money income distributions, still less to compare wage and salary structures. So it is not surprising that careful scholars hesitate to draw conclusions about relative degrees of equality. The writer's hypothesis—and it cannot presently be more than that—is that, as regards the urban population, distribution is noticeably more equal in the socialist countries. This is partly because of relatively lower white-collar earnings, partly because of the absence of property income, partly because of free or subsidized provision of basic consumption items. On the other hand, the gap between urban and rural incomes is probably wider in the socialist countries, where the rural population is also proportionately larger.

In this chapter we have tried to describe the socialist economies without professing to *evaluate* their performance. We have aimed at a neutral, unpolitical statement which might be considered fair in Moscow or Prague as well as in London or New York. This is not an easy task, and has no doubt been imperfectly performed. But any overtones of criticism or approval which may have crept in are unintentional.

To answer the question whether the socialist institutional structure is "better," in an economic sense, than the typical capitalist structure would require much more information than we presently have on various aspects of economic performance, plus a series of value judgments. It is not even clear that it is a very interesting question. We shall nevertheless return to it briefly in chapter 10.

4 LESS DEVELOPED ECONOMIES

The economies we have considered thus far can be labeled "socialist" and "modified capitalist." But what is one to do with economies which are neither? Are they precapitalist (or perhaps presocialist)? In the Marxian scheme, they would perhaps be considered "feudal." But these labels have little descriptive value.

The less developed countries differ greatly in size. There are many very small economies, such as Hong Kong, Singapore, Jamaica, Mauritius, and some of the tiny West African countries. These countries are extremely dependent on exports and imports, and can develop only as satellites of the larger economies with which they trade. It is perhaps more useful to look at the thirty to forty countries which are large enough to aspire to a more self-contained development. Most of these countries, however, are still small in terms of national output. India, with its large population and land area, is very atypical; and the literature of economic development has been unduly influenced by concentration on the "Indian model." Medium-sized countries such as Chile, Colombia, Ghana, Uganda, Ceylon, and Thailand are more representative of the group as a whole.

Even with this qualification, the less developed economies are more heterogeneous than the two groups already considered. Some have a long history of independent government, while others have recently emerged from colonial status. Some have an average per capita income, by conventional measures, of less than $100 per year, while others have an income level above $500. Some are densely populated relative to arable land area, while others are still thinly populated. In some, modern industry, is negligible, while in others it provides 15 or 20 percent of national output.

This heterogeneity raises questions which we should mention without professing to answer. First, what does it mean to say that these countries are "less developed" than those in the other two groups? Or to say that, among these countries, some are "more developed" than others? What dimension of measurement is implied in such statements? There is a natural tendency to rely on estimates of per capita income. But this is surely a superficial approach. Per capita income is symptomatic of other characteristics of the economy. But symptomatic of *what*, precisely? This is what we need to know.

Second, some countries in the group seem to resemble each other rather closely. This suggests the possibility of a useful typology, a scheme for dividing the universe of LDCs into subcategories. But there is no agreement at this point on what classification is most appropriate. Some have suggested that there is a "Latin American type," or a "tropical African type" of economy and society. Others have suggested a division between countries which are densely populated relative to their resource endowment and those which are thinly populated. The small, open economy is sometimes contrasted with the large, relatively self-contained economy. The "oil and mineral economies" are sometimes said to have a distinct family resemblance. Seers has suggested a classification scheme based on degree of specialization in primary products and consequent export dependence.[1] Diversified economies with a substantial manufacturing sector, such as India, Mexico,

1. Dudley Seers, "An Approach to the Short-Period Analysis of Instability in Primary-Producing Countries," *Oxford Economic Papers*, Feb. 1959.

Argentina, would appear at one end of such a spectrum, while at the other end would be the "banana republic" and the "oil sheikdom."

Setting aside these problems, we proceed to treat the less developed countries as a single group. We undertake, that is, to specify characteristics which appear *in some measure* in all members of the group, though more strikingly in some than in others. The following features seem to be of special importance: limited economic competence of government; dominance of subsistence production and self-employment; imperfection of markets; underutilization and low productivity of factors of production; marked dependence on export earnings and capital inflows; small public sectors and "modern" industrial sectors; low per capita income and very unequal distribution of income; low growth rates, with wide dispersion of individual country performance. These features are interrelated, in ways which are not yet fully understood. But they provide useful "handles" for analysis of these economies.

LIMITED ECONOMIC COMPETENCE OF GOVERNMENT

Political leadership in the LDCs does not have the unity, discipline, and drive characteristic of the socialist countries; nor does it have the support of a well-organized political machine. The stable, multiparty systems of the capitalist countries are also usually absent. One can think of only a half-dozen examples of Western-style democracy, and even these are precarious.

The typical pattern is either one-party civilian rule or military rule. Under one-party government, the ruling party tends to be an oligarchy heavily concentrated in the capital city, and with a thin base of popular support. The common man, and particularly the peasant farmer, normally views government with suspicion and apprehension. About half the LDCs are presently governed by military regimes, and these regimes differ considerably from country to country. In some countries the officer class is more open to boys from low-income families than is the civilian governing class, and may in fact be the main channel through which poor boys can move upward. Viewed in these terms, the recent advent of left-wing military governments in Peru, Bolivia, Libya, and the Sudan (and earlier in Burma and the UAR) is not as anomalous as might be thought.

Where there is no provision for orderly transfer of power, governments are necessarily unstable. The coup replaces the election. Thus the first concern of any government is to remain in power. This makes for a short time-horizon, and preoccupation with security and prestige objectives. There may be other reasons for government coolness toward economic development. A government dominated by the well-to-do is unlikely to push hard for changes which might disturb existing privileges. While there may also be prodevelopment forces in the society, they have to make their way against a strong current of inertia or opposition.

Apart from the *motivation* of government, its *competence* in economic management is usually limited. Except in India and other ex-British areas, where civil service traditions were thoroughly instilled, government jobs tend to be regarded as political prizes rather than steps in a professional career. Economic administrators often have no specific training for their positions. Where one does find an able man in a top policy position, he often has little supporting staff. There is a great lack of "middle management" between the top official and the clerk. Despite the importance of economic issues, the number of qualified economists is tiny, relative to the need, and supply is rising only slowly. Government salaries are usually low, relative to earnings in private business and the professions. So salaries are often supplemented by bribes. Whatever may be said about the usefulness of "constructive corruption" in getting things done, it does not make for systematic application of policy priorities. Low salaries and political insecurity also lead many able men to seek refuge in U.N. jobs or join the brain drain to the developed countries.

Weak staffing is compounded by two other difficulties: "statistical nakedness" and "poor feedback mechanisms."[2] The best economic measurements are those which arise as a by-product of administration, such as import and export statistics, or central government revenues and expenditures. But estimates of agricultural production, most other kinds of production, price and wage levels, household incomes; and so on are usually weak. The GNP estimates based on these shaky ingredients are correspondingly weak. By "poor feedback mechanisms" we mean that government is often unaware of the consequences of its actions. For examples, licenses are required for all imports, but no one bothers to keep a tally of who is getting the licenses. Budget allocations are made for road building, but when the next budget year rolls around no one knows how much work was accomplished under last year's allocations. Project analyses are prepared ex ante, but there is no auditing ex post. Poor feedback makes it difficult to correct even blatant misestimates and errors.

Some governments recognize their limited competence more clearly than others; and they adjust to it in differing ways. Some do little in any direction. Others overstrain their administrative systems, attempting to enforce a variety of economic controls which are beyond their capacity. In such cases nothing gets done very well, and the net effect on the economy may be negative. In still other cases, government is doing the wrong things—things which tend to blight private activity without substituting effectively for it. Such haphazard interventionism, unguided by clear economic analysis or a workable overall strategy, is common throughout the less developed world.

Finally, we may note the absence in most LDCs of a developed national consciousness. Most Western countries had a long period of national unity *before* the beginnings of modern economic growth. Nationalism was typically an en-

2. I owe these terms to Professor C. E. Lindblom, who has used them in seminar discussion.

ergizing force which supported economic modernization. But to a resident of Bali, Java is a foreign area. To a member of the Masai tribe, Kenya and Tanzania are virtually meaningless. Thus even if the central government were growth minded, and wished to mobilize the citizens for a national effort, it would have great difficulty in conveying such a message.

SUBSISTENCE PRODUCTION AND SELF-EMPLOYMENT

In most LDCs the great majority of the population live in the countryside. They allocate their time among producing food, largely for home consumption; producing "Z-goods"[3] (housing, furniture, clothing, personal services) for home consumption; and leisure. Purchased goods are a small part of total consumption, and are obtained by exchanging small amounts of food with village artisans.

From one standpoint, development consists in a gradual increase of marketed production relative to home production. Historically, this has usually occurred as a by-product of foreign trade. Myint has shown that the market economy may penetrate the subsistence economy through the opening of foreign markets for a peasant product, such as cocoa from Nigeria and Ghana, which is exchanged for imports of finished consumer goods. The new wants stimulated by the appearance of these goods induce the peasants to work more and to allocate more time to the export crop. Helleiner has shown that the rapid rise of Nigerian cocoa production after 1900 was accomplished without any reduction of food output, simply by increased inputs of labor time and of previously uncultivated land.

Another possibility is the appearance of foreign mining and plantation enterprises which employ local wage labor. These wage payments create a money demand for foodstuffs,

3. This concept is developed in S. Hymer and S. Resnick, "A Model of an Agrarian Economy with Nonagricultural activities," *American Economic Review*, Sept. 1969, pp. 493–506.

leading to a rise in food marketings. But such spillover effects are not inevitable. One can visualize a foreign-owned economic enclave, importing its own labor and foodstuffs as well as manufactures, which would have minimal interaction with the indigenous peasant economy. The British tea plantations in Ceylon, and the rubber plantations in Malaya, seem to have been of this type.

Dominance of subsistence production is accompanied by prevalence of self-employment. In the countryside, most people are either tenants or independent cultivators. In either case the family determines its labor inputs, and its income is a residual rather than a wage. In the cities, too, most people are "workers on own account": artisans, traders, providers of transport and personal services. Wage earners in government and "modern" business enterprises are a small, though sometimes a growing, proportion of the labor force.

Such an economy presents perplexing measurement problems. Consider the problem of valuing national output. What is the value of the "Z goods" which a rural household produces for itself? What is the product of an itinerant street vendor in the cities? Even if such questions were answerable in principle, the relevant data are certainly not collected by national statistical officers. Their GNP estimates must accordingly be given a low degree of credibility.

Unemployment figures also have little meaning in such an economy. Even where population pressure is severe, open unemployment may be small. Open unemployment is a luxury which can be afforded only in countries rich enough to have income-support systems. In a less developed economy, almost everyone will profess to be occupied at something; but he may produce very little at this occupation. Low-productivity employment, rather than open unemployment, is the heart of the matter. But where there are no good measures of output, the degree of labor-force underutilization is hard to determine.

There are nevertheless two ratios which are significant as development indicators. These are the number of wage and salary earners relative to the labor force, and the marketed share of agricultural output. If these ratios are rising over time, one can conclude that the economy is undergoing structural change.

IMPERFECTION OF MARKETS

There is no economy without markets, and in most LDCs markets are increasing in importance. But they remain far from the textbook vision of a comprehensive, interdependent market network, involving numerous and well-informed buyers and sellers, with prices tending toward uniformity and moving flexibly to provide correct signals for economic decisions. The absence of such a mechanism is a key feature of underdevelopment.

This can be documented in any IDC by reviewing the main types of market. Look first at *labor* markets. The wage differentials between the white-collar and manual levels, and between skilled and unskilled manual workers, are substantially wider than in either the capitalist or socialist economies. This may be due partly to cultural and traditional factors, such as the European-Asian-African layering of occupations and wage scales in East Africa. But it is due also to restricted training facilities for the higher occupations. Earnings of modern-sector employees are substantially above those of the self-employed in traditional urban activities and in agriculture. This gap, indeed, is often so wide as to suggest that it arises partly from political pressures. An interesting question is whether earnings in agriculture are above or below those in traditional urban activities, and whether migration serves as an important equilibrating force; but little can be said about this because of the lack of information on earnings in self-employment.

As regards *capital,* there are sharp cleavages between the rural economy, the monetized domestic economy, and the export-import sector. The rural economy traditionally depends on the village moneylender, and modern banking facilities are absent or poorly developed. In the domestic monetized sector, self-finance is the dominant technique. Initial capital is raised from family members, and the business grows through reinvestment of earnings. Public stockholding is important in only a few countries. The export-import sector often has its own sources of finance through local branches of foreign banks.

There is normally a central bank, serving mainly as financial agent for the government; and a few commercial banks, concentrated in the cities and lending mainly for trade rather than production. But there is nothing like the network of saving banks, insurance companies, investment banks, mortgage lenders, securities dealers, and so on which exists in developed countries. This makes it difficult to mobilize and transfer savings to the growth points of the economy.

Capital market imperfection is reflected in a wide spread of interest rates. There is often a legal ceiling on what the organized commercial banks may charge, below the rate which would prevail in a free market. The banks then ration credit within a limited circle of established customers. Other would-be borrowers must resort to the unorganized money market, at substantially higher rates. This is one reason why it is difficult for new enterprises to set up in business. The highest interest rates in the economy are typically those charges by rural moneylenders.

In product markets, the dominant fact is the small domestic demand for most goods relative to the optimum scale of production. Monopoly or "strong oligopoly" is pervasive, while markets approaching pure competition are virtually absent. Price-cost margins tend to be high, and are protected by high tariffs on most manufactured goods. Information flows are poor and business practices generally archaic. It is common to find wide and apparently erratic price variations for the same commodity of service.

Government intervention in price setting is typically more widespread than in the Western countries. Government has heavy influence on the wage structure through minimum wage legislation and through its own employment policies. It usually sets maximum interest rates. Foreign exchange rates, a key price in these economies, are usually maintained at nonequilibrium levels. Transportation, electric power production, and other utilities are normally operated by government. Government has strong influence on the prices of manufactured goods through its exchange rate, tariff, and import restriction policies. These activities tend to intensify the price distortions which would exist in any event.

ECONOMIC SLACK: FACTOR SUPPLIES AND FACTOR USE

The blame for low per capita output is often placed on resource scarcity. While there is something to this, two other observations are warranted. First, in most LDCs more resources are available than are being used—there is "economic slack." Second, the resources which are used have relatively low productivity. The development problem is mainly an *organization* problem rather than a *resource* problem.

We cannot enter into the complexities of defining and measuring "surplus labor"; but simple observation suggests that many able-bodied men in these countries are not working a full day or week. Labor force participation rates are also abnormally low. Thus there is substantial labor force slack. Economic historians have noticed the same phenomenon in some of the Western countries during the early period of modern economic growth.

It is more heterodox to suggest that capital shortage is not a major constraint on economic growth in the LDCs. But there is reason to think that this may be true. There is often unused saving capacity, both in the sense that many people are living above subsistence level, and in the sense that they are consuming more than they would choose to consume if savings could be put into secure assets at yields reflecting the scarcity of capital in the economy. Private saving apart, there is the fiscal mechanism. Lewis' dictum that no country is too poor to collect 20 percent of its national income in taxes may or may not be correct. But most countries could raise *more,* and could save a higher proportion of current revenue for capital formation, than they are presently doing. In practice, however, one could not raise taxation rapidly—say, by 5 percent of GNP—without giving rise to inflation, as the public sought higher money incomes to compensate for lower real consumption.

What about physical capital shortages? The transport-communications-power network of the LDCs is certainly meager relative to that of the Western economies. But it may still be adequate to the demands being placed upon it. In countries where the "directly productive" sectors are moving forward so rapidly as to put serious pressure on infrastructure, the IBRD and other foreign lending agencies will usually consider this a profitable investment opportunity. Probably a commoner situation is that in which infrastructure has already been pushed beyond immediate needs. Such a situation—"development via excess capacity," in Hirschman's terms—has so far not proven a very successful development path.

The capital shortage argument, then, reduces to an argument that machinery, fuels, and other requisites for manufacturing development must usually be imported in the first instance, and that exports plus foreign borrowing may not provide enough exchange for this purpose. This "foreign exchange constraint" is genuine, and will be examined in a moment; but the "domestic savings constraint" which usually accompanies it in foreign-aid models is distinctly suspect.

In retrospect, it appears that the widespread identification of capital as the major bottleneck to economic growth was a historical accident. It came about partly because the Harrod-Domar model, in which capital plays a pivotal role, was lying ready to hand when work on economic development began.[4]

4. The Harrod-Domar model assumes that output is generated by a technology which combines capital and labor in fixed proportions. When adapted to the development context with abundant labor the

Further, some of the early students of development were deeply involved in foreign aid policy; and this perhaps inclined them to overestimate the importance of the capital which they were seeking to provide.

It is often said that the LDCs suffer from a shortage of entrepreneurship. It would be more correct to say that business talent is usually present but underutilized. There is certainly no shortage of people interested in, and successful in, making money. They are accustomed, however, to make it from such traditional sources as landowning, moneylending, and trade. They are interested in quick turnover and high profits. Thus there is a problem of reorienting their interests from commerce and land ownership to manufacturing. In this area they will usually, at the outset, lack managerial skills. One has to discover how to manage a factory by learning from others and, in good measure, by actual experience.

The businessman, or potential businessman, faces special barriers in many LDCs. Ethnic distinctions are often important. Some Asian and African countries are trying to squeeze out their most experienced businessmen because they are members of a Chinese, or Indian, or other minority group. Businesses are normally closely controlled family concerns; and those who become executives by belonging to the "right" families are not necessarily most qualified for their jobs. The politico-economic environment is usually unfavorable to new enterprise. Access to such scarce inputs as bank credit, import licenses, and building permits depends on favorable decisions by government officials and bankers with close ties to the established business community. Such a system favors the insiders, the families which at some point got a head start in the economic race. To encourage new sources of entrepreneurship would discommode the present dominant groups. Why should they do it?

---

model suggests that the rate of growth of output is determined by the rate of growth of the capital stock. (This can be seen to be the fraction of income saved divided by the capital/output ratio.)

In addition to the failure to mobilize potential factor supplies, the factors which are in use typically have low productivity. The reasons for this differ from sector to sector. Where peasant agriculture predominates, low output per worker is associated with traditional production methods, accompanied by scarcity of modern inputs and (in some countries) a high labor-land ratio. But one cannot assume that there will be more enterprising management under a large landlord. The "improving landlord" of eighteenth-century England does not find many followers in today's LDCs. The large landowner, often an absentee operating through a hired manager, is interested in a secure and stable income; but he is not necessarily interested in income maximization or in innovation.

In urban trade and service activities, low productivity is associated with labor surplus. Rapid population growth, plus the attractions of city life, leads to cityward migration in excess of employment opportunities in the modern sector. More and more people crowd into retailing and services, where one can set up on a street corner with little or no capital. Like agriculture, this is a "spongy" sector, capable of indefinite labor absorption. But unless the volume of service demanded expands proportionately, output per worker will decline over time.

In some wage-earning employments, such as government and domestic service, there is strong social pressure to employ unnecessary people on essentially charitable grounds. Hence the staff of six household servants where three would do, and the government office crowded with clerks and messengers beyond any reasonable requirement.

In manufacturing and other "modern" industries, output per worker is substantially above that in traditional activities; but it is substantially below that of similar plants in the developed countries. This could be due partly to use of more labor per unit of capital, as a rational adjustment to relative factor prices; but this is probably a small part of the explanation. Most of the productivity difference seems to be due to such things as: traditional and unprogressive production management; poor policies concerning worker selection, training, and wage setting; poor first-line supervision; lower personal capacity of workers, arising from limited education plus nutritional and health deficiencies; and overstaffing of plants because of social or legal pressures.[5] Some LDCs have antilayoff laws which make it very difficult to discharge an employee once he has been hired.

TRADE AND CAPITAL MOVEMENTS

The ratio of exports to GNP varies widely among the LDCs, depending mainly on their economic size. In some very small countries it exceeds 50 percent. In India, it is below 10 percent. After adjusting for the size variable, trade ratios in the LDCs are probably no higher than in the Western countries. The composition of their trade, however, is quite different. Their exports are predominantly to the developed countries rather than to each other. They consist overwhelmingly of primary products, which are exchanged for manufactured goods, fuels, and industrial materials. Many countries, moreover, are highly specialized in one or a few primary products—they are "oil economies," "copper economies," "banana (or cocoa, or coffee) economies."

The consequences of this trade pattern have been extensively explored. Export proceeds fluctuate considerably from years to year because of fluctuations in crop yields, world prices, and foreign demand. Indeed, in the LDCs export fluctuations are the main source of economic instability, playing

5. The writer investigated this matter in detail for a sample of new manufacturing plants in Puerto Rico. Although most of these plants were owned by U.S. companies and designed to mainland standards, their initial productivity was typically much below mainland levels. After five to ten years of "learning by doing," however, most managements were able to achieve substantial productivity gains. For detailed documentation of how this was done, see Lloyd G. Reynolds and Peter Gregory, *Wages, Productivity, and Industrialization in Puerto Rico* (Homewood, Ill.: Richard D. Irwin, for the Yale Economic Growth Center, 1965).

somewhat the role of investment fluctuations in the capitalist economies. The rate of increase in demand for many primary products is less than the rate of increase in world GNP, due to low income elasticities in the richer countries for basic foodstuffs, and due to material-saving innovations and synthetic substitutes in the case of fibres and other industrial raw materials. It is also alleged that the terms of trade have tended to shift against primary products and in favor of manufactures, though there is no clear statistical support of this view.

The rate of growth of exports constrains the growth of imports, unless an excess of desired imports can be covered by borrowing. It is normal for a young, developing economy to be a net borrower. During the nineteenth and early twentieth century there were large flows of British capital to the United States, Canada, Australia, and South Africa. There were also substantial capital movements to some of the Latin American countries, especially Mexico, Chile, and Argentina.

Large capital movements still continue. But the character of the flow is now considerably different. While there is still some private investment, mainly in oil and mineral industries, capital transfers to the LDCs now come predominantly from foreign governments or from the World Bank group. Moreover, loans are made to governments in the recipient countries, so that the flow is biased toward financing public sector activities. These transfers are normally "commercial" in the sense of carrying interest and repayment obligations, though often at less than market rates. Since repayment must come from export earnings in the future, a borrowing country must assess its future repayment capacity realistically. Some LDCs, after 20 years of extensive borrowing since 1950, are already near the upper limit.

So the LDCs face a dilemma: they have achieved political independence, but without the economic independence which comes from high productive capacity. They are still subjugated in varying degree to the economic needs and political rivalries of the richer countries. They resent this situation. They occasionally hit back at one or other of the creditor countries. Peru denounces the United States; Cuba snubs the USSR. But in the short run they have no ready avenue of escape.

THE COMPOSITION OF OUTPUT

Little need be added to what has been implied in previous sections. The rural sector, including household subsistence production as well as marketings, usually produces more than half of national income. Government is a small sector, usually producing only 10 to 15 percent of national output, compared with the 20 to 30 percent in the capitalist economies. "Modern" industry, including factory-style manufacturing, mining and oil extraction, electric power, railroads, and other infrastructure industries, varies considerably in size from country to country. In the least developed countries, where infrastructure is weak and factory industry almost absent, it may amount to less than 10 percent of GNP. But in some semiindustrialized countries of Latin America, this rises to 25 or 30 percent.

There remains a residual of "traditional" urban activities, including handicraft manufacturing, house building, trade, personal services, and the like. In output terms, the size of this sector is difficult to judge because of the lack of income data. In employment terms, it is a large sector, though many of those nominally employed in it are underemployed in varying degree.

In economies at this income level, it is particularly important to distinguish between the sector proportions of *output* and the sector proportions of *employment,* because intersectoral differences in output per worker are wider than in more developed economies.[6] Output per worker in modern industry and government is substantially above the na-

6. The fact that intersectoral productivity differences decline as per capita income rises has been documented by Simon Kuznets in *Modern Economic Growth,* chap. 3.

tional average. (In the case of government, this amounts to saying that government wage scales are well above earnings in traditional activities.) Output per worker in agriculture and in traditional urban activities is well below the national average. Thus the proportion of the labor force employed in these activities is above the percentage of output produced, being as high as 70 to 80 percent for the least developed countries.

THE LEVEL AND DISTRIBUTION OF INCOME

These are poor countries. Per capita income is low. We note this fact at the end of the discussion rather than at the beginning because of its purely symptomatic character. It tells us nothing about the reasons for low incomes or about the possibilities of improvement. Low income per se is not necessarily a barrier to economic advance. All countries began somewhere.

It is not possible at this point to measure and compare levels of real per capita income in the LDCs at all accurately. The statistical staffs of these countries are very small. The writer has seen a two-man staff preparing national accounts for a country of fifty million people. What can actually be measured under such circumstances? Trade flows, because of licensing and taxing systems. Output of public enterprises and of large-scale private enterprises, which are usually subject to profit taxes. Government payroll expenditure, which by definition equals government output. But these components are a minor part of national output. Estimates of agricultural output are subject to wide margins of error. Household subsistence production is difficult to measure, and in any event is not measured; and neither is traditional urban production. Published figures of GNP per capita must accordingly be given a low degree of creditability at this stage.[7]

7. It has become almost as essential for every country to have a GNP figure as for it to have an airline, a university, and other prestige symbols. But the U.N. Statistical Department has done a disservice by publishing such figures at their present low level of reliability. The printed

Their widespread use in intercountry comparative studies is deplorable and wastes much research effort.

But must we stop with such an agnostic conclusion? People will insist on making comparisons among the LDCs and between them and the more developed countries. What can be done? First, *gross* differences are doubtless significant. Countries which in the conventional tabulations appear in the $100–200 range almost certainly are poorer than those in the $500–750 range. Comparative study of such clearly separable groups can yield useful results. But it is unsafe to use techniques which imply that one can measure small differences. Second, there is something to be said for physical indicators of real consumption levels, an enterprise on which the U.N. Institute for Social Studies in Geneva has been working. This would include such measures as caloric intake, housing space, shoe and cloth availability, school enrollment, infant mortality and other health data, radios, bicycles, and other consumer durables per capita. In more advanced countries, such a procedure would be considered crude. But in the absence of credible money aggregates, physical indicators may provide useful information on comparative income levels among the LDCs.[8]

Income comparisons between the LDCs and the MDCs are also difficult. The income gap is undoubtedly wide, but considerably less wide than it appears in conventional estimates. The reason is partly that subsistence production in the LDCs tend to be ignored or undervalued, partly that many of the

---

figure implies accuracy, though it may in fact be extremely flimsy; and it becomes the basis for subsequent statistical manipulations which are largely waste motion. It would have been wiser to concentrate for the time being on technical assistance in this area, hoping that national estimates would eventually achieve a degree of firmness justifying publication.

8. Dudley Seers once commented in a seminar discussion, "Whenever I go to a new country, I look first at people's feet. Are they barefoot? Are they wearing sandals? or cheap shoes of local make? or more substantial imported shoes?" This "shoe standard" of comparison may correlate rather well with overall real consumption levels.

things counted as "consumption" in Western GNP estimates
—military and police expenditures, urban and suburban
transport costs, environmental control activities—do not add
to welfare, but are really costs arising from highly industrialized and urbanized economies and from national power
struggles.[9] If adjustment could be made for such considerations, it might turn out that the true income differential between, say, the United States and Indonesia is 12:1 rather
than the 30:1 suggested by conventional measures. More
radically, one can argue that it is futile to attach any quantitative indicators to such very different patterns of life.

It is usually thought that income *distribution* is more unequal in the LDCs than in the Western economies. It is probably true that the top 5 percent of families receive a larger
share of household income in most LDCs than they do in the
West; and true also that the middle-income brackets are thinly populated because of the smallness of the business and
professional class. But in most LDCs we do not have adequate
income measures for the bulk of the population, which would
permit comparison of Gini coefficients or other measures of
household income distribution *as a whole*. The situation also
differs substantially from one LDC to the next. In the heavily
populated countries, income inequality is accentuated by the
high level of rents. But areas such as West Africa might show
a substantially more equal distribution.

After admitting the impossibility of precise measurement,
it remains true that the great majority of people in the LDCs
are very poor. But what do we mean by this? As one tours the
back country, one observes that people are eating—not very
well, but perhaps better than their fathers or grandfathers.
Their houses keep out the rain. Heating is no problem in
warm climates. Clothes cover the body and are adequate by
local custom. So in what sense are these people worse off than
the rural Italian or Russian? First, they are riddled by disease
which lowers their energy and shortens their life span. Sec-

9. This point has been argued by Kuznets. See also Ezra J. Mishan,
The Costs of Economic Growth (New York: Praeger, 1967).

ond, the great majority are illiterate. This produces a stunted mentality, a limited receptiveness even to simple ideas and calculations, an inability to participate in economic change. The decisive fact is not that they derive fewer "utils" of consumer satisfaction than the German or the Swede. They are poor *as human beings*.

This kind of poverty, plus the poverty of economic institutions and governmental capacity described earlier, is the root of their problem. Without changes at these levels, external capital must sink like water into sand.

RATES OF ECONOMIC GROWTH

If we cannot accurately measure GNP per capita, we cannot know how rapidly it is increasing over time. The same fog of uncertainty surrounds growth rates as surrounds point-of-time comparisons. We can nevertheless suggest several plausible hypotheses:

1. Actual growth rates are usually lower than officially published rates. One reason is that official estimates are unduly influenced by performance in the measurable sectors— modern industry, government, and foreign trade—and that output in these sectors is usually growing faster than output as a whole. The overall result for the economy will depend on the *weighting* of market output as against subsistence production. Since subsistence production is poorly measured, its proper weight cannot really be determined, and there is probably a general tendency to set it too low, thus inflating the aggregate growth rate. National income accountants must also have in mind the desirability of showing a high growth rate, and must realize that estimates which err in an upward direction will be better received by their superiors than those which err in the opposite direction. Thus without implying any deliberate "cooking" of the figures, there are psychological and political reasons for presuming some optimistic bias.

2. The median rate of GNP increase in the LDCs over the past two decades has been below that in the capitalist or so-

cialist economies. The median rate of increase in these other two groups since 1950 has been of the order of 5 percent per year. It is unlikely that the LDCs have attained such a rate on average, despite the strong performance of some individual countries.

3. The growth rate of GNP per capita in the LDCs has been *distinctly* lower than in the other two groups. This follows from hypothesis 2 above plus the higher rate of LDC population growth. For the higher-income countries, the rate of population growth has recently averaged about 1.4 percent per year, individual country rates falling mostly in the range of 1.0–1.5 percent. For the LDCs, the comparable average is about 2.9 percent per year, with country rates mainly in the range of 2.5–3.5 percent.

The LDCs, then, would have had to achieve a substantially *higher* rate of GNP increase merely to equal the rate of increase of GNP per capita in the other two groups; and this they have clearly been unable to do. The median annual increase of income per capita in the capitalist and socialist economies since 1950 has been between 3 and 4 percent per year. At a wild guess, the median for the LDCs has probably not been above 1 percent. The gap between richer and poorer countries is thus growing rather than diminishing.

4. *Dispersion* in national growth rates over the period 1950–70 was considerably greater for the Southern countries than for either of the other two groups. While small differences in performance cannot be measured accurately, gross differences are detectable. Thus one can say that, within Latin America, Mexico and Colombia have done better than Argentina and Chile. In Africa, Kenya and the Ivory Coast have done better than Guinea or the Congo (Kinshasha). In Asia, Taiwan, Thailand, and Malaysia have done better than Indonesia or Ceylon. In a certain number of LDCs, income per capita clearly is rising and the future outlook is promising.

CONCLUSION TO PART ONE

Thus far we have examined our three groups of economies in isolation. It will be useful now to summarize their key features, and to comment on how they interact in the world economy.

A Structural Comparison

The structural characteristics examined in Part One are summarized in table 4.1. This table attempts to describe, not to evaluate. The latter would be a hazardous task, since there are many dimensions of economic performance, and the question of how these should be weighted to arrive at an overall rating necessarily involves value judgments.

Note that almost all the items in the table are measurable, though existing measurements are not always precise. The verbal tags in the table suggest orders of magnitude. But there is much intercountry variation within each group, and there are also important time trends. These trends are related particularly to rates of increase in per capita output. As per capita output rises, the capital accumulation rate tends to rise, the population growth rate to decline, the agricultural sector to shrink relatively, and so on.

The level-of-development dimension, indeed, cuts across the capitalist-socialist dimension of comparison. Many characteristics of national economies are related more clearly to per capita income than to the ownership system.

Table 4.1 yields an impression that the capitalist and socialist groups resemble each other more closely than either resembles the less developed economies. The reason is perhaps that both groups are on a secure growth path. The European socialist countries, including the USSR, are relative latecomers to the development parade. Thus they have had time to reach only moderate levels of per capita income, and this is reflected in their economic structure. They are now in the mainstream of progress, however, and the benefits and

TABLE 4.1

A Comparison of Structural Characteristics

Characteristic	Capitalist economies	Socialist economies	Less developed economies
1. Political structure	Multi-party	One-party	One-party (or military rule)
2. Public administration	Well developed	Well developed	Poorly developed
3. Market structure	Extensive use of markets	Limited use of markets	Markets prevalent but imperfect
4. Population growth	Low	Low	High
5. Capital accumulation rate	High	High	Low
6. Agricultural sector	Small	Medium	Large
7. Public sector	Medium	Large	Small
8. Trade participation	High	Moderate	High
9. Employment of resources	Usually near full employment	Excess demand normal	Substantial underemployment
10. Inflationary pressure	Moderate	Strong	Zero to strong
11. Income per capita	High	Medium	Low
12. Growth rate	High	High	Low
13. Income distribution	Moderate inequality, diminishing	Relatively equal	Markedly unequal

penalties of continued growth may turn out not too differently from capitalist experience.

The Interaction of Economies

Myrdal has emphasized that before 1940, and more particularly before 1914, one could speak of a world economy—integrated in the sense that it had a "head" in Western Europe and North America, to which the rest of the world was attached as an economic (and often also as a political) appendage.[10] The two world wars, the rise of the socialist group, and the virtual disappearance of colonialism wrenched this structure violently apart. The ex-colonies are now on their own vis-à-vis the ex-colonial powers, which feel at most a certain sentimental obligation toward them. The socialist countries also, through choice as well as necessity, have tended to form a separate economic bloc—one should perhaps say two blocs, since the economic ties between the Asian and European socialist countries are tenuous. It is interesting to look briefly at the new patterns of trade and capital movements.

The strongest currents of trade are *within* the Western capitalist group and *within* the East European socialist countries. In both cases this consists largely of an interchange of manufactured and semimanufactured products. The less developed economies, on the other hand, have only a limited interchange with each other and look mainly outward to the other two groups. Economists have urged the merit of regional cooperation among LDCs, and there have been limited experiments in this direction. But the manufacturing sector, in which such cooperation would be most feasible, is poorly developed in most countries. Moreover, economic nationalism seems even more virulent in the LDCs than elsewhere, and often prevents cooperation which would seem feasible and efficient.

10. See in particular his *Beyond the Welfare State* (New Haven: Yale University Press, 1960); and *An International Economy* (New York: Harper, 1956).

East-West trade has risen rapidly over the past decade, though the United States remains largely outside this current. The rate of future expansion depends partly on progress in relaxing political tensions; but there are economic barriers as well. Many of the primary products which the socialist countries might export are already in surplus in the West; and the quality of manufactured goods from those countries will have to be raised substantially to compete in Western markets.

The less developed countries' exports of primary products to the capitalist countries confront rather low income elasticities of demand. Since GNP in the capitalist group is rising at about 5 percent per year, however, the growth rate of primary exports is still substantial. A more distant prospect is that the LDCs might be able to market a growing volume of labor-intensive manufactures. This would require not only more manufacturing expertise and higher quality standards in the LDCs, but also a receptive trade policy on the part of the developed countries. The recent movement in the United States toward quota restrictions on imports of textiles and certain other consumer goods are symptomatic of the difficulties which the poorer countries may encounter in trying to utilize their ample labor supplies.

The LDCs may be able to raise their exports to the socialist countries more rapidly than their exports to the West. The prevalent condition of excess demand and commodity shortages in the socialist countries would seem to provide a ready market. In addition, the socialist economies are more nearly complementary to the less developed economies than are the capitalist countries. Their backward agriculture tends to create food deficits, particularly in poor harvest years. Thus the socialist countries are able to absorb large quantities of rice, wheat, sugar, cotton, and other things which in the West would be redundant and unwelcome. In return, their capital-goods orientation permits them to supply the machinery and industrial supplies which the LDCs need for their industrialization programs. In view of all this, it is surprising that

LDC-socialist trade has not expanded even more rapidly. The answer may be partly that chronic excess demand in the socialist countries, which are themselves continuing to industrialize rapidly, makes them unwilling to release goods for export, and that this is the effective constraint on the volume of trade.

Capital movements are more highly politicized than they were in an earlier era. The main current of private capital movement, like the main current of trade, goes on within the circle of capitalist countries. In most LDCs the political situation is sufficiently unstable that private investment is warranted only for very high rates of expected return; and to permit such high returns is unpopular and politically difficult in the recipient countries. For the most part, then, capital movement to the LDCs takes the form of government borrowing either from the World Bank group or from individual lending nations. The World Bank group with its three "windows" for hard loans, soft loans, and private investment finance, will probably continue to increase its share of total lending. Bilateral "aid" programs have the familiar limitations of tied procurement, lack of continuity and long-range programming, and a frequent effort to attach political strings. There is substance to the chronic LDC complaint that the richer countries offer only limited amounts of aid, sometimes on rather stiff terms, while with the other hand they impose severe restrictions on LDC exports and decline to cooperate in stabilization schemes for primary products. Though the volume of government-to-government lending may continue to rise gradually, it seems unlikely to grow as fast as was hoped a decade ago; and since repayment obligations are now rising rapidly, the net capital flow will probably diminish. Thus exports may have to bear a growing share of the burden of financing import requirements.

The socialist countries, while their lower income levels may make them less able to "afford" aid, do have an advantage in the structure of their import requirements. Since they need precisely the foodstuffs and other primary products

which the LDCs can supply, they are able to accept loan re-
payments in local currency, that is, in goods. The capitalist
countries, on the other hand, typically require repayment in
hard currencies, which makes their loans less attractive to
the borrowing countries.

In addition to the economic interaction among the three
groups, there is interaction also at the political and intellectual levels. It is no doubt artificial to regard the capitalist
and socialist groups as coherent entities competing for the
allegiance of the Third World, and the latter as making a deliberate choice of politico-economic system. Politics is not so
simple and historical development not so rational. But as
political leaders and would-be leaders in the LDCs observe
the operation of the capitalist and socialist systems, as they
consider the business propositions and intellectual arguments emanating from those countries, as students go to both
Eastern and Western countries for advanced training, opinions and preferences are formed which will have some influence on the course of domestic politics. Some LDCs seem
set on a "mixed economy" development path, and some of
them will in time "graduate" from the less developed category via this route. Others will move in a socialist direction
and, as we shall argue in Part Two, there is no reason to
doubt that this is also a viable development path. Thus over
the very long run, one may expect the number of LDCs to
diminish gradually, and the number of countries in the other
two categories to increase.

The income gap between the capitalist and socialist groups
on one hand, and the less developed countries on the other,
will almost certainly continue to grow over the foreseeable
future. Nor is it clear that this tendency could be reversed
even by massive capital transfers, which the richer countries
thus far show no inclination to furnish. A country's development turns mainly on *internal* effort, and the number of
countries capable of such an effort is still limited.

PART TWO
ECONOMIC POLICY

5 CAPITALIST
ECONOMIES

We start from the premise that, within each of our categories of economy, the high-priority policy areas are broadly similar. Thus we can sensibly discuss policy priorities in the capitalist economies as a whole, as we propose to do in this chapter; and we can make similar catalogs for the socialist and less developed economies in the two chapters which follow. This should be taken for the moment simply as a working hypothesis. How far it is warranted can be judged better after we have tried it out.

By a *policy area* we mean something broader than a policy *objective* or *target* in the Tinbergen sense. A policy area typically involves a conflict among multiple targets. Determination of the trade-offs among objectives, and judgment of how much weight should be attached to each, is the essence of policy making. Thus full employment, price stability, and balance-of-payments equilibrium are *targets*. But the *policy area* is best described as regulating aggregate demand. Similarly, the policy area of income distribution involves a complicated choice among such objectives as efficient resource allocation, interpersonal equity, individual work incentives, and the aggregate savings level.

What is meant by asserting that a policy area is "important"? This can be interpreted as meaning that: (1) a large body of opinion holds that the economy is not meeting criteria of satisfactory performance in the area in question (in some cases, as during a severe depression, opinion may be virtually unanimous; in other cases, as in debates over income distribution, there may be wide division of opinion); (2) economic performance in the area has a substantial effect on the welfare of the citizens generally, or of substantial groups of citizens; (3) economic performance is susceptible of alteration through government action.

Why government? Cannot economic performance be improved by changes in the behavior of private groups? Obviously, it can be. But *responsibility* for stimulating desirable changes in behavior rests on government, and exhortations to private groups to behave differently will usually not suffice. To achieve results, government must reshape the legal and institutional environment so that it is to the advantage of private groups to behave in the desired way.

We suggested in chapter 1 that judgments of relative importance need not be merely subjective. One can estimate how many people would benefit (or lose) from a particular policy action, and how much they would benefit. The fact that such estimates contain wide margins of error should not deter one from making them.

One can also look at the matters on which legislators and administrators choose to spend time and one can sample informed opinion. If a dozen high officials in Washington, or Moscow, or Bangkok agree that a certain policy area is important, we may well give weight to their opinion. This is not to say that officials are omniscient. Their diagnosis of a problem may be inadequate, and their proposed remedies more or less erroneous. But they are probably pointing to an area which deserves attention.

An interesting effort in this direction has been undertaken by a team of economists, who analyzed contemporary economic policy in the Common Market countries plus the United States, the United Kingdom, and Norway.[1] Their

1. E. S. Kirschen, et al., *Economic Policy in Our Time*, 3 vols. (Amsterdam: North-Holland and Chicago: Rand-McNally, 1964). See esp. vol. 1: General Theory.

approach differs from our own, first, in that they sought a ranking of specific *objectives* rather than broader policy areas. Complex objectives, such as improved resource allocation, were subdivided into: improved allocation through internal competition; improved allocation through international trade; improved mobility of factors; and "coordination"— intervention by government to take account of externalities or otherwise to improve private allocation. Second, they were interested in the different priority rankings of different political groups. Parties in the eight countries were divided into "socialist," "center," and "conservative" groupings. Each party's objectives were determined from party programs and from party actions while in office. The resulting rankings, aggregated for the eight countries, are shown in table 5.1. Note that objectives which appear high on the conservatives list are usually low on the socialist list, and vice versa.

When the three columns are combined by a simple point weighting system, price stability, full employment, and economic growth (expansion of production) win out in the overall competition. Next in order come collective needs and international economic relations. Resource allocation, in the usual sense of competitive domestic markets, comes low on all three lists.

A policy area which gets high marks on tests of quantitative importance, and which also gets high marks from economic policy makers, can safely be put on our priority list. While we have tried to observe these broad guidelines, what follows should be taken as no more than the personal ranking of one reasonably informed observer.

Our own ranking of policy areas in the capitalist economies, in order of declining importance, is as follows: (1) regulation of aggregate demand; (2) the mechanism of international payments; (3) supply of public and quasi-public goods; (4) equality of economic opportunity; (5) personal income distribution; (6) economic growth; (7) improvement of markets.

Despite the Kirschen study and other efforts, this ranking contains an unavoidable subjective element. It will have

TABLE 5.1

Preferences of Political Groupings with Regard to Objectives of Economic Policy (Synthesis for 8 Countries)

Priority Ranking	Socialists[a]	Center[b]	Conservatives[c]
1	Full employment	Price stability	Price stability
2	Improvement in income distribution	Expansion of production	Collective needs (defense)
3	Collective needs (nondefense)	Full employment	Improvement in balance of payments
4	Expansion of production	Collective needs (defense)	Allocation (international)
5	Reduction in working hours	Allocation (international)	Protection-priorities[d]
6	Allocation (coordination)[e]	Improvement in income distribution	Expansion of production
7	Protection—priorities	Collective needs (non-defense)	Full employment
8	Price stability	Protection-priorities	Allocation (internal competition)
9	Allocation (international)	Allocation (internal competition)	Collective needs (nondefense)
10	Allocation (internal competition)	Improvement in balance of payments	Allocation (mobility of factors)

[a]Social Democrats and Labor.

[b]Christian Democrats and, in the U.S., Democrats.

[c]Radicals, Independents and French Gaullists, Conservatives in all countries, German and Belgia n Liberals, and U.S. Republicans.

[d]Special support for particular industries or regions, such as agricultural price supports.

[e]Government intervention to improve private resource allocation, as by public utility regulation o r city planning.

Source: E. S. Kirschen and others, Economic Policy, 1:227.

served some purpose, however, if it stimulates other economists to disagree and to prepare their own revised lists. In any event, the analysis under each heading does not depend on the order in which they appear.

The discussion is narrowly circumscribed; and these restrictions apply also to chapters 6 and 7. We are not attempting to evaluate the performance of the economies in question, neither are we attempting to prescribe solutions for their problems. We are trying simply to indicate areas in which there is considerable consensus that performance could be improved. This will lay a background for Part Three, in which we explore the descriptive and policy relevance of Western economic analysis.

To readers who are familiar with Western economies, the discussion of this chapter may seem quite superficial. But the symmetry of the discussion requires both that there be such a chapter, and that it be brief. For Western readers, it will serve mainly as a checklist of familiar problems. For non-Western readers, it may possibly provide new perspectives.

REGULATING AGGREGATE DEMAND

Since the 1930s, this area has usually been given top billing. The problem is to maintain a smooth expansion of output, at a ceiling rate prescribed by the "growth variables" of the economy, while at the same time maintaining reasonable price stability. In most countries, the policy preference as between price and output objectives is such as to permit mild secular inflation, which has in fact been the general rule since 1945.

Manipulating the steering wheel of aggregate demand requires short-range tactics and a longer-range strategy. In the short run, constant diagnostic attention is needed to detect potential economic slowdowns and to counter them by monetary and fiscal devices. The longer-range problem is to absorb a high rate of capital formation without unduly depressing the marginal yield of capital. The conventional prescription for this is rapid technical progress. But we do not know much about the nature and sources of technical progress, or how far it can be influenced by public policy. So, while short-run macroeconomic policy is now reasonably effective, we cannot be so confident about our ability to sustain high rates of capital formation into the indefinite future.

Considering the impressive performance of the Western economies since 1945, can we now put the aggregate demand problem on the shelf? I do not think so. Aggregate demand remains a problem in the sense that, without careful attention month by month, economic performance is likely to fall below acceptable standards. The fact that economic engineering in this area is now much improved does not mean that potential instability has vanished. Moreover, as short-range measures become increasingly effective, the long-range problem of sustaining the yield of capital is thrown into sharper relief.

Two other problems in this area have not been satisfactorily resolved. The first, often termed "incomes policy," is how to restrain the wage-price pressures which accompany sustained high employment. The literature in this area is remarkably frustrating, consisting largely of efforts to talk away the problem. Some economists maintain that a moderate rate of secular inflation does not injure the economy in "real" terms, and on the contrary may have a euphoric effect on business confidence. Others argue that the degree of wage-price pressure is not serious, or can be contained by mild measures of persuasion. Still others take the view that, while the problem is indeed serious, little can be done about it in a basically private economy.

These efforts to dodge the issue suggest that we have not made a mental adjustment to living with continuous full employment. But with reasonable skill in economic management, we shall be living under high-employment conditions for the foreseeable future. In this economic milieu, the problem of secular inflation is indeed serious. It will not go away, and no country has yet devised effective ways of coping with it.

THE MECHANISM OF INTERNATIONAL PAYMENTS

The second troublesome area is that of balance-of-payments adjustments. The proposition that free exchange among countries leads to specialization along lines of comparative advantage, with an increase in world output which makes possible gains for both parties, is one of the oldest in economics. While this proposition has been greatly complicated and qualified in recent years, there remains a prima facie case against trade restrictions.

Trade restrictions among the Western countries are substantially lower today than they were in the 1920s and 1930s, while the volume of trade is much higher. In most Western economies, trade as a percentage of GNP has been higher since 1945 than at any previous time. The most striking instance is the reduction of trade barriers between countries of the European Economic Community, which has intensified competition and stimulated efficiency in the production of tradeable goods, and has contributed to a rapid increase in trade volume.

But the extent and permanence of this progress should not be exaggerated. Considering the small profit margins on which manufacturing concerns operate, effective tariff rates of 10 to 15 percent (and rather more than this in the case of Japan) are still substantial. There is also a wide variety of quantitative restrictions on trade. This is most noticeable as regards agricultural products, where domestic price supports are buttressed by severe trade restrictions. But it occurs also where shifting comparative advantage threatens dislocation of a major industrial sector, as in the United States textile and shoe industries. So it is not yet certain whether the Western countries will move farther in the direction of trade liberalization, or whether they will retreat from the present high-water mark.

The issue is exacerbated by the fact that liberal trade arrangements, combine with a regime of fixed exchange rates and national autonomy in monetary-fiscal policy, leads inevitably to balance-of-payments problems. A country which inflates faster than its neighbors is likely to find its balance deteriorating. Even with all-round price stability, a country which succeeds in maintaining a higher growth rate may suffer an adverse balance through income effects. There are many other possible reasons for balance-of-payments shifts—changes in tastes, resource supplies, technology, and the rest.

There are several possible adjustment mechanisms, none of them entirely satisfactory. A country whose balance is deteriorating can improve its position by curbing aggregate demand; but this is unpalatable if it means unemployment and a reduced growth rate. Floating exchange rates, while supported by a considerable number of economists, have little support among central bankers and finance ministers. Still another possibility is economic integration, extending to a common currency and full coordination of central bank policies. The participating countries would then be (economically) regions rather than nations, rates of expansion in aggregate demand would necessarily be closely synchronized, and balance-of-payments concepts would have no more meaning than they do among Federal Reserve districts in the United States. This possibility—involving, as it does, substantial restrictions on national sovereignty—is still rather visionary even for the EEC countries; and there is no possibility of the entire Western world converting to such a system in the foreseeable future.

Meanwhile, we struggle on with ad hoc devices: the "adjustable peg," an asymmetric system under which a country with chronic deficits is permitted to revalue its currency downward, but one with chronic surpluses is not required to revalue upwards; "swap agreements" among the Western central banks, which permit massive transfers to meet speculative threats to a particular currency; and enlargement of international reserves through "paper gold" to permit greater freedom of maneuver. But the conflict between national sovereignty in monetary-fiscal policy and the requirements for international equilibrium is built into the system. Whenever a country runs into serious and continuing deficit, trade restrictions will be urged as one means of closing the deficit. Thus improved methods for balance-of-payments adjustment may be a necessary condition for permanence of liberal trade policies.

SUPPLY OF PUBLIC AND QUASI-PUBLIC GOODS

In the Western economies, private production and sale is deemed to work satisfactorily for most goods and services. But there are three types of exception: (1) public goods, to which the exclusion principle cannot be applied and which cannot be sold at a price; (2) quasi-public goods or, in Musgrave's terminology, "merit wants," where pricing is feasible but where there may be reasonable grounds for free or subsidized provision by government (education and health services are leading examples); (3) even for goods which are privately produced and marketed, there are cases in which the market does not yield fully satisfactory results and where some type of public intervention is warranted.

The key question about a public good is *how much* of it should be produced. By definition, demand for such a good cannot be revealed and tested in the market. Decisions on output level are reached in the "political market place," by the rivalry of parties contending for public favor. It is often contended a priori that the political mechanism is biased so that its results differ from what the adequately informed citizen would "really prefer." Galbraith argues that the bias is toward too low a level of public services, while economic conservatives often proclaim an opposite bias. But the truth is that we know little about citizens' demand for public services, the accuracy with which this demand is transmitted through political channels, and how this varies by type of service and level of government. Political scientists have paid little attention to these issues. They are now beginning to be investigated by economists, who have the advantage of being interested in *economic consequences* rather than in governmental procedures per se, and who are accustomed to quantitative analysis.

The problem of output level arises also with respect to quasi-public goods. To the extent that government intervenes to provide education, health services, and so on, below full cost, consumption will be larger than it otherwise would be. The case for subsidization rests partly on external effects—it is in my interest that my neighbor's child be healthy and well educated. Beyond this, it is often argued that consumers tend to buy less health care, education, and so on than they would do if they were better informed and more farsighted. The assumption of consumer ignorance and myopia is debatable, however, and even if correct, it could lead to a conclusion that more information rather than subsidized goods should be provided. Actual practice in the Western countries varies substantially, both as regards the *range* of goods which are accorded some degree of "public-ness," and as regards the extent of subsidization.

The third kind of situation—where market sale at a price reflecting private costs does not yield satisfactory social results—includes a complex array of subcases. The simplest analytically is that of divergence between private and social costs or benefits. These divergences are more substantial than the usual brief textbook references suggest. Factory smoke does not just dirty the laundry of the family next door. It can coat a whole metropolis wtih layers of grime and invade the lungs of millions of people. In densely populated areas, air and water pollution have reached a level calling for expensive programs of environmental control.

The decision to buy an automobile is a private consumer decision. But when large numbers of people do this, and when they try simultaneously to drive their cars through congested areas, they impose costs on each other. There is the direct inconvenience of traffic congestion and increased travel time. There is the derived demand for wider roads and streets, for off-street parking facilities, and for police to control traffic violations. Retailers in the core city, who appear to benefit from the customer's ability to drive directly to their door, may beyond a certain point lose out to the suburbs.

There is a clear need for collective decisions to strike a proper balance of costs and benefits. One possibility is to limit access to the central city by private automobile, perhaps by making it more expensive, and to divert traffic to more economical public transport systems.

Another example: the cost of maintaining a worker from retirement age until death can legitimately be considered a production cost of the industries in which he has been employed. But until recently it was not so regarded, and the costs fell haphazardly on individuals or on general government funds. More Western countries now have compulsory pension systems, supported by levies on employers and sometimes on employees as well. Altogether, then, the task of taking care of external effects which the market ignores is a large one.

Next, consider industries such as rail transport and electric power, which are subject to decreasing costs over a wide range, and in which marginal costs are much below average costs. Devising an optimal price-output policy for such industries is difficult, and applying it in practice may be even more difficult. Public ownership and operation of such industries, which is the practice in most Western countries, no doubt makes it easier to apply economically correct policies, but does not guarantee that this will be done.

The railroad case is complex in that railroads are in direct competition with motor transport, and to some degree in competition with air and water transport. These other forms of transport are also usually owned or subsidized in varying ways by government. Overall planning of the transport network is thus required to achieve least-cost movement of freight and passenger traffic. Many countries, including the United States, are barely beginning to think in these terms.

Finally, we may note the problems arising from urbanization. City populations have been growing faster than total populations since the beginning of the Industrial Revolution, and in the Western countries most people now live in metropolitan complexes. Growth has been guided by land values, locational advantages to industry and commerce, housing preferences of consumers, and other economic stimuli; but in some respects it seems decidedly haphazard. The outcome is that many large cities are not pleasant places in which to live and work.

To make large cities livable will require public action of a more innovative sort than has prevailed in the past. Beginnings have been made through city planning, zoning regulation, slum clearance, park and recreational development. But in many countries, notably the United States, these are still only minor skirmishes with a problem which will require decades of sustained effort.

Housing is a specialized problem within the larger problem. Central cities tend increasingly to be inhabited by the very rich and the very poor, while medium-income groups move to the suburbs. The private-housing market can doubtless continue to serve the affluent, who can afford the full cost of comfortable apartments on expensive sities. The poor, however, are crowded by the market into very congested quarters. The landlords do not earn good returns on their expensive but dilapidated property, so the property continues to deteriorate, and replacement costs in the private construction market are so high that rebuilding is not profitable.

Are there any "market solutions" here? A gradual increase in the incomes of the poor will help; but there is no ready way by which individual families who want better housing can accomplish the rebuilding of whole sections of a city. As incomes rise, more of today's poor will move out of the center. But surely it is not economically efficient for all to move—the central city must be good for something. So one comes back to the need for city-wide planning, systematic rebuilding, and (probably) subsidized rentals for low-income families, despite the *general* presumption that money transfers of "free purchasing power" are superior in welfare terms to tied transfers of specific goods.

EQUAL ECONOMIC OPPORTUNITY

Even in highly capitalized economics, labor is much the largest input to production. Labor markets are consequently a very important type of market. It is standard doctrine that labor is best allocated if each individual has full freedom to choose his occupation in the light of prospective returns, training costs, personal capacity, and personal preference. Labor supply curves derived in this way, in conjunction with market-specified demand curves, lead to a welfare optimum.

The capitalist economies presently depart from this norm in significant respects. Families in the lower occupational strata are usually poorly informed about possibilities in the higher occupations; and they tend on this account to have unduly low occupational aspirations for their children (or sometimes quite unrealistic, fantasy-like aspirations). Entrance to the upper occupational strata also requires extended general education and often specific vocational training. This is expensive, and most lower-income families either cannot or will not pay the price. Finally, training capacity for technical, professional, and administrative occupations often falls short of the number who would choose to enter those occupations given adequate information and financing. Removing the informational and financial constraints without enlarging training capacity would simply intensify bottlenecks in the educational system.

The class structure of the Western countries does not arise just from property inheritance, but also from educational-occupational inheritance. There is strong inbreeding in each occupational stratum and even in specific occupations. Doctors' sons become doctors, plumbers' sons become plumbers, business men's sons succeed to the family business. This is perhaps least true in the United States and Canada, where the channels of higher education are wider and the tradition of social mobility stronger. (On the other hand, the United States has its unique Negro problem, one element of which

is that Negroes have been denied the educational opportunities which would enable them to move into the higher occupations in proportionate numbers.)

Restrictions on access to education and hence on free occupational choice misallocate labor and reduce national output. But this is to put the case too mildly. Restraints on
occupational choice widen wage-salary differentials and increase the inequality of personal incomes. They also violate
widely held standards of equity and tend to undermine the
foundations of political democracy. Market inadequacy in
this area is peculiarly galling.

The central problem is equal access to educational opportunities, limited only by personal abilities and preferences.
But any such general formulation glosses over many issues of
detail. "Equal access" on what terms? Should would-be en-
trants to technical and professional occupations be charged
part of the training cost, on the ground that they will receive the higher incomes resulting from training? This would
argue for an enlarged educational loan system. Or should
technical and professional education be provided free? In
this event, does "free" mean only free tuition or does it include scholarships to cover living costs? The more generous
the financial terms, the more people will presumably apply
for these types of education. Should there be an effort to hold
admissions in line with estimated demand, and if so, by what
methods? To the extent that enlarged training facilities are
needed, how should the capital costs be financed? These are
important issues in applied economics.

This view of class structure in the capitalist countries
differs from the usual Marxist interpretation. Private ownership of property, which Marxists emphasize, is important in
that it increases the inequality of household incomes, which
in turn increases the inequality of educational opportunity.
But in our view social classes rest mainly on occupational
specialization, with associated differences in education and
income level. If this is correct, the class structure can be
loosened up through the educational system. In principle,

one could devise a system in which classes are sorted out afresh each generation on an ability basis. This will doubtless never be fully achieved. "Dumb rich kids" will continue to be educated. This may be socially wasteful, but it is the kind of waste about which one cannot be very excited. More serious is the waste of talent in low-income families. If able youngsters from these families can have unrestricted access to education, they will tend to outcompete the more privileged but less talented. Some movement in this direction is visible in most Western countries; and it seems likely that class lines will become increasingly permeable over time.

INCOME DISTRIBUTION AND REDISTRIBUTION

This is one of the oldest areas of economic theory and policy. Nineteenth-century British economists, grounded in utilitarian philosophy, asserted not only that a more equal distribution of income would increase community satisfaction but that they could prove it. Modern economists, warned off by strictures against interpersonal utility comparisons, decline to assert that one income distribution is demonstrably superior to another. Their private preferences, however, tend to be egalitarian and they often end up by making egalitarian recommendations while stoutly denying that these have any scientific basis.

It is useful to distinguish the problem of *inequality* from that of *poverty*. Since most income in the capitalist countries is now labor income, inequality arises mainly (though by no means entirely) from different rates of pay for different occupations. In most Western countries, these differentials have diminished considerably over the past half century. Given freer access to education and thus to the higher occupations, along the lines suggested in the last section, occupational differentials would shrink still further. It can be argued that unequal occupational opportunity, rather that income inequality per se, is the root problem.

Yet income inequality remains a problem in at least two

senses. First, a particular occupational group is often dissatisfied with its wage level relative to other groups which, for one reason or another, are taken as a point of reference. Collective bargaining negotiations resound with arguments that one group has lost ground relative to others, or that it should be entitled to gain ground because of special circumstances. This issue, termed "wage differentials" (United States) or "relativities" (Britain), is a major obstacle to winning union agreement for any sort of incomes policy. Few groups are willing to be frozen *in their present relative position*. Most are inclined to urge special circumstances which, they allege, should make them an exception to the general rule.

Second, distributional equity is a central issue in the framing of tax structures, particularly the schedule of personal income tax rates. People at all levels of income typically argue that their bracket is being taxed unfairly relative to others, and that the burden should be shifted upward or downward. The way in which this issue is resolved has a substantial effect on the distribution of spendable income.

Poverty obviously exists, but is by no means easy to measure. Conventional definitions, usually resting on a judgment of what items a household requires to achieve some "minimum level of health and decency," are arbitrary and subject to change over time. What was considered tolerable in 1900 is not so in 1970. A different approach, proposed by Victor Fuchs among others, is to define the poverty line for a family of specified size, and urban or rural location, as a percentage of the median income of all families in that class.[2] Thus the poverty line would rise with the general level of incomes, as it does at present, but in a more regular and systematic way.

To say that occupational wage differentials are diminishing is to say that the lowest rates of pay are rising faster than higher rates. This tends to bring more and more of the house-

2. Victor Fuchs "Comment" in Lee Soltow, ed., *Six Papers on the Size Distribution of Wealth and Income* (New York: Columbia University Press, for the National Bureau of Economic Research, 1969), pp. 198–202.

holds which contain at least one employable wage earner above the poverty line. There remains, however, a substantial group who for one reason or another are unable to work—the disabled, the aged, mothers in broken homes with small children. There is little disagreement in principle that such people should be provided for through transfer payments. Argument centers rather on the size of such payments, the level of government which should take responsibility for them, and whether any qualifying conditions should be attached. There is also the question of cash transfers versus subsidized provision of food, housing, health care, and other components of a basic standard of living. Despite the well-known argument that the latter approach is inferior in welfare terms, consumption subsidies are quite widely used in the Western countries.

ECONOMIC GROWTH

There are fashions in economic policy, and during the 1950s and early 1960s, "growthmanship" was strongly in evidence. In part, this may have been merely imitative. Since growth is in fact an important objective in the socialist and less developed economies, why not in the West as well? There was during this period a marked development of growth models, both positive and normative, by economic theorists; and it is natural to think that what one is speculating about must have practical relevance. At the peak of the cold war era, some were led to believe that the capitalist economies must participate in a growth race with the socialist economies, which were thought at that time to be advancing more rapidly. In the United States, there was the special circumstance of undercapacity operation from about 1958 to 1965, which focussed attention on diagnosis and remedies.

More recently this kind of concern seems to have subsided, and there has even been a certain revulsion against it. In some circles GNP is now termed "gross national pollution," the ascetic life style is glorified, and it is pointed out that growing urban congestion and larger military expenditure may raise GNP while reducing welfare. Moderate opinion would still hold, we think, that increasing productivity enlarges the options open to a society, including the options of leisure time, education, and cultural activity. But since productive capacity in the capitalist countries is already growing at better than 5 percent per year, it is not clear that there is need for special action to accelerate this rate. Confusion arises also from the fact that a "growth policy" might be interpreted in several different ways:

1. It might mean simply adequate attention to aggregate demand, which we have already recognized as important. If aggregate demand can be regulated so as to avoid serious lapses from full employment, which are mainly declines in investment activity, this will raise the average level of capital formation and the rate of increase in GNP. Success in this respect is probably the main reason why Western growth rates since 1945 have been well above these of earlier decades.

2. It might mean an effort to project the level and composition of national output for five or ten years ahead, with a view to revealing the implications for inputs of trained manpower, basic materials, imports, electric power and transport, and government services. Much work of this sort now goes on in all the capitalist economies. It is useful in averting potential bottlenecks and in planning the expansion of infrastructure facilities with a long construction period. It does not, however, constitute a growth policy in the sense of an effort to raise the GNP growth rate.

3. It might mean that government should aim to raise the values of certain variables which influence the growth rate, such as the amount of research and invention, or the rate of improvement in labor force quality through education and vocational training. There is no doubt that government should be active in such areas, and present expenditure levels in some areas may be less than optimal. This can be discovered, however, only by careful cost-benefit estimates for

specific government programs. Aggregative growth targets would not seem to add much in the way of decision criteria.

4. It might mean that government should try to raise the rate of saving and capital formation. Some increase, though probably only a moderate one, might be achieved through the fiscal mechanism. The conventional objection to doing this is that present savings levels measure consumers' time preference, and that there is no warrant for government interference with consumer choice. But given that most saving is now corporate or governmental rather than personal, that much of personal saving is institutionalized and habitual, and that individual decisions in this area have large and unrecognized external effects, this line of argument is no longer convincing. Actual savings may well differ from what a fully informed community would choose to save if confronted with a present versus future alternative in a national referendum.

It does not follow that we know the *direction* of the deviation between actual behavior and what might be in some sense optimal behavior. It is not clear that a fully informed community would choose to save *more* than they are now doing so that their grandchildren, who are going to be considerably richer in any event, may be richer still. (One Swedish economist has likened such behavior to "sending aid packages to our rich grandchildren in America!") Moreover, investment outlets would have to be provided. This, rather than the supply of saving, is the main constraint on investment in rich countries. Government certainly can encourage investment by favorable tax treatment, by stimulating research and invention, and other measures. But we do not know whether it can do enough in this respect to permit the gross investment rate in the United States to rise, say, from 20 to 25 percent of GNP, even if this were shown to be desirable.

In sum: the capitalist economies are already quite rich. Real per capita income is rising at a rate which, if maintained, will mean more than a doubling in each generation.

Scarcity remains a problem in the sense that people have an unlimited appetite for nonnecessities. But it seems myopic to regard this as a major problem, over which we must whip ourselves into a frenzy of accumulation. On this account we have placed growth rather low on our Western priority list.

MARKET REFORM

The issue of competitive versus monopolistic organization of product and factor markets has traditionally received much attention in Western economics. It is not clear, however, that the effects of monopoly—at least, the static resource allocation effects—warrant this degree of attention. Harberger has estimated, admittedly by rough methods, that restoration of pure competition in all product markets, with the resource reallocation resulting from this, would raise GNP by less than one percent.[3] In labor markets, too, the effect of unionism on wage structure seems less than might have been expected a priori. The summary of available evidence by H. Gregg Lewis estimates that, in the United States around 1960, the wages of unionized workers may have been raised by some 7 to 11 percent, and the wages of nonunion workers depressed by some 3 to 4 percent, compared with what would have happened in the absence of unionism.[4]

This is not to say that monopoly is unimportant, but rather that its importance lies in directions different from those commonly supposed. As regards producing monopolies, the most interesting question is the dynamic problem posed by Schumpeter: is monopoly or strong oligopoly more favorable than atomistic competition to a high rate of innovation and hence of cost reduction (or product improvement) over time? It is rather surprising that after several decades of

3. Arnold C. Harberger, "Monopoly and Resource Allocation," *American Economic Review,* May 1954, pp. 77–87. See also David Schwartzman, "The Burden of Monopoly," *Journal of Political Economy,* Dec. 1960, pp. 627–30.
4. H. Gregg Lewis, *Unionism and Relative Wages in the United States* (Chicago: University of Chicago Press, 1963), p. 5.

speculation and research there is still little consensus on this point. Other interesting unsettled issues are: (1) To what extent do monopolists and quasi-monopolists actually maximize? Are they lazy in holding down costs, compared with managers operating under the whip of competition? Are they satisficers as regards expected profit margins? (2) To what extent does cross-raiding by monopolists in different industries (to which Schumpeter attached much importance), plus the potentiality of international competition, provide an effective substitute for atomistic competition?

As regards unionism, too, an approach focused on its presumed wage-distorting effects misses several possibly more important issues: (1) Does collective bargaining worsen, or could it conceivably alleviate, the problem of achieving reasonable price stability under sustained high employment? (2) How serious is the output loss and public inconvenience caused by work stoppages in "essential" industries? (3) Are these losses clearly outweighed by the protective services which unions render to the individual worker? (4) Do unions function as adequately representative bodies, in the sense of providing equal and fair treatment to all members and would-be members, and in the sense of reflecting accurately the members' economic preferences?

It is quite wrong also to regard nonunion labor markets as adequately competitive. There are many possibilities of market improvement through such things as public employment exchanges, improved forecasting of labor demands, vocational training programs geared to demand estimates, improved counseling of young people, retraining programs for adult workers, and aids to geographic mobility. These things are quite independent of the "union monopoly" controversy, and tend to be obscured by undue concentration upon it.

In sum, there are important policy issues in the area of market organization; but many of these issues do not fit neatly into the framework of conventional microeconomics.

6 SOCIALIST ECONOMIES

Every socialist economy contains both *market elements,* that is, horizontal relationships among enterprises, workers, and consumers; and *planning elements,* that is, flows of information and instructions through a vertical administrative hierarchy. Within a context of comprehensive public ownership, the mix of these two control systems may vary widely. To attain an optimal mix may be regarded as the central problem of socialist economic administration.

The problem appears in many specific forms: control over current production plans, control over investment allocations, indicators of satisfactory enterprise performance, extent of central allocation of materials and components, methods of costing and pricing, locus of price determination. These questions are interrelated, all involving the broader issue of how much scope shall be allowed for market relationships and market-oriented enterprise behavior. This issue obviously has political overtones. While relaxation of central economic controls does not necessarily imply a proportionate reduction of party control over the governmental structure, neither are the two unrelated. Maintenance of party control is an overriding goal to which all other objectives are subordinated.

Since 1960 this complex of problems has been under active discussion throughout the socialist world, and most countries have experimented with new control techniques. These experiments will be our main concern in this chapter. In addition, however, we shall examine several other areas of policy concern: the choice of investment levels and growth targets; determination of the menu of consumer goods; improvement of agricultural performance; and rationalization of trade relations.

PLAN AND MARKET IN ECONOMIC MANAGEMENT

A decade ago there was a standard textbook picture of planning methods in socialist economies: producing enterprises guided by a multiplicity of physical targets; success indicators and bonus systems which did not lead enterprise management to behave in an optimal way; requirements and supplies of key commodities adjusted by the central planners through "the method of material balances"; administration of commodity flows through a rationing system; prices which did not accurately reflect resource scarcities and which played only a minor role in economic management. The author would then point out the economic deficiencies resulting from these arrangements, after which a Western reader could settle back in his chair with a feeling of superiority.[1]

But economic wisdom is not restricted to the West. The inefficiencies arising from centralized physical planning have long been evident to many Eastern economists and administrators. During the 1960s there was much experimentation with new techniques, varying in detail from country to country, but all tending in the direction of decentralization, flexibility, and enterprise autonomy. Experimentation was most active in Yugoslavia, Hungary, and (until 1968) Czechoslovakia, somewhat less active in the USSR and the other East European countries, where it took more the form of adminis-

1. The writer does not mean to criticize anyone else more severely than himself. This is essentially the picture of the Soviet economy presented in the first edition (1963) of my *Economics*. A quite different discussion will be found in the fourth edition.

trative streamlining than of any widespread resort to market devices.

In consequence, it has become more difficult to generalize about socialist planning methods. The only safe statements are of the type: "This is the system installed in Yugoslavia in 1965," or "These are the reforms introduced in Hungary in 1968." It is possible, however, to sketch the issues which are being discussed and the main kinds of institutional change which are being attempted.

Some Defects of Traditional Planning Methods

Let us be clear at the outset why many people have become disillusioned with the planning methods developed initially in the USSR, and transferred after 1945 with little change to the East European countries. We are not concerned at this stage with the final bill of goods. Let us accept "planners' preferences" as valid. At issue here are the problems which arise in achieving the desired bill of goods, and particularly those which arise at the enterprise level.

First, in an economy with hundreds of thousands of products, *everything* cannot be planned. Adequate information cannot be made available fast enough at the center, nor could the largest existing computers handle the necessary calculations. *Some* discretion in choice of inputs and assortment of outputs will always exist at the enterprise level. This creates a possibility, either that the manager will have no criterion for choice within his area of discretion, or that criteria will be imposed from above which lead him to uneconomic choices. The latter has tended to be true under traditional planning methods, which emphasized such physical criteria as weight (of metal products), yardage (of cloth), or volume (of petroleum products).

Second, measurement of performance by output rather than sales reduces the producer's incentive to meet buyers' preferences. A firm can be highly "successful" while unsold goods continue to accumulate. In addition, the traditional emphasis on gross output rather than value added encourages vertical disintegration, with possible losses in efficiency.

The fact that sellers have little interest in serving buyers, and have only limited contact with buyers, ramifies back through the supply chain from finished goods producers to raw material suppliers. When one adds overambitious output targets and chronic excess demand, the result is that enterprises have difficulty in obtaining even the inputs which have been allocated to them. Unofficial and extralegal methods of "expediting" become necessary; and even so, production is often interrupted by material shortages. The problem can be alleviated by reducing the tempo of growth; but this leads to a stop-go economy, with cycles of the type noted in chapter 3.

Multiplicity of a firm's output can be handled by aggregation in value terms. But the fact that the traditional cost-plus prices are not scarcity indicators reduces the significance of such totals. The fact that capital and land have not been assigned a scarcity price also distorts choice of production techniques.

Finally, we may note the difficulty of introducing technical change at the enterprise level. Major changes, while they may yield benefits in the long run, are apt to interrupt production in the short run, and they also involve risk. A manager who has a successful going concern, and whose horizon is bounded by the annual output plan, may not wish to gamble immediate performance against the possibility of future gain.

These are not carping criticisms by a Western "outsider." Everything said here has been said in even stronger terms by Eastern commentators. We say this much merely to suggest the background to which Eastern policy makers are reacting, and the reasons why institutional innovation is a major concern.

The Meaning of "Economic Reform"

In no country has there been a complete reconstruction of the control mechanism. The Hungarian reform might be regarded as approaching this. But in most countries the reforms are being grafted on to institutions and procedures carried over from the past. Equally important, they are administered by much the same people, so that change has to fight its way upstream against bureaucratic routine and inertia.

There is considerable disagreement concerning the appropriate speed and directions of economic change. Much of the impetus for reform has come from the pioneer work of economists such as Brus in Poland, Sik in Czechoslovakia, Kornai in Hungary, Liberman and Kantorovich in the USSR. Economic discussion has been freer and more penetrating during the 1960s than in earlier decades. But there are many conservative economists who distrust the new proposals. Administrators who have grown used to the existing system and feel secure within it also tend to lean against the winds of change. Because of this lack of consensus, and because of the possible instability of a half way reform, one must expect changes in the control structure to follow a zigzag course.

There is also a difference between issuance of new regulations and actual changes in economic behavior. A new procedure may or may not mean anything in practice, or it may turn out to mean something different from what was intended; and it takes time to find out. Thus any evaluation of reform measures must lag several years behind events.

Some countries have been more experimental than others. Yugoslavia has gone farthest, and has a special system of worker participation in management not found in any other country. Hungary installed a coherent, carefully planned set of reform measures at the beginning of 1968. Czechoslovakia installed a similar set of reforms in 1967 and 1968; but after the Soviet intervention, the most prominent advocates of reform were discredited and turned out of office, and many of their policies were reversed.

It will be useful to describe the new Hungarian system, which incorporates most of the ideas which have been tried out in one country or another during the 1960s. After that we shall examine the more limited changes which have been made in the other socialist countries.

Comprehensive Reform: the Hungarian Case

The main features of the new Hungarian system are:[2]

1. Detailed production planning is now carried out by enterprises rather than by central authorities. There are obviously some exceptions to this: new plant construction or major plant expansions; products of special export importance; military items; a few other commodities still subject to central allocation. In general, however, the enterprise is free to choose among outputs, inputs, and production methods with an eye to profitability. This enterprise autonomy operates within the broader framework of social ownership. Decisions to found, reorganize, merge, or liquidate an enterprise are made by higher authorities. The enterprise director is appointed by higher authorities, and removable by them for unsatisfactory performance.

2. Enterprise autonomy implies abandonment of administrative allocation of materials and intermediate products, and this has been done except for a short list of commodities which are of special export importance or which are in unusually short supply. In general, buyers and sellers now negotiate directly on quantities, specifications, and deliveries. There is also a new system of wholesale organizations for producers' goods, designed especially to meet the needs of small buyers. These organizations operate on ordinary commercial principles, making their profit from a trading margin.

An important ancillary objective of the new system is to break down monopoly positions. The fact that buyers can now shop around instead of being assigned to a particular seller should intensify competition in producer goods' markets. Agreements among sellers to subdivide the market or otherwise restrict trade are specifically forbidden.

2. The description below rests mainly on a set of papers included in István Friss, ed., *Reform of the Economic Mechanism in Hungary* (Budapest: Akadémiai Kiádó, 1969).

3. There has been a substantial decentralization of investment decisions. Enterprises are allowed to retain 60 percent of their depreciation charges and about 40 percent of their profits. They can also borrow from state banking organizations. It is estimated that this will allow about 40 percent of national investment to be decided on at the enterprise level, and that this proportion will rise within a few years to 50 percent. The investment proposals which will still be centrally approved and financed include: normal "public sector" (in the Western sense) investments; new plants, or plant expansions which will substantially increase capacity; and investments designed to serve numerous branches of industry, such as power, transport, or water networks.

4. Considerable reliance is placed on profit sharing as an incentive for all personnel, but especially for the higher levels of management. Enterprise profits are first divided into a *sharing fund* and a *development fund* for investment purposes, according to a formula based on the labor-capital ratio in the branch of industry concerned. The development fund is subject to a flat tax rate of 60 percent, while the sharing fund is taxed under a progressive schedule ranging from 0 to 70 percent.

The system initially established in 1968 related the maximum amount which an individual might receive from the sharing fund to his status in the enterprise: (a) general managers, directors, and deputy directors (less than 1 percent of the work force) could receive profit shares up to 80 percent of their regular salaries; (b) "the leaders of workshops, senior foremen, projectors, constructors, technologists, economists, etc." (4 to 12 percent of the work force in most branches of industry) could draw bonuses—as a group average—up to 50 percent of their salaries; (c) all other employees could receive a profit share up to 15 percent of wages and salaries, as a group average. Thus the people whose decisions were most consequential received largest rewards for a good profit performance.

This system has since been revised substantially by con-

verting part of the former bonuses to fixed salaries. The ratio
of fixed salary to total income is now considerably higher
than in the early stages of the reform.

5. A new costing formula has been adopted, and there has
been an effort to bring prices into closer (though by no means
full) accord with costs as thus calculated. In addition to labor, materials, and depreciation charges, each enterprise pays
a capital charge of 5 percent on the value of fixed and cir-
culating assets used in the business. It pays interest on loans
from state credit agencies; and land rents have been introduced on a limited basis. A net income corresponding to 12
percent of the wage bill plus 10 percent of the value of assets
used is also built into the cost estimates.

The next step was to bring producer prices into closer
agreement with the revised costs. Csikós-Nagy estimates that,
before the 1968 price reform, industrial prices averaged 24
percent *below* true cost, while after the reform they averaged
6 percent *above* cost.[3] In addition to realignment of individual prices, the general level of producer prices rose substantially. It was not considered desirable, however, to raise
the retail price level, since this would have precipitated large-
scale wage readjustments and other macroeconomic distur-
bances. So the gap between producer and consumer prices,
and thus the turnover tax revenue to government, is now
much smaller than before. Moreover, the gap varies among
products. Consumer prices have not yet been subjected to
the same thoroughgoing review as producer prices. The in-
herited structure of consumer prices is so distorted, and consumption habits based on this structure are so deeply in-
grained, that specialists consider it may take 10 to 15 years
to approach a situation of equal retail margins throughout
the economy.

6. The previous fixed prices have been replaced by four
categories of price: (a) fixed; (b) maximum or ceiling prices,
which under conditions of excess demand will tend to be

3. Friss, *Economic Mechanism in Hungary,* chap. 6. All references
below to pricing are from this source.

the actual price; (c) prices which may fluctuate between prescribed limits; (d) free prices. The mix of these devices varies
substantially as one moves from raw materials through to the
retail level. Prices are most flexible at the processing stage,
where about three-quarters of all prices are free of control.
But free prices exist for only about one-quarter of basic materials, which are typically in very short supply; and only
about 30 percent of consumer goods prices have been freed,
since inflationary pressure continues strong. The picture is
thus one of limited price flexibility, with an expressed hope
for growing flexibility over the years ahead.

7. The cost and price revisions have produced a different
composition of national income and a different structure of
government revenues. In industry, wages now form about
two-thirds of value added, with capital and rent charges
forming one-third. For the economy as a whole, the proportion is about three-quarters to one-quarter. This ratio is not
far from that observed in capitalist economies at a comparable level of development.

In the state budget, turnover tax revenue has dropped
dramatically from 53 percent of total revenue before the reform to 7 percent after it; and most of this is absorbed in sub-
sidizing consumer goods whose retail price is now below the
new producer price. About three-quarters of government
revenue now comes directly from enterprises in one form or
another: the profit tax, the capital and rent charges, the government share of depreciation allowances, a 25 percent tax
on payrolls, and social insurance contributions.

8. The loosening of central controls has increased the possibility of wage-price inflation and has compelled greater attention to macroeconomic policy. The instruments used are
familiar: fixed or ceiling prices on most consumer goods; an
"incomes policy" which, for example, provided that in 1968
the general wage level in industry might rise by no more
than 4 percent; monetary policy, involving variation of both
interest rates and credit availability, depending on the social
importance of the proposed investment as well as the level

of aggregate demand; and varying the timing of centrally planned investment programs. Tax variation does not seem to be visualized as an important short-term device.

9. Two standard exchange rates, based on the estimated cost of earning foreign exchange, have been established, one for trade with the socialist countries and one for trade with other countries. Exporting concerns are now paid the foreign price of their products, while importers are charged the foreign price for their imports, converted at the appropriate exchange rate. This is an effort to align domestic with foreign prices, to strengthen export incentives, and to use imports as a means of strengthening competition in the domestic market. Even though competition is now viewed with favor, the possibility of domestic competition is limited by the very scale of enterprises, which creates a monopoly or oligopoly situation in most markets.[4] Intensified foreign competition may serve to alleviate this situation.

This in broad outline is the new economic structure. So what has happened? Experience in the first two years of operation has been generally encouraging.[5] Enterprises have found it possible to manage their affairs without detailed directives. Industrial output has continued to rise, though the price level has also risen moderately. Decentralized investment has been somewhat larger than was projected, but the central authorities have been willing to accommodate this by cutting back their own projects. There seems no

4. Pryor finds that the average scale of enterprise is considerably larger in the socialist countries than in the West, and is largest of all in Czechoslovakia and Hungary despite their relatively small markets. In the mid-1960s, the percentage of mining and manufacturing employment in enterprises with more than one thousand employees was as follows: Czechoslovakia 92 percent, Hungary 86 percent, Poland 71 percent, USSR 64 percent, U.S. 63 percent, Italy 32 percent, West Germany 27 percent (Frederic L. Pryor, "Barriers to Market Socialism in Eastern Europe in the Mid 1960s," forthcoming in *Studies in Comparative Communism;* this paper contains a good comparative analysis of the economic reforms in all the East European countries through the late 1960s).

5. In addition to the Pryor study, see Richard D. Portes, "Economic Reforms in Hungary," *American Economic Association Proceedings* May 1970, pp. 307–13.

present disposition to reverse the trend of the reform—indeed, there has been a modest additional freeing of prices and allocations.

Soviet Economic Reform

While these reforms have been relatively modest, they are important because of the size of the Soviet economy and because they indicate a more experimental attitude than prevailed in earlier years. While the reforms were in a sense "completed" during the years 1965–67, there is a continuing discussion of their accomplishments and deficiencies, and a certain amount of continuing experimentation.[6] The main steps taken in the mid-1960s were:

1. Wholesale prices were thoroughly revised. Capital charges, at a standard rate of 15 percent, were included in cost calculations; and price-cost margins were considerably increased. No branch of industry now shows an overall loss, and the number of enterprises showing a loss has been much reduced. A side effect is that capital charges plus enterprise profits remitted to government are now the largest source of public revenue, outweighing the formerly dominant turnover tax.

2. Enterprise plans are in principle to be less detailed and less physical. Within approved financial totals, enterprises are to have greater flexibility in adjusting inputs to reduce costs and in adjusting outputs to meet customer requirements. Retained profits and bank loans are now an important, though still minor, source of investment funds for the enterprise.

3. The key success indicators are now value of *sales* (rather than *output*), and overall *profitability*. The percentage of plan fulfilment is calculated by a complicated formula, which

6. Good recent articles include: A Kornin, "Economic Reform and Tasks in Further Improving Price Formation," *Problems of Economics,* December 1968, pp. 39–46; M. Garin and A. Druzenko, "Plant Engineers," *Current Digest of the Soviet Press* 21, no. 29: 14–17; "Next Steps in the Reform: One Plant's Viewpoint," *Current Digest of the Soviet Press* 20, no. 39: 19–22.

includes both these elements and which varies somewhat among industries. This percentage is then applied to the wage fund of the enterprise in order to compute the "incentive fund" from which bonuses are paid to workers and management.

4. Enterprises are encouraged to take more initiative in seeking out customers and sources of supply and negotiating directly with them on quantities, specifications, and deliveries.

Recent Soviet literature suggests that, while these are generally regarded as steps in the right direction, there are troublesome unsolved problems. There seems still to be much petty tutelage of enterprises by the supervising ministries. Detailed lists of physical targets are still issued, and are often revised—usually upward—at frequent intervals. Freedom of interenterprise negotiation is restricted by the continued central control over material flows. Even after enterprise A has agreed to sell certain quantities to enterprise B, it may take several months for the necessary papers to be reviewed and approved by central procurement officials.

There is criticism of the inflexibility of prices, and proposals for more frequent price revision and some decentralization of price-setting authority. There is criticism that the system still provides little incentive for introduction of new or improved products. An interesting suggestion here, reminiscent of Schumpeter, is that firms should be allowed to set a high initial price for new products, which would be reduced gradually over the course of time. There is complaint that the formula for determining the incentive fund is unduly complicated and can readily become counterproductive. For example, the fact that the wage fund forms the base of the calculation reduces the firm's incentive to economize on use of labor. There appears to be substantial overstaffing in Soviet industry—usually referred to euphemistically as "internal labor reserves"—which intensifies the general labor shortage in the economy.

A more technical criticism, advanced by proponents of

rational pricing such as Kantorovich, is that profit rates still differ widely among branches of industry. Thus in 1967 the profit rate was 38 percent in light industry, 20 percent in machine building and metalworking, 14 percent in lumber, woodworking, pulp and paper, and 7 percent in electric power.[7] There is also substantial variation in the norms of expected profitability applied to new investment proposals. Thus proposals are being approved for electricity projects yielding only 10 percent, while textile investments are expected to yield 33 percent.[8]

The fact that such criticisms are advanced freely and from authoritative sources suggests that further reforms may be in the offing. Indeed, piecemeal and pragmatic reform may possibly become habitual.

The Feasibility of Halfway Reform

As between conservative reforms of the Soviet type and the more thoroughgoing Hungarian reforms, most of the East European countries are probably still closer to the Soviet pattern. Limited changes have been made in the areas of cost calculation and pricing, success indicators, enterprise self-financing, and greater enterprise autonomy in other directions. But these changes are embedded in a system of centralized physical planning, fixed prices, and controlled allocation of materials. This effort to graft limited reforms onto a structure which is rather inhospitable to them creates difficulties which deserve brief comment.

The blending of old and new may well create a situation in which some of the powers nominally granted to lower administrative levels cannot be exercised effectively, or in which exercise of those powers produces unintended results, leading possibly to pressure for recentralization. First, in such a

7. N. Garetovskii, "The Role of Profit and Profitability Under the New System for Economic Stimulation of Production," *Problems of Economics,* Aug. 1969, pp. 3–30.

8. L. Vaag, "When is Innovation Advantageous?" *Current Digest of the Soviet Press* 21, no. 40, 7. See also V. Bogachev and L. Kantorovich, "The Price of Time," *Problems of Economics,* Feb. 1970, pp. 3–27.

mixed system it is not easy for firms to exercise their nominal authority to vary inputs and outputs. With continued excess demand maintaining a sellers' market for inputs, the firm may have to use what it can get rather than what it would prefer. To the extent that physical output targets are maintained for major products, firms may be similarly constrained in their output choices. Further, an increase in profit need not indicate improved economic performance, since neither product nor factor prices necessarily reflect resource scarcities.

Second, it is difficult for a quasi-market system to function when market-clearing prices are not permitted. Suppose enterprises were given full freedom (as they usually are not) to trade directly with each other in materials, intermediate products, and capital goods; but suppose that prices of these goods were fixed below the market-clearing level. The result is general "shortages," haphazard deliveries, inventory hoarding, and interruptions of production. This leads naturally to pressure for reinstitution of rationing to maintain an orderly materials flow.

Third, suppose that decentralization of investment decisions produces a level of planned investment above the capacity of capital goods industries. Not only will inflationary pressure be intensified, but some planned projects will be squeezed out (or find their construction periods much delayed), and the surviving projects may not constitute an optimal mix. This seems to have happened, for example, after the 1967 Czech reforms. Enterprise profits, retained earnings, and planned investments turned out to be considerably higher than had been projected. Moreover, the enterprises were nimble enough to get many of their projects in ahead of the centrally planned or "government" projects, so that the squeeze came mainly on the latter group. Such an outcome may be economically undesirable, and at any rate unacceptable to the central economic authorities.

Fourth, some countries have grouped the enterprises in each branch of industry under a "trust," a supervisory level intermediate between the enterprise and the central au-

thorities. This can create problems, depending on how the
trusts exercise their nominal powers. At one extreme, they
might function merely as letterboxes, passing on the directives received from above. In this case there has not been any
real decentralization. At the other extreme, they might attempt to operate as monopolies, asserting the interests of
their industry against other sectors of the economy. Such
policies, which in the West might lead to efforts at "trust-
busting," are in the East more likely to lead to proposals to
curb the power of the trusts by reasserting central controls.

The emergence of such difficulties after a partial reform
could lead one to argue either that the reform went too far
or that it did not go far enough. Both lines of argument are
frequently heard in the socialist countries. Those who were
never in favor of reform can now say "We told you so. The
problem is that the anarchy of the market has been allowed
to intrude into our orderly planned economy." They will advocate curbs on enterprise autonomy and tightening of central controls. "Liberal" economists, on the other hand, may
argue that, if one chooses to rely on market instruments, one
must use them in a thoroughgoing way. The problems have
arisen, not because producing units were given too much
freedom, but because they were given too little. This line of
argument, however, is apt to be regarded as both "academic"
and unorthodox. The combination of ideological antipathy
to "the anarchy of the market," bureaucratic preference for
traditional routines, and party leaders' fear of a weakening
of party control is a powerful one, and in the end the proponents of recentralization will often prevail.

But strengthening of central controls leads back into the
difficulties noted earlier; and when these difficulties become
glaring enough, there will be pressure for new experiments
in decentralization. Institutional evolution in the socialist
economies may thus follow a dialectical course, with any
strong movement toward either central administrative con-

trols or market controls setting up in time a movement in the opposite direction.[9]

Decentralization Versus "Computopia"

A quite different view is that the computer may have arrived just in time to make full central planning a feasible proposition. Since the politics of the socialist countries work against a "market socialist" utopia, why not work toward a different kind of utopia, in which market processes are replicated in the computer and detailed production orders issued on the basis of these calculations? Peter Wiles has termed this "perfect computation in lieu of perfect competition," while others have termed it "planometrics" or "computopia."

The rationale of this approach has been worked out mainly by mathematicians rather than economists, including in the USSR Nemchinov, Novozhilov, and Kantorovich.[10] Mathematicians have an advantage in being relatively free of ideological preconceptions and thus able to take a straightforward efficiency approach to economic problems. Moreover,

9. This point has been emphasized by Montias: "Experience has shown that when the planners seek to embrace too many activities, they fail to keep them within their grasp. 'Spontaneous' activities go on at lower levels, without regard to approved programmes, because the plans are too inaccurate to regulate the detailed operations. . . . There are also forces making for re-centralization in a partially decentralized system. In part, these forces stem from the upper echelons of the administration, intent on neutralizing the negative effects of uncoordinated decisions taken at lower echelons, and in part from the enterprises themselves, which are constantly appealing to superior authorities against adverse decisions on the part of their suppliers or of their functional organizations. The dynamics of a bureaucratic organization kept under political pressure are such as to cause a larger share of these detailed decisions to be referred all the way to an ultimate decision-making authority. In short, *the natural equilibrium of a command economy tends to be repelled by both extremes of centralization and decentralization*" (John M. Montias, "The Czechoslovak Economic Reforms in Perspective," in George R. Feiwel, *New Currents,* pp. 508–09).

10. A basic source is L. V. Kantorovich, *The Best Use of Economic Resources* (Cambridge: Harvard University Press, 1965). See also V. S. Nemchinov, *The Uses of Mathematics in Economics* (Cambridge: M. I. T. Press, 1964); and John P. Hardt et. al., eds., *Mathematics and Computers in Soviet Economic Planning* (New Haven: Yale University Press, 1967).

sheltered by the prestige of physical science and by an esoteric language, there are not as subject as the "political economists" to criticisms of unorthodoxy. They have thus been able to work in relative freedom, though at a very abstract level and (as yet) with little visible influence on economic affairs.

The central insights come from linear programming, which was developed more or less simultaneously by Kantorovich in the USSR and Dantzig, Koopmans, and others in the United States. In Western writings the standard linear programming problem is to maximize the output value of two or more products, whose prices are given, on the basis of given quantities of productive resources and given linear transformation relations. In Kantorovich, the problem is turned around. The bill of goods to be produced is given by a planning decision. The problem is how to produce this menu at minimum resource cost. Solution of the problem yields both an allocation of inputs among products *and* a valuation of each input—"objectively determined values" in Kantorovich's terms, "shadow prices" in Western terminology—which are analogous to market prices in a perfectly competitive economy. The essence of Kantorovich's view is that such prices, reflecting both scarcity and productivity, must be substituted for present pricing practices to yield optimal economic results.

Linear programming was developed as a tool for solving micro problems, and its main applications have been at the plant level. (Kantorovich's initial experiments involved allocation of logs among stripping machines in a Leningrad plywood factory so as to maximize the throughput of logs per unit of time; and most of the illustrations given in his book are of similar character.) The question is how extensible these methods are to economy-wide planning. Note first that the final bill of goods is taken as given, without reference to "utility," "consumer preference," and so on. No one proposes to admit the computer to output decisions. So planometrics could at most solve only part of what Western economists would regard as the optimizing problem.

Within these limits, the problem is whether all the things the central planner should know for efficient decision can be reduced to quantitative terms, whether a vast amount of detailed information from all corners of the economy could be transmitted accurately and rapidly to a central point, and whether the subsequent calculations are within the capacity of available computer systems. The problem could perhaps be mitigated by "computer decentralization," that is, by establishing subcenters to process information from particular sectors of the economy, which would then feed information to and receive instructions from the "big machine" in Moscow. One can even imagine a "far out" planning system in which the present hierarchy of economic administrators would be replicated by machines sitting in the offices presently occupied by bureaucrats.

It seems unlikely, however, that the administrators will agree cheerfully to their own euthanasia. Nor does it appear that the informational-computational problems are soluble even on technical grounds. The prevalent opinion among experts seems to be that computopia is for the time being an entirely fanciful idea.[11]

In fairness to Soviet proponents of "optimal planning," it should be added that they do *not* advocate this kind of utopia as a practical proposition. On the contrary, what they claim to have demonstrated is that a system of rational prices can be used for *indirect* guidance of the economy. They are much concerned with relations among different levels of the hierarchical control structure, with appropriate levels of decision making, with ways of combining central control in the large with enterprise autonomy in detail (which they believe can,

11. See, for example, comments by Abram Bergson, "Market Socialism Revisited," *Journal of Political Economy,* Oct. 1967, pp. 655–73; Egon Neuberger, "Libermanism, Computopia, and Visible Hand: the Question of Informational Efficiency," *American Economic Review Proceedings,* May 1966, pp. 131–44; Alec Nove, "Planners' Preferences, Priorities, and Reforms" in George R. Feiwel, *New Currents,* and Ward, Montias, and others in the Hardt, *Mathematics and Computers* symposium.

given correct pricing, produce socially optimal results). What they are mainly urging is a rational approach to calculation of economic efficiency, as against the doctrinaire approach of the old-style "political economists."[12]

Interesting work along these lines has been done in Hungary by Janos Kornai.[13] While Kornai believes in the usefulness of programming methods and has been instrumental in applying them to Hungarian planning, he has never been an advocate of computopia. Rather, he regards the computer and the market as *complementary goods.* The purpose of programming calculations is not to substitute for the market but rather, in areas where central decisions are necessary, to make those decisions more efficient.

THE TEMPO OF ECONOMIC GROWTH

The overriding objective of socialist economies is expansion of output capacity. The main instrument is a high rate of capital accumulation, though there is also strong emphasis on human resource development.[14] High investment implies austerity in consumption—a "classical" growth strategy. Real wages lag the rise in per capita output, permitting heavy investment in producer goods' industries.

The form which this strategy takes varies with the size and openness of the economy. In the largely autarkic Soviet development, it consisted of massive transfers of labor and other domestic resources into infrastructure industries and heavy manufacturing—"machines to build machines." This has been true also in the even more self-contained economy of

12. For a review of recent work by this school of Soviet economists, see Michael Ellman, "Optimal Planning (A Review Article)," *Soviet Studies* 20 no. 1, 112–36.

13. See his *Mathematical Planning of Structural Decisions* (Amsterdam: North-Holland, 1967); and Janos Kornai and T. Lipták, "Two-Level Planning," *Econometrica,* Jan. 1965, pp. 141–69.

14. The Pryor study cited in chap. 3 found that socialist countries' expenditure on education is as high as, and expenditures on research and development is rather higher than, that in Western countries of comparable per capita income.

China. In smaller economies such as Romania, underemployed labor and other domestic resources were directed partly toward export production, the proceeds being used to import machinery and industrial supplies from Czechoslovakia, East Germany, and the USSR. As Romania after 1945 rebuilt its capacity to produce foodstuffs, forest products, and crude oil, these *could* have been directed toward consumption needs. Food could have been eaten, timber could have been put into housing. Instead, food, timber, and oil were transformed into capital goods via foreign trade.[15]

It is commonly said that socialist economies differ from others in that their growth rate is a matter of deliberate choice. This does not mean, however, that objective restrictions on the growth rate are absent. In the short run, there are limits on the capacity of domestic capital goods industries, on import possibilities, and on availability of raw materials, fuels, and power. In small economies, particularly, an effort to press too hard against these restrictions leads to bottlenecks and an enforced reduction of the growth tempo. Moreover, since economic performance cannot be perfectly anticipated and controlled, ex post increases in GNP will deviate—typically, in a downward direction—from the ex ante targets. Such shortfalls are not distributed evenly over the whole of national output. Target fulfilment is typically higher in such activities as power, metals, and machine building than in consumer goods industries, housing, and services. The reason is that, as input shortages become apparent, the former category is given priority in the rationing process.[16] Much of consumer goods output, indeed, can be regarded as a residual.

15. This case is documented in Montias, *Economic Development of Communist Rumania.*
16. The relative ease with which this can be done under centralized physical planning is an important reason for resistance to decentralization. The central economic authorities naturally wonder: "If everyone is allowed to compete for resources in the market, can we any longer be *certain* that what we regard as high-priority industries will get the supplies they need?"

The objective limits on growth rates at any time are some-what uncertain. There are also differences of opinion about how much austerity the population will accept, or should be asked to accept. Thus the choice of a growth tempo some-times becomes a matter of factional rivalry within the Party. Leaders tend to get classified as "hard liners," favoring a high investment level, or "soft liners," who are willing to reduce investment targets in order to offer consumers more in the short run. Even soft liners, however, favor investment rates which are high on a world scale.

The choice of an investment level does not dictate a specific allocation of investment. Further choices are required, and socialist economic literature provides few clues as to how these choices are made. There is frequent reference in Soviet sources to "the law of planned proportionate development of socialist economies," but this formulation seems to have little concrete meaning. A more specific principle is that output of capital goods industries should grow more rapidly than that of consumer goods industries. A heavy industry-light industry sequence of industrialization is preferred to the op-posite sequence. In the Soviet case, this made good sense in terms of the size of the economy and the predominance of defense considerations. It is less clearly appropriate in the smaller East European countries, which have tended never-theless to follow the Soviet model.

Investments in heavy manufacturing, electric power, and so on are large and "lumpy," and it is not feasible to spread a limited annual budget evenly over all claimants. This must be partly responsible for the jerky, unbalanced pattern of Soviet economic growth ("unbalanced," that is, over any 5–10 year period, though perhaps eventuating in a "balanced economy" after 50 years). During each planning period, a few industries are singled out as prime constraints on future growth. Resources are channeled into these "leading links," to the temporary deprivation of other industries. As the chosen industries expand, however, capacity shortages ap-pear in related industries, that is, in other parts of the input-output matrix. These new bottlenecks are then attacked during the next planning period.

Growth in the socialist economies has been unbalanced also in the sense of emphasis on "directly productive activities" to the relative neglect of "infrastructure." True, power production has been greatly expanded. But in the transportation field, preexisting roads and railroads have been used more and more intensively, with relatively little investment in new construction and repair. Housing, the major item of social infrastructure, has also received relatively small allocations. In Hirschmanesque terms, the strategy has been one of "development via shortages" (of infrastructure) rather than "development via excess capacity."

This strategy works in the sense that the socialist economies have grown and are growing. The industrial base is being laid. But will not any one of numerous expansion paths "work" in this sense? Is there any basis for regarding one (temporarily unbalanced) path as preferable to another? The question whether Western conceptual tools are of any use in analyzing such problems will be raised in chapter 9.

MEETING CONSUMER REQUIREMENTS

In any economy, capitalist or socialist, one can classify national output into investment goods, community consumption, and "private" consumer goods. Under traditional socialist planning the investment share is centrally decided. Even where enterprises have some autonomy in investment, government has macroeconomic instruments for holding the investment total within prescribed limits. In neither case does the time preference of households enter directly, though it may enter indirectly via political pressures for higher consumption. Socialist planners have a bias toward high investment, implying a low rate of time discount. (This is probably a bias of planners in any economy, the difference being that socialist planners have superior tools with which to implement their preferences.)

Actual socialist and capitalist economies do not differ as much as a comparison of ideal types might suggest, either in the size of the investment allocation or the mechanism by which it is decided. In capitalist countries, too, most saving is done by business corporations and government agencies, with household saving a minor part of the total. The Fisherian picture of individual time-preference maps meeting capital productivity schedules in the market is quite far from contemporary reality. Capitalist governments also influence the level of national saving and investment through the tax structure, monetary controls, support of research and development, and other policy instruments. The investment allocation comes out, on the average, a few percentage points lower in the capitalist than in the socialist economies; but the difference is not dramatic.

Does the socialist political mechanism tend also to allocate more resources to public goods than do Western political systems? This may be true for some types of public good, but certainly not for all. In chapter 3 we note Pryor's finding that, for some types of public expenditure, the country's per capita income level is the most important determinant and "systems" differences are not significant. In the special case of military expenditure, the size of the country and its role in strategic alliances are dominant considerations. Both the United States and the USSR "overallocate" to the military, compared with their smaller allies.

What can one say about the 60 percent or so of output which consists of "private" consumer goods? At first glance, the production apparatus in the socialist countries does not seem very consumer oriented. Shortages and (less frequently) surpluses are endemic, the price-cost gap varies widely from product to product, the size of the gap seems to have no direct influence on output decisions, there is little effort to ascertain consumer preferences by market research of market experimentation. It is sometimes said that the output pattern reflects planners' preferences rather than consumers' preferences· but this may or may not be a useful concept. As Nove points out, "Planners prefer to be able to prefer."[17] Beyond this, it is not clear why they should prefer one menu of consumer goods to another, still less specific details of assortment and design. Even if they had definite preferences, it cannot be assumed that these correspond with the outputs actually appearing on retail markets, which may reflect varying degrees of miscalculation and error. What actually happens may be something which nobody would have preferred ex ante. This leads back to difficulties already described: chronic excess demand and sellers' markets, inferior position of retail enterprises vis-à-vis manufacturers, "success" indicators for enterprises which pay inadequate attention to quality, styling, and design, and an ideological bias against service outputs.

It is clear that the category of "merit goods" (and of "demerit goods") is wider in the socialist economies. Even capitalist governments subsidize school lunches, medical care, and low-income housing, while penalizing alcohol and tobacco. But in the socialist economies, systematic price discrimination extends (on the low side) to all housing, to basic food and clothing items, to books and other educational materials, to both local and long-distance passenger transport, and (on the high side) to a wide array of "luxury products."[18]

17. "Planners prefer to be able to prefer. . . . they have a vested interest in a decision-making structure that gives them power to make decisions. It is also a socio-economic fact that, for various reasons, public authorities in charge of resource allocation often do not seem to care much for the convenience of the citizens. But this is quite another question. It does not mean that the planners prefer any particular bill of goods. They do not consciously desire that the customer be unable to obtain what she wants, though the institutional arrangements are such that she may be unable to do so" (Alec Nove, "Planners' Preferences, Priorities, and Reforms," *Economic Journal,* June 1966; reprinted in Feiwel, *New Currents,* p. 286).

18. A Soviet economist, after noting the relatively low price of basic foodstuffs, proceeds: "Moderate prices are fixed for consumer goods as well: for overalls and shoes, domestic electric appliances, watches, goods for children, textbooks, school copy books, medical drugs, sanitation articles, and many other goods. These prices, as a rule, are fixed at the level close to prime cost. . . . The rent for a separate, two-room flat with a kitchen, including payments for electricity, gas, and hot and cold water totals no more than 10–12 roubles per month. Rent in the USSR

One consequence is widespread shortages and queuing for the subsidized goods, particularly urban housing.

The object of such widespread subsidization is to bring a menu of basic necessities within the financial reach of every household, thus establishing a minimum level of consuption. Differential pricing is used in lieu of cash transfers and progressive income taxation to alter the distribution of real income in an egalitarian direction. Most Western economists would probably say that, while this may be a feasible technique of income redistribution, it is in welfare terms an inferior technique. The most efficient method of redistribution is to provide money transfers, leave consumers free to choose among goods according to their preferences, and maintain a (generally) neutral price system which reflects resource costs.

But this argument is not watertight. It assumes a degree of consumer information, foresight, and rationality which may well be absent even in economies where advertising distortions are absent. It overlooks interdependence and external effects in consumption. Moreover, where the object of policy is to raise the welfare of a *particular group*—families with children, or the ill and disabled—a case can be made for measures aimed directly at this objective, such as low-cost children's food, clothing, and school books or low-cost medical care.[19]

At any event socialist planners, even after a lecture course

---

accounts for approximately 5 percent of a working family's budget. . . . On city transport, one-way fares are from 3 to 5 kopecks. . . . It is natural that in the USSR there are certain goods where the State tries to limit demand by imposing a sales tax on them and imposing a higher price level; such goods are vodka, other strong drinks, tobacco. . . . The prices fixed for jewelry, perfume, fine fabrics, and some other goods are relatively high" (R. Belousov, "Price as a Means of Planning the National Economy," in Douglas C. Hague, *ed., Price Formation in Various Economies* [New York: St. Martin's Press, 1967], pp. 143–44). Automobiles might have been included in the high-price category, while trucks are low priced.

19. This and the possible arguments for differential pricing are well developed in Maurice Dobb, *Welfare Economics and the Economics of Socialism* (Cambridge: Cambridge University Press, 1969), chap. 10.

on the principles of ideal pricing, might not want to adopt them as a universal rule. The reason may be that their approach to the problem of serving the consumer, and their vision of the eventual "affluent society," differs from that prevailing in the West. We visualize a golden age in which the marginal utility of income to each consumer will be very low and his total utility very high. Receipt of money income, and allocation of this income by consumers on retail markets, will remain the central mechanism for commodity distribution. But as the level of real purchasing power rises higher and higher, an extra dollar will eventually have little significance.

Marxians also aim at a millennium of "high mass consumption." But the path to it consists in *steadily enlarging the sphere of free distribution* of goods. Since free distribution of most things is not yet feasible, low-cost distribution of consumption necessities is regarded as a step in the right direction. Since the subsidized goods are available to all—or all who can work their way to the head of the queue—this is also a step toward equalization of real household incomes. A basic reason for lack of interest in perfecting consumer markets is that they are regarded as a second-best mechanism, whose role will diminish in the decades to come.

This line of reasoning, however, is most applicable to goods which are generally regarded as necessary elements in a decent standard of living, and of which everyone desires some minimum amount.[20] Provision of this minimum, on a subsidized

---

20. Dobb *(Welfare Economics,* pp. 218–19) suggests an interesting technical point in this connection. When consumer incomes have reached a certain level (and assuming a rather egalitarian distribution of income), some new item of consumption—a bicycle, a radio, a refrigerator, eventually an automobile—will come to seem both necessary and attainable. Every family will want one unit of the good, but rarely more than one. Thus demand will be very elastic up to the satiation point, but highly inelastic beyond that. "This . . . means that no market equilibrium exists between zero (or some very low) output and a satiation (or near-satiation) output. . . . the crucial planning decision will be whether to put the item into production at all, and if so whether the community

or eventually a free basis, may be a sensible policy objective. But as the productive power of the economy grows, and as basic wants are increasingly satisfied, consumer desires spill over increasingly into luxuries and semiluxuries. These will form a growing proportion of total output. Instead of the "full communism" of Marxian theory, it may be more plausible to visualize a "split-level economy," with free distribution of a basic menu of necessities and market distribution of other goods. For goods on the market list, equalization of price-cost margins would seem a sensible rule. And for all goods, output should be responsive to consumer preferences concerning quality, assortment, and design.

So there is a genuine problem of ascertaining and meeting consumer preferences, which will grow in importance as the socialist economies become richer. This is recognized by many socialist economists and administrators. It underlies efforts to establish closer links between manufacturers and retailers, to give the latter greater voice in quality and design, to substitute sales for output as a success indicator. It is inherent in discussions which are beginning to appear on demand elasticities and the need for market research on consumer preferences and intentions.[21] Moreover, pricing and investment decisions may be influenced increasingly by revealed preferences. In the USSR, for example, output capacity for some products—watches, cameras, radios, bicycles—is now large enough so that, at traditional turnover tax markups, these goods have begun to back up in distribution channels. This has led to price reductions for some items, to "clearance sales," to introduction of time payment. The implication is

---

can afford to produce it on a scale sufficient to satiate demand: a decision that can scarcely be a market-guided one, still less decided according to marginal rules."

21. See, for example, B. Gogol, "Problems Pertaining to the Study and Evaluation of Public Demand," *Problems of Economics*, Jan. 1970, pp. 43–58; B. Davidovich and E. Chertikhina, "Mathematical-Statistical Methods in the Forecasting of Demand," *Problems of Economics*, May 1968, pp. 18–26; and V. I. Raitsin, "Planning the Standford of Living According to Consumption Norms," a monograph published as *Problems of Economics* 11, nos. 6–7 (1968).

that investment allocations for such products can be cut back, and this message will surely not be lost on Soviet planners. Adjustment of investment and output plans to sales figures may be more sluggish than in a market economy; but there is no reason to think that feedback is entirely blocked.

THE LAGGING AGRICULTURAL SECTOR

In the socialist countries, agriculture has typically been a lagging sector, whose slow growth has retarded the general economic advance. How to accelerate the increase of agricultural output is one of the most basic and intractable of policy problems.

The form of the problem differs, depending on whether agriculture is privately or collectively organized. In some socialist countries, most land remains for the time being in private hands. This is regarded as a transitional stage, since collective cultivation is considered correct in principle; but the transition may last for a long time. Here the problem is to provide the training, the modern inputs, and the cash incentives which will call forth increased output from a multitude of small cultivators. The problem is similar to that of raising agricultural productivity in the LDCs, which will be examined in chapter 7.

The problem of raising output levels on collective farms has several facets:

1. What is the optimum scale for a collective? The average size of Soviet collectives has risen substantially over time through mergers and consolidations, reflecting an apparent belief that costs never rise as scale is increased. Whatever the case in industry, this proposition seems doubtful in agriculture, where the problem of supervising spatially dispersed activities is inherently more complex. It is possible that most collective and state farms are beyond optimum scale, and that this accounts for part of their production difficulties.

2. Agricultural progress requires a variety of "modern" inputs, produced outside agriculture and organized by gov-

ernment: agricultural research and education; extension services; modern power-driven machinery; electric power; fertilizers; improved seeds and breeding stock; pesticides; and a
variety of other supplies. Moreover, because of the synergistic
character of agriculture, improved inputs should be provided
in the correct proportions. An optimal "package" of improved
seeds, fertilizers, pesticides, cultivator methods, and water
supply will raise output by more than the sum of the addi-
tions which would result from each of these inputs if applied
separately.

Soviet agriculture has been starved for inputs, while urban
industries have been favored.[22] There has been an unwilling-
ness to allocate sufficient investment funds to farm machinery
production, fertilizer production, and other agricultural inputs. The sellers' market in these things has made manufacturers inattentive to quality and design characteristics which
would best meet farmers' needs. There has been little attention to providing new inputs in optimal proportions. Inputs
have also been unevenly distributed among parts of the country—some regions have fared much better than others. Extension services have usually been weak or missing. Government representatives on the collectives tend to be viewed as
procurement people, charged with extracting the planned
amounts of food, rather than as sources of information.

Some of the most heavily agricultural countries of the socialist group, however, have shifted their priorities during
the sixties. In the early sixties China announced a policy of
giving first priority to agricultural development, with consumer goods industries second and heavy industry last—just
the reverse of policy during the fifties. Cuba, too, after a
period of striving for rapid industrialization, has reverted to
a primary emphasis on sugar and other agricultural products.
In Poland, agriculture's share of fixed capital investment has
risen from 10 percent in the early fifties to 16 percent in 1968;

22. On this and related matters, see D. Gale Johnson, "The Environment for Technological Change in Soviet Agriculture," *American Economic Review*, May 1966, pp. 145–53.

and in the USSR, agriculture's share rose from 15 percent during the fifties to 18 percent in 1966–68. The other East European countries, however, show no such upward trend. Agriculture's share is typically of the order of 15 percent, compared with 45–50 percent allocated to industry.[23]

3. The level of farm prices is important. If the rural-urban terms of trade are markedly adverse to agriculture, as has been true in some countries at some times, production is injured in several ways. The best trained and ablest young people have an incentive to move to the cities, leaving agriculture with an inferior labor force. Those remaining in agriculture have only a limited incentive to produce marketed output, and may work less or direct their work toward subsistence production. Low collective farm income also reduces the amounts available for investment in machinery and other modern inputs, which hampers improvement of productivity.

In the Soviet case, while the general level of agricultural prices is now considerably more favorable than it used to be, the price structure leaves much to be desired.[24] Some products are much more profitable than others. Nonstaples such as sugar beets, sunflowers, fiber flax, and tobacco have typically been most profitable, with grain products next, and meat and livestock products least profitable. This must have contributed to the well-known lag in livestock production. There are also wide cost differences among farms, arising from variation in natural conditions. While this is partially offset by variations in government procurement prices, interfarm differences in net income and return to labor remain substantial. There is little indication of any effort to concentrate production of particular crops in the areas best suited to them.

4. How are production decisions to be made? At one extreme, agriculture can be treated like the heavy machinery

23. UNECE, *Economic Survey of Europe, 1968*, pp. 150–51.

24. For recent analyses of pricing and other aspects of Soviet agricultural planning, see I. Lukinov, "Prices and Planned Economic Regulation of Agricultural Production," *Problems of Economics*, May 1969, pp. 67–90; and Morris Bornstein, "The Soviet Debate on Agricultural Price and Procurement Reforms," *Soviet Studies*, July 1969, pp. 1–20.

industry. How much acreage shall be planted to each crop, and how this shall be distributed by regions and individual collectives, may be decided at higher supervisory levels, with the farm free to submit proposals but not to make final decisions. At the other pole, government might prescribe prices at which it is prepared to buy agricultural products, and leave each farm free to choose its production pattern in the light of these prices. If the resulting national totals do not correspond to desired outputs, relative prices for next year could be adjusted to curtail output of "surplus" products and encourage filling of shortages. Over the years, a desirable output mix could be approached experimentally.

Past practice has tended toward detailed central planning. But a price-guided system would seem well suited to the peculiar production conditions of agriculture. Agricultural production functions are highly specialized. Each piece of land has a unique combination of topography, soil characteristics, plant nutrients, moisture, sunshine, and growing season which determine its comparative advantage for various crops. These things cannot be known in sufficient detail at higher levels to permit central determination of optimal production plans. The local farm manager is more likely to know what is feasible in his particular circumstances.

In the case which has been most studied, that of the USSR, it seems clear that agricultural planning has been overcentralized and that mistakes have been made, sometimes on a massive scale. While hybrid corn is good in proper circumstances, Premier Khrushchev's crusade on behalf of this crop led to its being planted in areas where it should not have been. His strong antipathy to oats hampered the development of efficient corn-oats-wheat rotation.

5. Workers on state farms are wage earners, and the members of collectives are also essentially wage earners. Part of their income, to be sure, is a bonus which depends on production results for the farm as a whole; but such group bonuses are notoriously unreliable as a stimulus to individual effort. So the state or collective farm manager has a problem familiar

to many American farmers—how to get the "hired man" to perform effectively in return for his wage. It seems unlikely that one can ever develop incentives for a farm wage earner which will be as strong as those of the owner-operator of a "family farm." But the incentive structure could perhaps be better than it has been in the past.

RATIONALIZING TRADE RELATIONS

The term "rationalizing" should be construed in a modest way. All countries restrict trade in one degree or another. All governments show some preference for home production over foreign production, and for across-the-board development where specialization might yield higher income. Moreover, since governments are more patriotic than individual business men, these tendencies are accentuated in a socialist economy. But as Harry Johnson has argued,[25] it serves no useful purpose to stigmatize them as "irrational." The economist can try to estimate the resource cost of self-containment; but he cannot say that a government which chooses to bear this cost is wrong.

There is clear evidence that, given the small size of the East European economies, their manufacturing sectors are overly diversified; and that, in consequence, they are failing to realize potential benefits of specialization and economies of scale.[26] In principle, these benefits might be realized either through supranational planning or through market coordination. In the late 1950s Premier Khrushchev proposed that COMECON be converted into an agency for coordination of national economic plans. Investment plans would be adjusted to permit a complementary development of the various economies, and it was even contemplated that investment funds would be transferred among countries as needed for a bal-

25. Harry Johnson, "A Theoretical Model of Economic Nationalism in New and Developing States," *Political Science Quarterly*, June 1965, pp. 169–85.
26. See Balassa, "Growth Strategies in Semi-Industrial Countries," pp. 24–47.

anced overall development. But some of the East European countries, in particular Romania, interpreted this as an effort to subordinate their development to the interests of the Soviet Union. The proposal fell through, and there seems no likelihood of its being revived.

There is no prospect either of a free trade utopia, in which trade flows would be guided by a unified network of markets and prices. The movement toward greater use of markets *within* some of the socialist countries, however, has been accompanied by some loosening up of foreign trade arrangements. This tendency seems to have gone furthest in Hungary, East Germany, and (abortively) in Czechoslovakia.[27]

The modest innovations to date include, first, changes in foreign trade organization. In some countries the number of entities permitted to engage in foreign trade has been increased considerably. Large enterprises producing for export have been allowed to enter into direct negotiations with foreign buyers instead of working through the state trading enterprises. In other cases, specialized trading firms have been set up for a particular branch of industry, operated jointly by the producing enterprises in that branch. This has been accompanied by a loosening of plan restrictions on trade. Profitability is emphasized increasingly, and targets are couched in terms of overall export volume rather than detailed commodity lists.

Second, in the course of revising internal producers' prices, there have been efforts to align prices of traded goods with those prevailing on the world market, so as to obtain a clearer indication of comparative advantage. These efforts are still quite limited, but potentially are of great importance.

Third, Hungary has adopted a single conversion rate for trade within the socialist group, and another rate for trade with convertible currency countries. Poland and (abortively) Czechoslovakia have also moved in this direction. The

27. For detailed discussion, see UNECE *Economic Bulletin for Europe* 20, no. 1 (Nov. 1968) 43–55.

Hungarian rates are intended to be "realistic" in the sense of reflecting the actual cost in domestic currency of earning foreign exchange. Since the calculations are based on average rather than marginal costs, however, it can be argued that the forint is still overvalued. It is planned that there will be a gradual withdrawal of subsidies from enterprises which are unable to break even at the new exchange rates. This will doubtless be slowed down, however, by resistance from enterprise managements as well as workers threatened with displacement.

Fourth, there have been limited steps toward multilateralization of trade among the COMECON countries. After each annual round of bilateral trade negotiations, there is a clean-up session in which an effort is made to trade off uncleared balances. There is also a COMECON-affiliated bank which can lend within limits to countries in an overall debtor position. The amounts presently involved in such transaction are only a few percent of intra-COMECON trade, but the machinery would permit enlargement in the future.

Finally, there have been steps toward a reduction of East-West trade barriers. Poland in 1967 became a member of GATT, of which Czechoslovakia was a founding member. The problem of how countries which depend mainly on tariffs can trade concessions with countries which depend mainly on quantitative controls was solved in this case by Polish concessions in volume terms. In return for specified concessions by the Western countries, Poland agreed to increase its import volume from those countries by not less than 7 percent per year for several years ahead. The Western countries retain severe restrictions on agricultural imports, however, while for most manufactures the Eastern countries have a major problem of raising product quality to an internationally competitive level.

The total impact of these recent changes should not be exaggerated. Bilateral barter, with the attendant difficulties described in chapter 3, is still the central trade mechanism; and protectionist sentiment remains strong. There has been a modest movement in the direction of trade rationalization; but the rate of future movement is clearly linked to the pace of internal economic reform. An important consideration is that trade rationalization is less important to the USSR than to the smaller East European economies. So Soviet policy makers may be lukewarm toward proposals for greater trade flexibility and convertibility, particularly if these are linked with intracountry liberalization measures toward which their attitude is generally conservative. Having failed to achieve coordination by a supranational system of physical planning, they will scarcely rush to embrace coordination through market devices.

7 LESS DEVELOPED ECONOMIES

Many of the less developed countries face special difficulties of identity and unity. Old colonial boundaries, which separated the jurisdictions of the European powers, have now become national boundaries. But this does not mean that the population identify themselves with the supposed nation. They are more likely to think in terms of their village. There are long traditions of tribal rivalry and internecine warfare which a slight spark can renew. Effective central government is established only gradually and with frequent setbacks. In some of the Latin American countries, government is still precarious and unstable after a century and a half of independence.

The first task, then, is nation building. Some measure of political unity and stability, internal peace and law enforcement, competence to administer simple government activities such as public works and tax collection, is a prerequisite for sustained economic growth. The following discussion pertains only to countries in which this requirement is met—countries where, when one advocates some line of action by "the government," one is not talking nonsense.

It should be emphasized that we are *posing* policy issues rather than solving them, and even this at a quite general level. The specific character of these issues varies from country to country. Even economists with long experience in the

LDCs are often in disagreement on the analysis of a particular problem and on appropriate lines of action. The information needed for a reasoned choice of policy is often lacking. We shall try, therefore, to avoid statements of the type "Such-and-such ought to be done," of which there are already far too many in the development literature.

The issues which impress us as deserving high priority are: (1) reducing the rate of population growth; (2) raising the rate of increase in agricultural output; (3) developing human skills, partly through the educational system; (4) creating modern economic institutions; (5) creating physical infrastructure; (6) raising the rate of domestic saving; (7) stimulating manufacturing development; (8) managing foreign economic relations; (9) reducing unemployment and underemployment. The last item is by no means least important. We put it last only because employment summarizes one aspect of total economic performance; and what we have to say about it will draw necessarily on the discussion in earlier sections.

POPULATION GROWTH

The rate of natural increase in most LDCs is in the range of 2.5 to 3.5 percent per year, and it has been rising over time. These rates are much higher than anything observed in the Western countries during the eighteenth and nineteenth centuries, and they have burst upon the world much more suddenly.

The long-term population experience of the older industrial countries is familiar. They entered the modern industrial era with birthrates of the order of 35 per thousand. Death rates were close to birthrates, and population increase was slow. During the nineteenth century, improved water supplies and sewage systems, systematic garbage and refuse disposal, a growing number of medical practitioners and hospitals, improved techniques for controlling epidemic diseases, and the progress of medical research reduced the death

rate gradually but steadily. Since birthrates for the time being showed little change, there was a large "population
bulge," lasting in most countries for fifty to one hundred
years. Eventually, however, the birthrate followed the death
rate downward for a variety of familiar reasons: urbanization,
higher income levels and a changed pattern of life, increased
knowledge of contraceptive techniques, a shift of social con-
vention from the large to the small family. Thus after a
"once-for-all" population spurt, these countries settled down
to a new demographic equilibrium: birthrates near 20 per
thousand, death rates near 10 per thousand, population
growth of the order of 1 percent per year.

The LDCs, with the latecomer's advantage of being able
to borrow advanced medical technology, have reduced death
rates much more rapidly. The case of Ceylon, where DDT
spraying and other measures of malaria control brought the
deathrate down from 21.5 in 1945 to 14.0 in 1947, is doubtless exceptional. But many LDCs have reduced their death
rates to the range of 10–20 in less than two decades. Meanwhile birthrates remain at the biological maximum of 40 -50,
with little tendency to decline. The result is natural increase
of the order of 3 percent per year.

This does not always present an immediate problem. Many
countries of Africa and Latin America, and even some areas
of Asia, still have unused cultivable land; but even here the
end of the frontier can be visualized within two or three
decades. For countries which are already densely settled,
population pressure poses a grave threat. To increase food
production fast enough to maintain a rapidly growing population at the same nutritional level requires a major effort;
and this means just keeping one's head above water, without
economic progress. Some countries have not been able to accomplish even this, and have turned from food exporting or
self-sufficiency to food importing. A country forced to import
food can import less machinery and raw materials, and must
find the goal of industrial development receding from its
grasp. Rapid population growth also puts heavy pressure on

the educational system and other public facilities, intensifies urban congestion, and contributes to a rising level of unemployment, which in some countries has already reached politically explosive proportions.

Attitudes toward the population problem range from black pessimism to moderate optimism. Possible reasons for optimism include: survey results indicating that most families in the LDCs do not *want* large numbers of surviving children; a consequent possibility that, as the number of births required to produce a given number of survivors declines, this will be reflected, with some lag, in a decline of actual birthrates; and the reasonable expectation that urbanization, increased education, and rising per capita income will have a negative though gradual effect on birthrates. But these are rather weak reeds on which to lean. There is a consensus among experts that vigorous family planning programs are in order. A number of countries have formally adopted such programs, though the scale of activity under them is still quite limited.

What are the main obstacles to success of family planning programs? The problem is not mainly a technical problem, since a variety of dependable techniques are either available or in sight. (In this respect, it resembles agricultural productivity—all the experts know what *could* be done, though no one may actually be doing very much.) Nor is it primarily a budgetary problem. The material inputs are not large, and can often be secured under international aid programs. Cultural and religious resistance constitutes a more serious problem; but there is considerable evidence that religious considerations do not weigh as heavily in families' actual reproductive behavior as might be expected a priori.

The main bottleneck is the physical shortage of doctors, nurses, midwives, and other health practitioners, which cannot be overcome in the short run by larger budget allocations. A second difficulty is the low status of women in most of the LDCs. Many husbands are neutral or even negative toward family planning, as in Latin America where production of many children indicates possession of the much-prized "machismo" (virility). So while women may be receptive, the men may negate their efforts. Family planning may progress only to the extent that women become socially and economically emancipated, as they increasingly are in the capitalist and socialist countries.

PRODUCTIVITY IN AGRICULTURE

The need for some minimal rate of agricultural progress is easily demonstrated, analytically and historically. In the Western countries, it appears that an agricultural revolution typically preceded or accompanied the industrial revolution, and that a sustained rise in output per acre and per farm worker has characterized their subsequent development. Most of these countries, indeed, now have a burdensome surplus of agricultural capacity. Analytically, the "Ricardian food bottleneck" has been familiar for a century and a half. In a closed economy with rising per capita income, food output must rise fast enough to prevent a shift of the internal terms of trade against industrial products, which by reducing their profitability would eventually choke off industrial expansion. In an open economy, agricultural products usually bulk large in national exports, and an increase in such exports is urgently needed to raise import capacity.

How can the necessary output increases be achieved? Without professing to answer this question, we can suggest the main areas which require the policy maker's attention:

1. In some cases, progress may require a redesign of agricultural institutions, and particularly of *land tenure* arrangements. Tenure reform is often urged on grounds of income distribution, economic opportunity, and social justice; but it may be warranted also by its output effects.

One cannot say that a tenancy system is necessarily unfavorable to high productivity. Where tenancy prevails, however, good performance requires that the landlord take an active interest in cultivation, and that he be prepared to invest, to innovate, and to organize the flow of material inputs to agriculture. Tenancy should be stable, rents moderate, and the tenant should receive a large enough share of output increases to provide adequate incentive. At best, tenancy probably does not provide as strong incentives as exist on the owner-operated farm, and at worst it can be a guarantee of agricultural stagnation.

2. There is usually a need for agricultural *research and experimentation*. Production functions for various crops, regions, soil types need to be analyzed. New strains of seed or livestock have to be domesticated. Research into pest control and weed eradication is necessary. There is also need for economic research: studies of what farmers are doing with their time, how much they are producing, what they are doing with it, how income is divided between consumption and reinvestment, whether there are indications that farmers would respond to greater income opportunities; and also studies of optimal output and input combinations. Shrewd as the peasant may be, systematic observation may reveal ways in which he could do better, even with traditional techniques, and substantially better with modified techniques and output patterns.

3. Research results have to be communicated, which requires an effective *extension service*. Some countries now have virtually no agricultural field staff. In others, the government agent is viewed as a tax collector and a natural enemy. Another common difficulty is that the extension agent is an educated civil servant from the city, who will not dirty his hands in the field. The farmer must be shown what to do by working alongside him, and even better, by the successful experience of his friends and neighbors. He must also be insured insofar as possible against risks of failure from new crops or techniques, which can be disastrous for families at subsistence level. Rational risk aversion probably accounts for much of the peasant's supposedly blind conservatism.

4. There is need for an adequate *flow of inputs* to support new outputs and techniques. The build-up of fertilizer production is a key problem almost everywhere. Improved tools,

seeds, pesticides, and the rest must be distributed equitably and at reasonable cost. This need not necessarily be done by government—indeed, inefficient government distribution has become a bottleneck on occasion—but government initiative and support is often required.

5. *Pricing, marketing, tax, and rent arrangement* should be such that the cultivator can count on receiving a substantial share of increases in farm output. How much is enough to provide adequate incentive for innovation and effort is a matter for analysis. "Substantial" need not mean 90 percent; but it certainly means more than 10 percent. Schultz has argued persuasively that government policy in many LDCs tends to depress the farmer's income while raising the prices of the things he buys, and that this policy bias is an important reason for agricultural stagnation.[1]

In outlining these problems, we do not mean to imply that governments have been inattentive to them or that no progress has been made. After an initial burst of enthusiasm for industrialization, most governments have tended to upgrade agriculture in their development programs. Much progress has been made in introducing new seed varieties, such as Mexican wheat and IRRI rice, and adapting them to local conditions. Fertilizer output and use is rising, irrigation schemes and double cropping are being extended. As a result of these and other developments, often termed "the green revolution," the rate of increase in food output today is substantially higher than it was a decade ago.

DEVELOPMENT OF HUMAN SKILLS

The LDCs are deficient in human capital as well as physical capital. The supply of technical, professional, and administrative personnel is often tiny relative to potential needs. Many manual and clerical skills are also in short supply. Since capital formation requires complementary inputs

1. See in particular T. W. Schultz, *Economic Growth and Agriculture* (New York: McGraw-Hill 1968).

of trained manpower, this skill constraint limits the rate at which capital can be created and managed.

Many manual skills, to be sure, can be learned on the job. But some measure of education almost certainly increases capacity for on-the-job learning; and from clerical workers upward through the professional ranks, increasing amounts of formal education are required. The educational system thus becomes the main instrument for training the labor force; and to devise an optimal educational strategy is a central development problem.

The problem appears superficially as one of allocating financial resources between education and other claims on the government budget, and of suballocation among different levels and types of education. Most of the costs, however, are costs of teachers' and students' time. These are the major costs even in Western countries; and they bulk relatively larger in the less developed countries, where warm climates reduce the cost of physical plant. So it is useful to view the educational structure as a system of manpower flows. Outputs at lower levels of the system become available as inputs (students) at higher levels; and part of the output at higher levels is fed back as inputs (teachers) at lower levels.

The educational pyramid is typically narrow relative to the numbers in each age cohort, and tapers rapidly toward the top. Thus even though 50 percent of children may enter the school door in Grade 1, only 10 percent may complete high school and less than 1 percent may finish college. The flow relations just mentioned limit the rate at which the pyramid can be widened—for example, the number of high school graduates going on to college plus the number "fed back" as primary school teachers cannot exceed the number of graduates available. By attaching values to the inputs and outputs at each level, one can derive an optimal expansion path. Programming methods have been applied to this problem by Tinbergen, Bowles, and others. A difficulty, however, is that educational expansion itself changes the value relations. It reduces the relative price of the higher skills by making them more readily available. Unless this is borne in mind, and a shifting scale of values is applied to future years, the educational plan may miscarry.

Estimates of the return to education are crude even in advanced countries, and very crude in the LDCs. A major unknown is the value of primary education. How much does five or six years of schooling add to the productivity of a farmer or a factory worker? What additional allowance should be made for the consumption value of education, and for external social and political effects? This will influence the decision on how rapidly to enlarge the intake of primary schools. An important practical consideration is that if the intake is expanded beyond the capacity of the system—say, by unduly increasing class sizes—the retention rate will fall. It may be better to have a slowly expanding system in which most of those admitted stay on to graduation, rather than a crash program which touches more of the population superficially, but in which pupils drop out after a few years and relapse into functional illiteracy.

Secondary education is typically a major bottleneck. There is an intense demand for secondary school graduates—for employment in government and industry, as inputs to an enlarged university system, and as school teachers, whose availability is the main constraint on educational expansion. But in many LDCs, secondary education has been the prerogative of an elite. Training facilities have been limited, and often organized by churches and other private groups, whose tuition charges have limited admission to higher-income families. In terms of percentage rates of enrollment increase, the main push usually has to be made at this level.

University education also usually needs to be enlarged, opened to children of nonelite families, and turned in a more vocational direction. Traditional high-prestige subjects such as law and humanistic studies need to be deemphasized relative to engineering, science, medicine, agriculture, economics, and administration. As a short-run measure, shortages of domestic training capacity can be met in part by importing teachers and exporting students. It would seem that both the capitalist and socialist countries could make a larger contribution in this direction than they are presently doing, and a contribution which would have a high yield relative to that on transfers of physical capital.

The economics of such a foreign trade in education presents interesting analytical problems. How can an LDC enlarge its supply of university graduates at minimum cost? Will programs which are optimal for the LDCs impose training costs (or displace domestic students) in the advanced countries to a degree which the latter are not willing to bear? To what extent would increased educational interchange lead to a larger "brain drain," and how might this be held in check? In addition to short-run optimizing, each LDC needs to devise a time path for movement to a self-sustained university system, that is, for educational import substitution. Japanese educational borrowing from the West, which still continues on a substantial scale, could usefully be analyzed in this connection.

It is possible to overeducate? The unemployed Indian arts graduate is a familiar problem, and even Indian engineers seem now to be in surplus. In West Africa unemployment is appearing at the high school level, as graduates migrate to the cities insisting on white-collar jobs which the economy is not yet able to provide. While these developments give one pause, they do not necessarily indicate that too many people are being trained. One should consider the possibility of: (1) modifying curricula to bring the output of particular skills more closely in line with visible demand; (2) improved vocational information and counseling for high school students, designed to aid them in their choice of curriculum and to modify unrealistic expectations; (3) making teaching jobs in primary and secondary education more attractive, to draw more of the educated manpower in this direction. In the Indian case, there is a severe shortage of teachers in rural areas while at the same time many thousands of university graduates prefer to sit unemployed in the cities.

INSTITUTIONAL INFRASTRUCTURE

Most LDCs are committed, by decision or by default, to substantial reliance on private decision making. But private economic activity does not spring up and flourish unaided. It requires complementary activity by government to create what may be termed *institutional infrastructure:* protection of property rights and enforcement of contracts, a body of corporate law and practice, a banking system and other financial intermediaries, strengthening of markets throughout the economy. Such economic institutions, which in Western countries are taken for granted, are often fragmentary or missing in the less developed countries.

The importance of *legal systems* is obvious and sometimes takes startling forms. It is surprising, for example, to discover countries in which it is not feasible to sue for collection of debts. In such countries, a man will enter a business partnership only with someone on whom he has strong moral claims, usually a near relative; this sets limits to the feasible scale of enterprise. To move from this stage to the large, widely held corporation requires legal reforms as well as economic change.

Key *markets* throughout the economy need to be created or improved. This is most obvious in the case of agriculture, where ill-informed peasants and rapacious traders cannot be relied on to devise efficient and low-cost marketing systems. But it is true also of labor markets, and of wholesale and retail markets in the cities. Financial markets often have to be created from scratch, and are almost necessarily government inspired in the first instance.

Improvement of markets involves also provision of improved *economic information:* forecasts of export markets for particular products, market or feasibility surveys for new industrial enterprises, accurate data on current performance of the economy, estimates of the rate of increase in domestic demand. One value of development plans, if realistic and validated by performance, is to give private investors an assurance of expanding markets in the future. They can be an important informational and risk-reducing device.

Government is often in the best position to initiate large new *corporate organizations*. Initiation, however, may or may not mean permanent government control. The Japanese government initiated numerous modern enterprises in the 1880s and 1890s, many of which were later sold off to private investors. More recently, development corporations in Pakistan and elsewhere have used a similar technique. Government must also decide how far foreign private companies should be allowed to participate in development of the economy, and on what terms.

Finally, there is a problem of ensuring that *economic controls* are deployed in a way which stimulates instead of repressing private economic activity. Preeminent here is the tax structure, where incentive effects need always to be weighed along with revenue effects. But credit facilities, tariff protection, foreign exchange controls, and other devices can be used in helpful ways. A good part of wisdom in economic policy consists in what government does *not* do, in avoiding actions which are merely meddlesome, in not trying to supersede the profitability estimates of private parties where these are likely to be better informed. The exhortations of Smith, Mill, and others on this point can still be read with profit.

Some may feel that problems of institutional design are "not economics," in that they do not involve quantitative issues of resource supplies, allocation, and pricing. This is too narrow a view even for developed economies, and much too narrow a view under conditions of underdevelopment. Institutional structure can be crucial for economic performance. Economists, who are specialists in evaluating economic performance, are in the best position to analyze these structure-performance relations.

PHYSICAL INFRASTRUCTURE

A geographic area becomes an *economy* only when goods, people, and information can move about the area at reasonable cost. This implies railroads, highways and feeder roads, coastal shipping where appropriate, telephone, postal, and radio communications. Electric power development is needed to make possible modern living standards in the towns and cities, and to supply the growing needs of industrial establishments.

Because these investments are large and expensive, and because of external effects which require central coordination, there is general agreement that they must be undertaken by government; and this raises several policy problems. First there is the question whether to build ahead of immediate demand or whether to wait until pushed by demand pressures. Building somewhat ahead of demand may be sensible on two counts. Many infrastructure projects are large and "lumpy," and there may be a substantial cost advantage in building a large installation at one stroke rather than adding on to it piece by piece. Moreover, construction periods are usually long, and to delay initiating a project until capacity shortages are already apparent may seriously hamper growth in other sectors. On the other hand, building far ahead of demand involves a risk of resource waste arising from errors in the demand estimates, and also the possibility that facilities will deteriorate before they are brought into use. By weighing such considerations one might determine an *optimal timing* of particular projects, and the problem is best posed as an optimizing one rather than as a choice between opposing strategies.

Second, there is normally an allocation problem. Government finances are limited, and so is the capacity of the construction industries. Only a certain number of infrastructure projects can be launched at any one time. Should a major highway program be pushed through at the cost of holding back power and irrigation development? Should resources be channeled into feeder roads or into coastal shipping? In a large country, regional allocation also becomes a problem. Should the investment budget be spread evenly over the whole country? or should one push hard in the economically more advanced regions to the temporary neglect of others?

Cost-benefit analysis is applicable here, though because of data deficiencies and the magnitude of structural changes in the early stages of development, its application is necessarily less precise than in more mature economies.

Where a public enterprise sells its output at a price, as do railroads or electric power corporations, what price policy should be followed? Should marginal cost pricing be used and, if so, how should the resulting deficits be covered? Should a public enterprise cover operating costs, plus a sufficient profit to meet investment requirements? Should it earn more than this, and make a contribution to general revenue? These are complex questions. There is evidence that public corporations, both in the LDCs and elsewhere, incur substantial operating deficits on balance, though there is considerable variation among countries and among types of industry.[2] But the reasons have been little explored. To what extent does deficit operation represent deliberate application of economic criteria? To what extent, on the other hand, does it stem from poor management plus political pressure for low prices, high wages, and overstaffing?

DOMESTIC SAVING AND CAPITAL FORMATION

Early economic growth normally involves a rise in capital formation as a percentage of national product; and while some of the finance for increased investment may come from abroad, most of it usually comes from domestic saving.

In principle, the government budget can be used for capital accumulation. The rate of increase in current expenditure can be held below the rate of increase in current revenue, to create a growing savings gap.[3] Thus the marginal rate of

2. Andrew H. Gault and Guiseppe Dutto, "Financial Performance of Government-Owned Corporations in Less Developed Countries," *International Monetary Fund Staff Papers*, March 1968, pp. 102–142.

3. The conventional division between current and capital expenditure, of course, does not coincide with that between growth-inducing expenditure and public consumption. Part of current expenditure on education, public health, and so on contributes to future productive capacity. Thus some countries include items of this sort in a "develop-

government saving will exceed the average rate, so that the latter rises gradually over time. This prescription is difficult to apply, however, and in some LDCs the government savings rate has been falling rather than rising. The difficulty is not merely that it is hard to increase tax revenues—many countries have done quite well on this. But as rapidly as revenue is raised, it tends to be swallowed up by pressure for larger military budgets, for increases in education, health, and welfare expenditures, and for increases in government salary scales.[4] Public corporations, too, usually draw subsidies from the general budget instead of contributing to it.

We can say little about private saving, because in most countries the data are fragmentary and the determinants of saving are obscure. As business corporations grow in importance, retained earnings provide an important potential source of investment finance. But corporate profits, particularly those earned by foreign firms, are a tempting target for taxation and sometimes for union wage pressure. The problem of devising appropriate tax and wage policies in such circumstances is complicated. It requires consideration of trade-offs among competing policy objectives, and also requires economic information, which is often unavailable.

As regards household savings, it is plausible to assume that people engaged in business—as farmers, traders, artisans, and so on—have a higher savings propensity than do wage and salary earners at the same income level. The reason is that the former have direct access to investment opportunities, often with a high yield. The prospect of a 30 percent return on a business venture calls forth more saving than does a 5 percent interest rate on a postal saving account. This stimulus

---

ment budget," which is broader than the conventional capital budget. But there is much intercountry variation in classification practices, so that one tends to fall back on analyzing capital expenditure instead of the preferable concept of growth-inducing expenditure.

4. For more detailed analysis of the government saving problem, see L. G. Reynolds, "Public Sector Saving and Capital Formation," in G. Ranis, ed., *The Public Sector in Economic Development* (New Haven: Yale University Press, 1970).

is operative, however, only to the extent that small business men (including farmers) are allowed to exploit investment opportunities and to keep a share of the proceeds. The problem of stimulating household saving thus overlaps with the larger problem of encouraging small business activity.

Saving by wage and salary earners who lack direct investment outlets can be stimulated through development of savings banks, insurance companies, government savings systems, and other financial intermediaries. It could be aided also by interest rates approaching the true value of capital in the economy, instead of the low (in inflationary economies, often negative) rates actually offered.

INDUSTRIAL DEVELOPMENT

An increase in manufacturing output as a percentage of GNP is a normal accompaniment of economic growth. This is partly because *consumption* of manufactured goods has an income elasticity greater than unity, use of capital equipment tends to rise faster than income at this stage, and partly because over time a growing share of the country's requirements for manufactures is supplied by domestic production rather than imports, that is, there is *import substitution*. The "natural" pace of import substitution depends heavily on the minimum efficient scale of production relative to the size of domestic market. Small-scale industries tend to appear early in the industrialization sequence, large-scale industries later. This tendency has been documented by Hoffman, Kuznets, Chenery, and other quantitative students of economic growth.

The main question about industrial development policy, then, is why there should *be* any policy. Why need government do more than encourage business men to respond to profit opportunities as they appear in the normal course of economic growth? Many answers have been given to this question, some more convincing than others. There is first the traditional "infant industry" argument. Labor in a LDC is untrained in industrial operations, management is inexperienced, and the initial costs of a new manufacturing concern will be high relative to costs in developed countries. But if the enterprise is protected for five or ten years, costs will gradually be reduced and domestic prices will become competitive with world prices. Not all industries, however, have potential comparative advantage in this sense, and there is clearly a danger of this argument being stretched to cover cases where it is inappropriate.

Second, it is argued that market costs of factors in a LDC are often a poor indicator of social cost. In particular, the social cost of (presently underutilized) labor may be much below its market price. Calculations based on social costs and returns, then, may show a particular industry to be profitable even though it would not be attractive to a private entrepreneur.

Third, there is the argument based on external effects and industrial linkages. Development of industry A, which supplies materials to industries B and C, may lower their production costs. Simultaneous establishment of all three industries may thus be profitable even though none would be so in isolation. Moreover, the amount of capacity which it pays to build in each industry will usually be larger when interdependencies are considered. These possibilities, to be sure, might conceivably be visualized by a private entrepreneur. But if the capital requirements are large, as in a coal-iron ore-steel complex or a petrochemical complex, government initiative and financial support may be needed.

Along such lines one can make out a qualified case for government support of industrial development, which may accelerate its pace beyond what would result from "spontaneous" private initiative. But experience in Argentina, Pakistan, and elsewhere has shown that this involves the possibility of serious error and waste. It is easy to foster industries whose social profitability is low or negative, and which cannot become viable in any foreseeable future. This means that other sectors, and particularly agriculture, are being taxed to support high-cost domestic manufactures, with a discouraging effect on output in those sectors.

FOREIGN ECONOMIC RELATIONS

Most of the LDCs are deeply involved in foreign trade, and face a variety of well-known policy problems. An initial problem is to raise traditional exports of primary products, which will be a major source of foreign exchange for a long time to come. While some primary products face low price and income elasticities in the developed world, this is not invariably true. Some products are more promising than others, resources can often be shifted among products, and some LDCs have done well with primary exports over the past generation. Export promotion is not necessarily competitive in resource terms with industrial development and other lines of domestic policy. It does require tax and exchange rate policies which do not discriminate heavily against export production, as well as efforts to lower production costs and to maintain the country's competitive position.

Foreign exchange proceeds from primary exports fluctuate considerably from year to year, and this is an important source of economic instability in the LDCs.[5] The impact of these fluctuations can be cushioned to some extent by domestic policy. Beyond this, there has been some degree of international collaboration to stabilize prices of particular export products (coffee, wheat, and so on), and to set up systems of supplementary finance to cushion temporary drops in export receipts. How far to move in this direction remains an important policy issue both for the LDCs and the developed countries, whose support is usually essential to success.

A permissive policy by the developed countries is needed also if the LDCs are to move further into exports of light manufactures, for which their abundant supplies of inexpensive labor would seem to give them a natural advantage. Some of the smaller Asian economies—Taiwan, Hong Kong, Singapore—have expanded substantially in this direction; but most

5. It is not clear, however, that diversification of primary exports reduces instability, or that export proceeds are more volatile for the LDCs as a whole than for the Western countries. Both hypotheses seem plausible, but have not stood up well to statistical tests.

of the developed countries maintain tariffs and quantitative controls designed to limit penetration of their markets. The struggle to protect the United States textile industry, which is doubtless losing comparative advantage over the long run, is a striking example.

On the import side, a key issue is how far it is wise and feasible to accelerate the natural rate of import substitution in manufactured goods. The grounds on which this might be justified were outlined in the previous section. The research literature suggests, however, that import substitution programs have been overdone in some countries, and that the high costs involved have retarded rather than advanced development. The selection of industries for support seems often to have been quite haphazard, relative to what would have been indicated by careful economic calculation.

It seems obvious that the viability of new manufacturing industries could be enhanced if groups of LDCs could agree on "common market" schemes. This has been done in the Central American countries, and has been discussed actively among the Southeast Asian and South American countries, thus far with only limited action. A major difficulty is that the LDCs differ substantially among themselves in degree of manufacturing development. The least developed tend to regard common market plans as a prescription for permanent subjection to the somewhat more developed. The discussions resemble the Romanian-Czechoslovak debate mentioned in chapter 6. Peru does not want its market for manufactures to be taken over by Argentina. Uganda does not want to remain a hinterland for an industrialized Kenya. Thus plans for economic integration tend to founder on the rocks of political and economic nationalism.

Another major policy area involves exchange rates and exchange control systems. Most LDCs have overvalued currencies in the sense that, at the present exchange rate, the demand for imports exceeds export earnings plus capital transfers. This foreign exchange gap is typically closed by exchange rationing. Exchange allocation then becomes a mechanism for detailed control of economic activity, with possible harmful effects on development. The artificially high exchange rate tends also to distort domestic economic priorities—for example, by reducing the profitability of agricultural production for export and raising that of "hothouse" manufacturing production. Some LDCs have accordingly shifted to a "liberalized" regime, typically involving some combination of: currency devaluation vis-à-vis the dollar and other hard currencies; abandonment of detailed exchange allocations in favor of competitive bidding; and strengthening of hard currency reserves by borrowing from the International Monetary Fund, the United States, and others, to ease the transition period.

Finally, most LDCs face a problem of "borrowing policy," the obverse of the "aid policy" problem in the developed countries. The LDCs are quite naturally chronic borrowers at this stage. So were the United States, Canada, Australia, and others for a long period. But a borrower must keep its rising repayment obligations in some reasonable relation to its prospective export receipts. There is also the problem of allocating one's borrowings by type and source in such a way as to minimize the real repayment burden. Efficient "debt-manship" is a tricky matter because of the numerous dimensions involved: grace period, interest rate, length of repayment period, whether payment can be made in goods or local currency, whether the loan is "tied" to procurement of goods from the lending country, whether political strings are also attached to the loan. Happy the country in which both the United States and the USSR perceive a strategic interest, which nevertheless manages to avoid allying itself with either country, and which cheerfully secures funds on good terms from all comers.

EMPLOYMENT AND UNDEREMPLOYMENT

In many LDCs underutilization of the labor force is a substantial and growing problem. It is quite possible for output per capita to rise, and for industrial output to rise rapidly, while underemployment also increases. As this has been borne in on students of development economics, they have tended increasingly to emphasize employment criteria as well as output criteria of economic progress.

The root of the problem is rapid population growth. When the rate of natural increase stabilizes at, say, 3 percent, then after a lag of fifteen years or so the labor force will also be growing at 3 percent. There is usually substantial migration from rural to urban areas, so that the urban labor force grows even faster. But the rural labor force also increases, though at a slower rate. In Latin America between 1950 and 1960, for example, the urban population grew at a rate of 4.5 percent per year, while the rural population grew at 1.4 percent.[6]

In a fully settled country with stagnant agriculture, the growth of the rural population tends to depress the average and marginal product of labor. The work available may simply be divided among more and more hands, hours per worker declining with total hours unchanged. Or, if the input of hours is increased, average and marginal productivity per hour decline. In either case, family living standards tend to decline as more and more people must be supported from the same land.

Those who move to the cities often do so in the hope of securing "modern sector" jobs at relatively high wages. To absorb all these migrants plus the natural increase of urban population, however, would require a very rapid increase of modern sector employment. Suppose that one-third of all urban workers are employed in modern industry, including government. Then if the urban labor force is growing at 5 percent per year, modern sector employment would have to grow at 15 percent per year to accommodate the newcomers.

Actual employment growth rates are much below this. In most of the African countries, between 1953 and 1963, non-

6. Ralph H. Hofmeister, "Growth with Unemployment in Latin America: Some Implications for Asia," mimeographed (Paper presented to AID Conference on Employment, Kathmandu, July 1970), p. 4.

agricultural employment rose by 1 percent a year or less.[7]
The exceptions were Ghana (4.0 percent), Sierra Leone (3.5
percent), and Nigeria (2.5 percent). In Latin America, over
the decade 1950–60, the number of manufacturing jobs increased only 29 percent, and all industrial jobs increased 33
percent. Experience in manufacturing has been particularly
disappointing. Rates of increase in employment have been
much below the rates of output increases. Between 1953 and
1963, for example, manufacturing output in Argentina rose
by 3.8 percent per year while manufacturing employment *fell*
by 3 percent per year. In Brazil, output rose 9 percent per
year, employment 1.8 percent.[8] There is similar evidence
from many other countries.

The gap between output and employment growth rates indicates a high rate of productivity improvement. New factories in the less developed countries, even when physically
identical with similar plants in the advanced industrial countries, usually have at first much lower output per worker. But
management and workers can and do learn from experience,
and labor requirements per unit of output gradually shrink.
Thus at the same time that new investment is creating additional jobs, the number of jobs in older plants is shrinking,
and this retards the growth of total industrial employment.

The tendency to economize labor, even in labor-surplus
economies, is often intensified by overpricing of industrial
labor. Through a variety of political and social pressures,
wage rates are pushed well above the level of earnings in
traditional activities, and above the level which would be
adequate for labor recruitment. Business enterprises, which
respond to market rates rather than shadow prices, act to curtail employment; and so does government, most of whose
budget goes for labor services.

Urban workers who cannot find employment in the modern
sector crowd into petty trade and service activities. Like agri-

7. Charles R. Frank, Jr., "The Problem of Urban Unemployment in
Africa," mimeographed (Paper presented to AID Conference on Employment, Kathmandu, July 1970), Table 2.
8. Hofmeister, *"Growth with Unemployment,"* p. 8.

culture, these are "spongy" sectors which can absorb an indefinite amount of labor. But they cannot do so without depressing output per worker. To revert to Latin America, it is somewhat alarming that the most rapid growth of employment between 1960 and 1965 was in "miscellaneous services" (4.2 percent per year) and in "unspecified activities" (9.4 percent per year).[9] Much of this must have been very nominal employment, odd jobs picked up by the fringe members of the urban economy.

The problem is not mainly one of open unemployment, though in most LDCs this is also growing. Scattered data from cities in Latin America and Africa show full-time unemployment rates in the range of 10 to 20 percent. But quantitatively more important is the underutilization, the low output per hour and per day, of those who are nominally employed. There is doubtless also much "hidden unemployment" of the sort which occurs even in the developed countries during recession periods, that is, reduced labor force participation rates reflecting the low level of demand for labor.

We cannot undertake to prescribe solutions, which would come close to prescribing for development policy in general. It does seem clear that increased employment in manufacturing and other "modern" activities can bear only a minor part of the burden. The main push must be toward population control on one hand, and toward creation of productive employment in the rural sector (including, but not limited to, direct employment in agriculture) on the other. Without more effort on these fronts, the employment situation will continue to deteriorate in most LDCs over the next generation.

CONCLUDING COMMENTS

1. We have said nothing explicitly about *development planning,* which in one form or another is now practiced in most of the less developed countries. This sort of planning

9. Hofmeister, *"Growth with Unemployment,"* p. 10.

differs substantially from that prevailing in the other two groups of economies. LDC plans are quite highly *aggregated*, they are largely *financial* plans rather than physical plans and their control power is limited mainly to the *public sector*. They serve several operational purposes: *First,* the projection of foreign exchange availabilities and requirements is a necessary step in formulating borrowing strategy. Indeed, the insistence of creditor nations that would-be borrowers present an overall picture of their economic situation and prospects has been a major reason for the growth of development planning. *Second,* within the public sector, the effort to draft a long-range development program forces individual departments of government to look further ahead and to set their annual budget requests in a multiyear framework. The result is an improvement in project preparation and justification, and greater rationality and consistency in capital budgeting. The minister of finance and the various spending ministries, however, usually retain considerable "countervailing power" vis-à-vis the planning organization.

Third, in the private sector, the "plan" is more nearly a projection. It is not just a dream, but neither is it a reality; and there is often substantial deviation between projections and performance. Even so, the planning exercise is useful in revealing inconsistencies between what is being projected for different sectors of the economy; and it will often suggest policy measures by which government can increase the chances of the projections being realized. *Fourth,* not the least valuable by-product of planning activity is improvement of basic economic data. As necessary data inputs turn out to be missing or inaccurate, there will be pressure to allocate more resources in this direction.

For these reasons the planning exercise is clearly *useful;* but it is equally clearly not *critical.* Some countries, such as Mexico, have developed quite successfully without an overall plan. Others, which we had best not mention, have impressive paper plans whose impact on the economy is minimal.

2. What if a LDC chooses a socialist rather than a mixed-economy path of economic development? By this we mean, not the mild and mainly verbal socialism professed by some of the African and Asian countries, but Marxist-inspired, Communist-led socialist à la China, North Korea, or Cuba. Do its policy problems then suddenly change shape and become different from those outlined in this chapter? If forced to answer yes or no, one would probably say "No." Infrastructure still has to be laid down, the educational system expanded, agricultural productivity raised, new industries organized and managed.

But the "soft state" has now become a "hard state." There is a government with a fighting creed and strong disciplinary power, capable of enforcing austerity in consumption and full mobilization of resources for investment. The strategy of development will doubtless veer toward the Soviet model, emphasizing a more rapid build-up of basic industrial capacity and greater autarky than under nonsocialist conditions. The sources of capital goods and industrial materials will be Eastern rather than Western. The subsequent need to import replacements and spare parts, and the exports required for loan repayment, will tend—ideological considerations apart—to attach these countries to the Eastern trading zone.

Whether this route offers firmer assurance of sustained economic development than the mixed-economy route is a most interesting question. The experience of China, Cuba, and other socialist countries starting from a really low level of per capita income is still too brief to provide clear evidence. But it would be unsafe, would indeed be merely prejudiced, to rule out the possibility of higher growth rates via the socialist route. Whether this is also in some sense a more expensive route, or whether possible economic advantages are outweighed by political and social disadvantages, would lead one into value judgments outside the scope of this essay.

3. With this chapter we have finished sorting out policy priorities for our three groups; and it is useful to set these

TABLE 7.1

A Comparison of Policy Priorities

Capitalist economies	*Socialist economies*	*Less developed economies*
1. Regulation of aggregate demand	1. Optimal decentralization of economic management	1. Reducing population growth
2. Supply of public and quasi-public goods	2. Growth strategy: tempo and pattern	2. Raising agricultural output
3. Equality of economic opportunity	3. Adapting production to consumer requirements	3. Managing foreign economic relations
4. Income redistribution	4. Raising agricultural output	4. Developing infrastructure: physical, human, institutional
5. Balance of payment problems	5. Rationalizing trade relations	5. Raising domestic saving
		6. Absorbing labor force slack

side by side, as we have done in table 7.1. An interesting conclusion emerges from this exercise. There are areas of overlap among the three sets of problems; but more striking is the extent to which the lists diverge. Each group of economies attaches high priority to areas in which, for one reason or another, it performs poorly; and these areas differ in the three cases.

Thus maintaining a steady expansion of aggregate demand through monetary-fiscal policy is a key problem in the "Keynes world" of the West. But it is not a key problem in the "Marx world" of the East or the "Say world" of the less developed countries. Implementing a detailed production plan is a central problem in the socialist countries; but the LDCs are not able to do this, and the capitalist countries do not need to do it. Laying down economic infrastructure—physical, human, institutional—is a central issue in the less developed economies, but not in the other two groups where such infrastructure is already more highly developed. Nor do the capitalist and socialist economies face the high rates of population growth which plague the LDCs.

Given this difference in problem sets, and given that economics is at least in part a policy science, one would not expect the same analytical tools to have equal relevance in all parts of the world. The relative usefulness of different Western tools will change as one moves to the socialist economies, and change again as one moves to the less developed economies, as compared with their usefulness on their home ground. Some of the problems of these other economies may require a good deal of new tool construction. These possibilities will occupy us throughout Part Three.

PART THREE
ECONOMIC THEORY

8 THE USEFULNESS OF WESTERN ECONOMICS. I

How far Western economic theory is transferable to other types of economy is a controversial question, on which it is easy to form strong opinions. It is also a complex question, on which simple statements are certain to be inaccurate. We must begin by describing some of the complexities and how we propose to handle them. What do we mean by "Western economics"? What do we mean by its "usefulness" in a different institutional setting?

The Array of Analytical Tools

Modern economics, as Joan Robinson remarked a generation ago, is best regarded as a tool-kit. In some sense, or at some level of generality, these tools form an interrelated whole. Any attempt to classify them is necessarily arbitrary; but we believe that the arrangement suggested below will be found convenient for working purposes. It begins with the most microeconomic concepts, those which relate to a single decision-making unit. The second group is of mixed character—macro in the sense of covering the entire economy, but micro in the sense of maintaining the identity of particular products, markets, and prices. The final group includes highly aggregated tools, which group all of economic activity into a few broad categories.

A. *Tools of Micro Character*
1. Microeconomics proper: the firm, the household
2. Normative microeconomics: operations research, management science, cost-benefit analysis

B. *Tools of Mixed Character*
1. Market economics; "price theory"
2. Interindustry analysis
   a) Overall programming models
3. General equilibrium theory
   a) Welfare economics
4. Trade theory

C. *Tools of Macro Character*
1. Short-run macroeconomics; monetary theory
2. Growth theory: positive variant
   a) Growth theory: normative variant

This schema does not attempt to cope with the numerous branches of applied economics. In most cases it is clear how these subjects tie into the core of economic theory. Labor economics, for example, ties in mainly through headings A.1 and B.1 above. Money and banking ties in mainly through heading C.1 but also, in its micro aspects, through A.1 and B.1. Public finance, which ramifies throughout the economy, draws on almost all the tool groups. Thus our conclusions on the transferability of tools will bear also on the question how far courses in applied economics may need to be reconstructed to "fit" a particular kind of economy.

The Meaning of Usefulness
We start from the proposition that economics is an *empirical science,* whose central purpose is the explanation and prediction of economic events. Positive economics is the heart of the discipline. The primary test of usefulness, then, is explanatory and predictive power. To be useful in this sense, a theoretical structure must take account of the actual structure of the economy to which it is being applied. Thus we should not expect that a particular piece of apparatus will be equally useful at all times and places.

Economics is also in some measure a *policy science*. A body of theory may be said to have "relevance" if its predictions lie in an area which is important for public policy. Since policy priorities differ in different kinds of economy, as we noted in chapter 7, a particular branch of theory will not have equal relevance in all circumstances.

Realism and relevance are clearly somewhat different criteria; and at the end of our discussion we shall rate our tools separately on these two counts.

We do not assume that all the items in our tool-kit have a high degree of realism and relevance on their "home ground," that is, in the Western capitalist countries. Some may have little usefulness in other kinds of economy because they also have little usefulness in our own. We shall make side comments on this point from time to time.

Usefulness to Whom?

In all the non-Western economies, and particularly in the socialist countries, the transferability of economic ideas is a touchy subject because it carries ideological overtones. The suggestion that socialist countries might make greater use of some Western concepts implies that socialist economic institutions are somewhat similar—or are even becoming more nearly similar—to capitalist institutions. But socialist texts in "political economy" assert flatly that the economic principles of a socialist system necessarily differ from those which prevail under capitalism. Explicit borrowing of Western concepts is discouraged. Even implicit borrowing encounters ideological resistance, and must usually be presented as a fresh discovery.

A similar sensitivity is often found in the LDCs. It is thought that use of Western economic tools implies a particular *policy stance,* an idealization of the market mechanism and an antipathy to government activity. This view, as we shall hope to demonstrate, confuses the policy preferences of some Western economists with the logic of their analytical tools. Micro theory does *not* imply uncritical admiration of private markets, or exclusive reliance on such markets for economic development, or a laissez-faire role for government. But the belief that it does is a confusing element in the discussion of possible tool transfers.

When we speak, then, of the "usefulness" of some Western tool in a particular economy, do we mean its *actual* use in economic discussion and policy formation, or do we mean *potential* usefulness? In the latter case, potential usefulness in *whose eyes*—an outside Western observer, or economists in the country concerned? It might be thought that we should focus on actual use, by economists and administrators, in the economy in question. We shall not limit the discussion this narrowly, and will at times express judgments of potential usefulness which might not be fully accepted in the LDCs and the socialist countries. We do so, not in a spirit of intellectual imperialism, but in the hope of stimulating constructive controversy.

Degrees of Generality and of Adaption

It is useful, and not at all original, to think of a hierarchy of theoretical constructs, ranging from the completely general to the very specific. Some concepts are so general that they must be true at any time or place—true, perhaps, because they are entirely empty, that is, definitional or tautological. But as theory comes closer to grappling with a definite body of phenomena, its structure becomes more elaborate, specific, and empirically oriented. One ends up with, say, a model of investment decisions in the United States steel industry in the 1960s. Most economists would agree, however, that at some point the labor involved in constructing a detailed model for particular cases outweighs any possible benefit. It is not the task of theory precisely to replicate reality.

We are interested here in an intermediate level of generality—models which are specified sufficiently to have predictive power for a particular economy at a particular time, but which are still couched in rather general terms. Now suppose one has such a model—say, a model of urban markets for manual labor in the United States. We are considering the possible transferability of the model to socialist economies or to the LDCs. One can imagine two polar situations:

1. The model might be completely transferable without modification. Its predictive power in the new milieu would be exactly the same as on its home ground.

2. The model might have zero transfer value, that is, having studied it would be of no help whatever in analysing the non-Western economy in question. (It is sometimes argued, particularly as regards the LDCs, that certain branches of Western theory have negative value, in the sense that preoccupation with them distracts the Western-trained economist from key aspects of the less developed economies and reduces his ability to analyze them.)

One would expect these polar situations to be rare in practice. The usual situation is one in which a Western tool has *some* transfer value, but it is not fully transferable "as is." It requires some degree of reshaping and adaptation. By this we mean something more than mere reestimation of parameter values, which will naturally differ from country to country. By adaptation we mean a rethinking of the questions to be answered, the variables to be included in the behavioral relations, and the hypotheses which can be derived from the revised model.

Adaptation in this sense may be slight or far-reaching. The revised model may bear a close or a rather distant resemblance to its Western prototype. This leads us to the kind of "scorecard" which will be used for the Western tools. At one stage of the work we tried to imitate the Michelin rating system for French restaurants. A particular tool, with respect to a particular type of economy, was given one, two, or three stars as judgment dictated. But this does not reveal the degree of adaptation which may be required; and a single rating also blurs the criteria of realism and policy relevance. Our "realism" scorecard, therefore, will be marked off in terms of "slight adaptation needed," "moderate adaptation needed," and "much adaptation needed"; policy relevance will be treated as a separate issue, requiring a scorecard of its own.

With this preview of where we are going, let us get started on the task.

MICROECONOMICS PROPER

We define microeconomics proper as the analysis of individual decision-making units: on one hand the business firm, including public enterprises selling at a market price; on the other hand the consumer and worker or, perhaps more correctly, the *household* to which these individuals belong.

We must begin by admitting that this body of concepts remains controversial even on its home ground. Progress has consisted mainly in more elaborate definition of the *meaning* of maximizing behavior. From this it seems a short step to *assuming* such behavior as a foundation of price theory and of general equilibrium systems. It is rather surprising that so many economists have been willing to take this step without reviewing the evidence on actual behavior. Their willingness to do so may be ascribed to such things as: (1) some kind of maximizing assumption seems logically necessary in building a general equilibrium system and trying to draw welfare conclusions from such a system. If taxed with unrealism, the theorist may well answer "What else am I to do"? (2) An econometrician studying the behavior of firms or consumers in the mass may feel that statistical regularities are enough, and that the motivation underlying these regularities is not an interesting problem. (3) Related to this is the line of argument that "assumptions don't matter," provided the theorems deduced from them have predictive power.

Another wing of opinion, however, holds that deviations of actual from assumed behavior are important. Galbraith and others have emphasized the systematic manipulation of consumer opinion by producers, which casts doubt on the proposition that pursuit of "given" wants will maximize consumer satisfaction. Another line of attack emphasizes the emulative and competitive character of consumption. If one assumes that consumer A's satisfaction depends solely on his consumption *relative* to that of some defined peer group, one reaches conclusions different from those of the standard model. Still another line of criticism is directed at the static character of existing models, in which the household seeks only an equilibrium adjustment to given preferences. This avoids the question of how new wants are developed, and the role of increasing education and increasing leisure time in this connection.

There has been less attention to the individual as supplier of labor, and to the satisfactions associated with work rather than consumption. The former might be judged equally important in welfare terms;[1] and there are encouraging signs that this is beginning to be recognized.[2] In an increasingly affluent economy, in which the occupational structure is being upgraded continuously, more and more people probably live to work instead of (as usually assumed) working to live.

Our theorizing about work and consumption may also be regarded as unduly individualistic. First, the individual is separated from the household of which he normally forms a part. Next, he is split down the middle and his reactions as producer are separated from his behavior as consumer. All this does violence to well-known features of reality. We know that individual willingness to seek overtime work or take a second job is related to household responsibilities. We know

1. As Peter Wiles points out, "The marginal disutility felt by workers is from every point of view as important as the marginal utility felt by consumers. If workers are forced into jobs they do not like, welfare diminishes. . . . If consumers want things that are unpleasant to produce they must pay high prices. Consumer's sovereignty unopposed by workers' sovereignty would be a curious form of tyranny, over man in one of his aspects by himself in another of his aspects. The freedom to 'sack the boss' . . . is . . . an integral but normally neglected part of welfare economics" *(Political Economy of Communism, p. 97).*

2. At a conceptual level, see Gary Becker's pioneer article, "A Theory of the Allocation of Time," *Economic Journal,* Sept. 1965, pp. 493–517. On the empirical side, see William G. Bowen and T. Aldrich Finegan, *The Economics of Labor Force Participation* (Princeton: Princeton University Press, 1969).

that labor force participation rates, particularly for women, are related to family income and family composition. We know that purchases of housing and consumer durables are related to where people stand in the life cycle of marriage, child rearing, and eventual retirement. But we do not yet have an integrated theory of the household as purchaser, supplier of labor, and asset holder.

Turning to the business firm, the implications of profit-maximizing behavior have been elaborated in detail, and are enshrined in countless textbooks. But while we teach the received doctrine, few of us are entirely happy with it, and there have been efforts to break out of the conventional mold in one direction or another.

First, the profit-maximization hypothesis has come under sustained attack. Alternative models have been developed in which the firm tries to attain some conventional profit target ("satisficing"), or to maintain its established market share, or to maximize the growth rate of sales, or to maximize the security and perquisites of management. Implicit in these models is some departure from purely competitive conditions which permits the firm to have a policy.[3] There is a considerable research literature in which business behavior is used to test one or another of these models.

Second, a number of economists have taken up the Schumpeterian challenge that the firm's most important activity is not optimal adjustment to given conditions, but rather an effort to change those conditions by inventing new products and technology. There has been an increase of theorizing and research on such problems as: the motivation of research and development activity, and the measurable output of such activity; the diffusion of new technology, among firms within

3. Most readers will be familiar with the Alchian-Friedman argument that, under purely competitive conditions, the assumption of profit maximization is warranted quite independently of what businessmen think or say they are doing. Only the firms which turn out—perhaps on a stochastic basis—to have been maximizing profit will be able to survive over the long run. The response of many recent theorists of the firm would be to deny that any close approximation to pure competition occurs in reality.

the innovating country and across national lines; and the "learning curve" pattern by which the cost of producing a new output is reduced gradually over time.

Third, there has been increasing attention to the fact that business decisions are made under conditions of imperfect foresight; and this has produced a large literature on decision making under uncertainty. Fourth, there has been much work on the way in which decision making in large firms is influenced by *the internal organization* of the firm; by the routing of information flows, the degree and type of decentralization of decisions, and so on. Kornai, in his penetrating critique of present microeconomics, advances a view of the firm as battleground.[4] Different functional groups, in charge of production, marketing, product design, finance, and so on are striving for quite different objectives. Their views clash in discussions within the management hierarchy, and a compromise of interests is reached. No one individual is in a position to optimize in the conventional sense.

Finally, in the Western countries we have little positive economics on the operation of public corporations. There is a large normative literature on how such enterprises *should* be managed—rules for investment calculation, marginal-cost pricing, and so on. But this is different from asking how public enterprises *actually* operate. A recent IMF study suggests that most public enterprises in most countries make operating losses, so that part of operating costs and all of capital costs have to be covered by budget transfers.[5] Is this an intended result of applying optimizing principles? Or does it result from politically induced decisions and managerial inefficiency? We do not know.

Socialist Economies

The notion of an economic mechanism responding to spontaneous expressions of consumer and worker preference is quite heterodox in the socialist countries. Perhaps on this

4. Kornai, *Anti-Equilibrium,* chap. 7.

5. Gault and Dutto, "Financial Performance of Government-Owned Corporations" pp. 102–142.

account, there is little explicit discussion of such preferences in the economic literature, and socialist thinking has to be inferred from observation of economic management.

In the area of consumption, there is a tendency to regard "necessities" and "nonnecessities" as distinct categories rather than as different ranges of a spectrum. For necessities, it seems often to be assumed that each household will want or need a fixed physical amount—so many square yards of housing space of specified quality, a certain caloric intake, so many suits, dresses, pairs of shoes, and so on per year. (Note that this is not unlike the procedure of the United States Bureau of Labor Statistics in defining consumer budgets which are thought to provide a "minimum level of health and decency." The cost of such budgets is widely used as an argument in setting minimum wages and in collective bargaining negotiations.) These physical amounts, multiplied by the number of individuals or households, become output targets for the economy.

This approach can perhaps be rationalized along lines suggested by Maurice Dobb.[6] Assume that consumer income is rather equally distributed among households, and that consumers' demand schedules for a particular good are similar. When average income in the community is low, commodity A is regarded as an unobtainable luxury, and planners may feel that they need produce only a token amount. As incomes rise, however, a point is reached at which commodity A seems both obtainable and in some sense necessary. Demand then becomes highly elastic over a wide range of quantities. But when output reaches a point corresponding to "full usage" of the commodity (for example, one watch per adult, or one TV set per household), demand becomes inelastic once more. Under these conditions it might make reasonable sense to treat demand as a *quantity* rather than a *schedule*. The key question is whether to include commodity A in the basic consumer menu. If it is included, there is no reason to produce less than the amount corresponding to "full usage."

6. Dobb, *Welfare Economics.*

Ideally, such a strategy would imply sufficient predict-ability of demand to permit appropriate upward adjust-ments of output, plus use of market-clearing prices. We have already indicated that in practice prices are often too low (or incomes "too high," relative to commodity availabilities), leading to large expenditures of consumer time in searching for goods and in queuing. The fact that socialist planners do not seem much concerned about this problem implies a low valuation of housewives' time, which seems odd in a system where labor is scarce, female labor force participation rates are high, and the value of an hour is presumably rising over time as development proceeds. Only recently, however, has the value of time been given much consideration in Western economics, and then mainly in connection with queuing theory and other problems in operations research rather than as part of demand theory.

Where does consumer demand come from? How are pref-erences shaped? What are the significant differences in this respect between capitalist and socialist economies? Under socialism, producers' efforts to sway consumer tastes are less in evidence, partly because in a suction economy there is little need to court consumers. (But this is not an unmixed bless-ing. The other side of the coin is lack of interest by producers in product innovation, variety, and quality—things from which consumers would stand to gain.) On the other hand, government efforts to influence tastes are greater in the so-cialist countries. Not only are basic consumption items sub-sidized, but so are books and periodicals, theatrical and other cultural performances, outdoor recreation, passenger travel, and vacation trips. Government promotion of such "merit wants" occurs also in the West, but not on such a substantial scale.

In the area of worker preferences, too, several presupposi-tions are evidenced in action. First, work is evidently good and to be encouraged. Idleness is frowned on in early-Puritan fashion. Not only are women encouraged to work in a wide variety of occupations, but child-care centers and other institutional arrangements have been devised to make such work feasible.

While work is good, too much work is not good. It is taken for granted that, as the productive capacity of the economy rises, the benefits will be divided between consumption and leisure. Reducing the work day and week is an important policy target. This will result, however, not from marginal calculations by individual workers in the market but from transmission of median worker preferences through party and trade union channels. In this sphere, one reason for limited emphasis on market mechanisms may be that the political mechanism is regarded as an adequate registering device.

The wage structure of the socialist economies implies that workers have a system of job preferences, and that they respond mainly to material incentives. (The notion that socialist enthusiasm alone can provide adequate incentives is confined to countries which, like China and Cuba, are still experiencing the early euphoria of socialization under the leadership of "old revolutionaries" to whom this is an article of faith.) Thus it is necessary to pay more to induce people to undergo prolonged training, or do heavy work in a coal mine or steel mill, or live in Eastern Siberia. The fact that, at least in the USSR, wage differentials are rather wide and are changed only infrequently suggests that they are not based on a nice calculation of the transfer price of the marginal man. They probably contain a safety factor which is judged adequate to make *certain* that important jobs will not go unfilled. It would not be difficult to formalize these ideas into a theory of labor supply; and such a theory might not look very different from corresponding theories in Western economies.

Turning from the household to the firm, it is clear that new theory construction is needed. One reason is that there are several varieties of socialist firm, each of which might be expected to have its own laws of motion. The Yugoslav worker-owned firm, in which profits are available for distribution among the members, is a special kind of creature.

Benjamin Ward's attempt to model such a firm has aroused discussion in both Eastern and Western circles.[7]

The Hungarian firm, in which different levels of employee are eligible for differing sizes of bonus, is another special case. So is the present Soviet firm, in which profit is a key success indicator, and a part of profit may be set aside for bonus payments and workers' housing and recreational benefits. The old-style Soviet firm, constrained by a variety of physical targets, was again quite different. In the socialist countries, then, one would need several theories of the firm rather than the unitary theory which we supposedly have for the capitalist business.

This would be true even on the assumption that socialist firms follow some simple optimizing rule. But this assumption is as questionable in socialist as in capitalist countries. The personal objectives of the managers as well as the institutional interests of the firm must be considered. It has sometimes been suggested that, in traditional Soviet firms, the manager tended to maximize his *personal security* by not doing anything for which he could subsequently be blamed. It seems likely, too, that different groups within the enterprise (and at supervisory levels above the enterprise) are pursuing rather different objectives, and that Kornai's picture of the firm as battleground is not farfetched.

Less Developed Economies

Here we must first take account of the argument that personal behavior is markedly less "economic" in the LDCs than in the more industrialized nations. This, it is said, undercuts the whole structure of microeconomics, in which rational calculations and material incentives play a prominent role.

This line of argument is ambiguous, and can be interpreted in several ways. It could mean that behavior is uncal-

7. For a recent critique, see Pavel Pelikan and Rudolf Kocanda, "The Socialist Enterprise as a Participant in the Market," *Czechoslovak Economic Papers*, vol. 9 (1968): 49–64.

culated or irrational, hence unpredictable; but few scholars
would defend such a strong assertion. More plausibly, it
could mean that behavior is routinized and traditional, and
must be explained in terms of established custom rather than
individualistic calculations. Thus there is the hypothesis of
the "inert peasant," who continues year after year to grow
traditional crops by traditional methods. Recent research,
however, casts considerable doubt on this hypothesis. Sample
studies of peasant farmers suggest that, given the known
technology and the resources available, their production
behavior is quite economic. They continue to apply labor
and capital until the marginal yield of these inputs falls to
a low level, at which point they sensibly stop short.[8] There
is also a large literature indicating that peasants respond to
the opening of new opportunities for cash sale of produce;
and that, where alternative crops can be produced on the
same land, they respond in the normal way to shifts in the
relative prices of these crops.[9]

A third interpretation might be that, in many cultures,
nonmaterial goals enter individuals' preference functions to
a greater extent than in the West. But this is not an objection
to economic analysis, as Robbins and others have demonstrated. Economic analysis requires that people *have* preference functions, but their admissible content is completely
general. The goals among which people allocate their resources can include aesthetic satisfaction, family or tribal
solidarity, spiritual progress, and many other things in addition to personal consumption.

A more substantial interpretation is that, because of cultural and institutional differences, preference maps will often
differ from their Western counterparts. One can imagine an
extended-family situation in which the incentive to earn addi-

8. This point is emphasized in T. W. Schultz, *Transforming Traditional Agriculture* (New Haven: Yale University Press, 1964).

9. See, for example, the discussion of agriculture in Jagdish N.
Bhagwati and Sukhamoy Chakravarty, "Contributions to Indian Economic Analysis: A Study," *American Economic Review*, Sept. 1969, supp.
pp. 29–59.

tional income, which will have to be shared with many relatives, is close to zero. One can imagine a "satisficing peasant" who, beyond some level of real income, becomes unresponsive to income incentives. African migratory laborers have traditionally gone to the city to save some "target" amount required for a bride price, or to put a tin roof on the house, or to acquire such highly valued consumer goods as bicycles or radios. When the target has been reached, the worker returns home; and the higher the daily wage, the sooner he may return. But such situations are not outside the realm of economic analysis. The backward-bending labor supply curve is a familiar creature in Western textbooks. Economists are surely ingenious enough to bend their curves in all sorts of strange ways, as may be required for descriptive accuracy in a particular context.

To argue that one can reason about micro behavior in the LDCs in an economic way is not to deny that much new theoretical work is required. A major reason is the different production organization of these countries. In both the socialist and capitalist countries, most of national output comes from large enterprises employing wage labor. Under these circumstances it is feasible to separate the economics of the household from the economics of the firm. And the economics of the firm, which as late as Marshall rested on the motivation of a small owner-manager, has become increasingly an analysis of the motivation of *hired executives,* running the enterprise on behalf of absentee owners.

In the LDCs, however, large "modern" enterprises produce only a small part of output. The economic landscape is dominated by very small enterprises, in which the owner contributes simultaneously capital, labor time, and management. This is the general rule in agriculture, in handicraft manufacturing, in traditional trade, transport, and service activities. In such enterprises decisions are being made simultaneously on inputs of labor time, allocation of this time between production for sale and for home use, reinvestment of income in the enterprise, and withdrawal of income for consumption.

One can still distinguish between "production" decisions, "consumption" decisions, and "labor supply" decisions; but these decisions form an interrelated system. The economics of the firm and the household are intertwined, and a useful theory of enterprise operation is bound to look different from Western theories of the firm.

An especially interesting task is to construct better models of production behavior in agriculture. Such models are important in themselves, and as components of overall growth models. LDC growth models sometimes fail clearly to specify the structure of the agricultural sector. In other cases, when one looks closely at the model, it turns out to be assuming a special organization of agriculture. Thus while the model may look completely general, it is in fact a special case, and inserting a different kind of agriculture would lead to different conclusions.

Agriculture can be organized in a variety of ways. There is collective farming. There is plantation or estate farming, in which a large landowner operates with hired labor. There is the owner-operated farm, "family farming" in the United States, "peasant farming" in LDC parlance. There is tenant farming, on a cash rent or sharecropping basis. Thus a variety of models, rather than a single model, is required. Some work has already been done, particularly on the owner-operated farm allocating family labor time among food production for home use, production of other things for home use, and production for market. But this line of theorizing is still at an early stage of development.

NORMATIVE MICROECONOMICS

Economic analysis usually assumes that the business firm minimizes cost at each point in time. But while we assume cost minimization in one mental compartment, in another we realize that cost minimization is difficult to achieve. This is one reason why we have schools of business administration. Over the past half century, business administion has become a much more complex subject, based increasingly on applications of logic, mathematics, economics, and psychology as well as on engineering knowledge. "Old scientific management," or Taylorism, has been succeeded by "new scientific management." The new techniques go by such names as "managerial economics," "management science," and "operations research." Subsumed under these broad headings are more specific techniques such as queuing theory; programming, linear and otherwise; information theory; general systems analysis; inventory models; transportation models; simulation; and game theory.[10] Use of these techniques has been facilitated by the development of electronic data processing equipment. Complex calculations, which would have been expensive or even impossible by older hand methods, are now feasible at moderate cost.

The structure of problems in operations research is broadly as follows: there are certain objectives—normally more than one—to be accomplished, and certain trade-offs among these objectives, from which one can derive an "objective function" or "measure of merit." There are certain variables which can be manipulated to attain these objectives. This enables the analyst to model the problem.[11] The model is

10. For a general survey, see Robert Dorfman, "Operations Research," in *Surveys of Economic Theory*, vol. 3 (New York: St. Martin's Press, 1966). See also William J. Baumol, *Economic Theory and Operations Analysis* (Englewood Cliffs, N.J.: Prentice-Hall, 1961); and Henri Theil, John C. G. Bost, and Teun Kloek, *Operations Research and Quantitative Economics* (New York: McGraw-Hill, 1965).

11. As Dorfman points out, "Operations research is not a subject-matter field but an approach or method. . . . the operations analyst, in contrast with the conventional business analyst, has a strong predilection for formulating his problems by means of formal mathematical models. . . . more than 40% of operations analysts are engineers by training, another 45% are mathematicians, statisticians, or natural scientists. . . . The essence of this point of view is that a phenomenon is understood when, and only when, it has been expressed as a formal, really mechanistic, quantitative model, and that, furthermore, all phenomena within the purview of science . . . can be so expressed with sufficient persistence and ingenuity. . . . These characteristics I take to be the style of operations research, and I define operations research to be all research in this spirit intended to help solve practical, immediate problems in the fields of business, governmental, or military administration" *(Surveys of Economic Theory,* 3: 31).

particularized by using statistical techniques to estimate the parameter values. It is then solved for explicit relations between the parameters under the control of management and the measure of merit, from which one can derive optimal values of the parameters and hence a basis for recommendations.

There has now been sufficient work on some types of problem so that a relevant model can be lifted off the shelf. Examples are the optimal use of two or more material inputs to produce two or more outputs (the "oil refinery problem"); the optimal location of two or more service facilities—steel mills, fire stations, or what not—to serve geographically dispersed customers (the "transportation problem"); an inventory policy which balances the cost of holding inventories against the potential losses from running out of stock (the "inventory problem"); the optimal number of check-out stations in a supermarket (an application of queuing theory). But for novel or complicated problems, the analyst may have to develop an ad hoc model, or may have to abandon hope of a general solution and fall back on the vicarious experience derived from simulation experiments.

This is all very necessary and useful. But is it economics? Or is it more properly a branch of business administration? One might argue that the internal operations of micro units are something about which the economist makes assumptions, but which he does not try either to explain or to improve. One might also point out that decisions which are optimal for the enterprise may not be at all optimal from a social standpoint. On such grounds, the "political economist" has tended to look down on the "business economist" as a promoter of private interests, and has consigned his activities to an intellectual underworld.

But there are counterarguments. Operations analysis applied to a grocery store might be considered trifling. But when applied to truck production at General Motors, or to location of new plants for the French electricity network, or to a large weapons system in the Department of Defense, the effects on resource allocation are clearly important. In the socialist countries, where the area of decision making is typically wider than under capitalism, these techniques have been applied to problems of substantial size.

A related body of techniques goes under the title of "cost-benefit analysis." This term tends to be applied to evaluation of public-sector projects, or of private activities having important external effects. Multiple outputs are usually involved, external effects are often involved, and the time period may extend several decades into the future. The earliest work of this kind in the United States related to multiple-purpose river development projects. But the approach has now been extended to many other areas, including highway construction, urban redevelopment, retraining programs for the unemployed, educational expenditure, and antipollution measures. This work has multiplied rapidly, and cost-benefit studies now form a substantial branch of our economic literature.[12]

Cost-benefit analysis involves both wrestling with conceptual issues and trying to reduce accepted micro concepts to operational form. Future outputs are necessarily uncertain. Further, where the output is not marketed at a price, its valuation becomes a matter of judgment. What is the social value of a high-school diploma, or of the time saved to commuters by quicker access to an urban center, or of lives prolonged by a public health program? Even where the product is marketed, private and social benefit may not correspond because of external effects. Valuation of purchased inputs is somewhat easier, but again, market prices of factors may not correspond closely to opportunity costs. How long in the future can the stream of outputs resulting from a given investment be expected to continue? What rate of return should be expected on a public project: the government borrowing rate, prevailing rates in the private capital market, the return to equity capital in private industry?

12. For a review of the literature through the mid-1960s, see A. R. Prest and R. Turvey, "Cost-benefit Analysis: a Survey," in *Surveys of Economic Theory* vol. 3.

Because of such difficulties, cost-benefit estimates are necessarily imprecise. But this in no way denies the value of the technique. Even rough estimates are superior to sheer intuition. Cost-benefit analysis reveals areas of ignorance, encourages collection of additional data, and forces the project maker to specify the basis for his eventual recommendation.

Socialist and Less Developed Economies

The techniques just described, being relatively narrow and "practical," are amenable to transfer across "systems" lines. The techniques of operations research or management science seem as useful to socialist enterprises as to any other. Indeed their potential usefulness is probably greater, since the organization of the socialist economies makes it easier to apply them to whole industries, regions, or transport networks. In the capitalist economies, the segregation of production into ownership units restricts scientific management to the confines of a single firm.

A recent study of Soviet practice, in addition to applications at the enterprise level, described several broader applications of programming methods: (1) calculation of least-cost transport of coal from mines to consumption points; (2) a similar study of allocation of cement from plants to consumption points in the Ukraine; (3) location of new ceramic construction materials factories in Kazakhstan so as to minimize the total cost of factory construction, production, and transportation while at the same time meeting expected demand at each consumption center; (4) a variety of applications within agriculture, including choice of a minimum-cost livestock diet, and an output plan to maximize feed production subject to constraints on the use of land, labor, machinery, and other inputs.[13]

Proposals for additional applications appear frequently in the Soviet press. Thus a recent article pointed out that

13. Benjamin Ward, "Linear Programming and Soviet Planning," in Hardt, *Mathematics and Computers.*

the number of construction projects underway at any time is excessive relative to the capacity of the construction industries, and that this means an inordinate stretching-out of construction times.[14] It was suggested that gains could be made by concentrating resources in each locality on a limited number of projects, while "mothballing" others for the time being; and that computer storage of relevant information and application of programming methods could be useful in this connection. The same article noted large losses from excessive inventory holdings, and suggested that computerization could help to rationalize inventory policies within each branch of industry. Experiments in this direction are apparently projected for several branches of metalworking.

While discussion naturally runs ahead of practice, it seems clear that application of operations research techniques in the USSR is increasing. This is true also in Hungary, and probably in the other East European countries as well.

In less developed economies, too, operations research techniques are potentially useful, but their actual use will probably spread only slowly. Even in the West, they are found mainly in enterprises large enough to afford specialized technical staffs; and the number of such enterprises in the LDCs is still limited. Such large enterprises as exist are often government operated. While these might seem at first glance a fertile field for scientific management, the absence of a profit constraint and, indeed, the frequent lack of any clear guidelines for enterprise performance works in the opposite direction. Moreover, technicians capable of using operations research have to be trained and in most LDCs training facilities are very limited.

Considerable progress has been made in cost-benefit analysis, which in the LDCs is often termed "project evaluation." In the 1950s, the rationale of public investment projects was often flimsy indeed. Costs, benefits, and construction times

14. V. Trapeznikov, "What is the Value of Time Lost and Time Saved?" *Pravda*, July 24, 1969. Reported in *Current Digest of the Soviet Press* 21 no. 30, 10–12.

were estimated haphazardly or not at all, and ex post results often differed greatly from the ex ante proposals. Pressure for better estimates was gradually brought to bear by lending agencies such as the IBRD and USAID and by planning commissions and budget agencies within the LDC governments. At the same time special training courses in project evaluation were established by the Economic Development Institute of the IBRD, the UN regional economic commissions, and other agencies. This has brought a progressive improvement in standards of project preparation and appraisal.

At best, however, cost-benefit analysis remains a more difficult task in the LDCs than in the industrialized nations. Relevant economic data are less available. Factor prices may not correspond closely to opportunity costs, and product prices may also be biased in various ways. If the project under consideration is large, its very completion will alter the price structure, so that the problem of whether to use present or estimated future prices is unusually serious. Criteria for choosing an appropriate discount rate for future benefits are even fuzzier than in developed countries.

Problems of external effects and of time sequence are also more important in the LDC setting. A cluster of interrelated projects must often be evaluated together. Even if the bundle of projects appears profitable, the resources available in any budget year are limited. This poses a problem of what to do first, what to leave until later—a strategy problem which cost-benefit techniques alone cannot handle.

MARKET ECONOMICS

By this we mean "Marshallian economics," "supply-demand economics," "price theory." It examines behavior at a semiaggregative level, in terms of the markets for particular goods, particular kinds of labor, particular financial instruments. While it rests on what we have termed microeconomics proper, it is somewhat less open to objection. One can predict that product demand curves typically slope downward and that labor supply curves (in a fully employed economy) typically slope upward, without asserting that most consumers or workers make a careful calculation of net advantage. One can predict that producers will respond to a permanent increase in demand, first by increasing output, and subsequently by net investment, without believing that they attempt to maximize profit at each moment in time.

Despite its long tradition, the relevance of market economics to research and policy in the capitalist economies is often questioned. Some regard it as mainly a demonstration that a network of purely competitive markets can produce static allocative efficiency. It is then pointed out that, in the capitalist economies, the output loss from resource misallocation is apparently not very large. Indeed, in chapter 5 we agreed that the "monopoly problem" in this sense is not a high-priority issue. Should we not conclude, then, that market economics has lost the central importance which it once seemed to have?

We would not at all agree with such a conclusion. We believe that market economics remains important in the Western context, though *not for the reasons usually given*. The reasons for continuing to study and teach this branch of economics lie in other directions. More specifically:

1. The main point of market economics is *not* the definition of equilibrium positions. The main point is comparative statics, that is, prediction of responses to changes in factor supplies, preferences, and technology. It is difficult to imagine how one could make such predictions without the apparatus of market economics, which is so much in our blood that we tend to forget how much we rely on it.

2. Suppose it is true, as it seems to be, that capitalist economies perform well in terms of static resource allocation. Surely it is of some interest to understand why this is so. It is also interesting to explore why it is not always so in other kinds of economy.

3. There is much evidence that what Leibenstein has labeled "X-efficiency (failure of firms to operate near their

production frontier) is quantitatively more important than static allocative efficiency. But X-efficiency is surely not unrelated to market structure and degrees of competitive pressure.

4. Perhaps the most interesting aspect of firm behavior is the degree of innovativeness in new products, improvements in product quality, and cost-reducing changes in production methods. While Schumpeter's hypothesis that monopoly is more favorable to innovation that atomistic competition may or may not prove correct, the problem is surely important; and it is a problem in market economics.

5. Part of the disinterest in market economics may arise from the fact that applied work has been concentrated so heavily on manufacturing. Steel, aluminum, and automobiles can eventually become boring. There is greater interest at present in the education industry, the health industry, output of public goods, efforts at environmental control. But these are all areas to which price theory is highly relevant.

6. The techniques of operations research and cost-benefit analysis are workable only if one assumes that price relations are reasonably correct, or that there is some basis for adjustment where they are not. As a mental experiment, try working through a cost-benefit problem without drawing in any way on your training in price theory.

7. National income accounting and macroeconomic theory also depend on a substructure of price theory, as will become apparent in later sections.

To say that, for all these reasons, *some kind* of market economics is a key component of the Western tool-kit is not to say that our present apparatus is fully satisfactory. In its purely static and purely competitive variant, it can look remarkably bare and empty. We shall have more to say about this in connection with general equilibrium theory, where these defects are particularly apparent.

Socialist Economies

Operating officials in the socialist economies already make implicit use of market concepts. The fact that these

may have been invented de novo rather than taken from
Western economic thought does not alter their practical importance.

The most conspicuous examples are found in labor markets. While there have sometimes been legal restrictions on
movement, and while housing shortages constitute an important practical barrier, these markets seem to function not
very differently from their counterparts in capitalist countries. The persistent excess demand for labor makes it easy
for qualified workers to find a new job. Labor turnover is
high and geographical migration is large. Discussions of
manpower policy read much like corresponding Western discussions, stressing the need for enlargement of the public employment service, more systematic registration of job va-
cancies with this service, better vocational counseling in the
secondary schools, closer adjustment of vocational training
programs to prospective demand.[15]

The existence of supply curves to particular occupations
and areas is recognized in wage schedules. Higher wages are
offered for more laborious work, for work involving greater
training and responsibility, for work in remote or unpleasant
areas, for work in high-priority industries whose recruitment
needs must be met. In the Soviet case, at least, the wide occupational differentials which existed from about 1930 to
1955 have been systematically reduced as supplies of the
higher skills have increased—a "market adjustment" which
has been occurring also in most Western countries. Demand
for particular skills, to be sure, tends to be interpreted as a
quantity rather than as a function of price; and labor supply
programs are geared to these point estimates. This is common practice, however, among physical manpower planners
in other parts of the world.

In consumer markets, the existence of a sloped demand

15. See, for example, a penetrating article by the chairman of the
Russian Council of Ministers State Committee for Utilization of Labor
Resources, Mr. K. Novikoo, "Problems of the Efficient Utilization of
Labor Resources," *Kommunist,* Sept. 1969, reported in *Current Digest
of the Soviet Press* 21, no. 38, 3–7.

schedule is recognized in efforts to set prices not too far from market-clearing levels. Where prices are set deliberately below this level on distributional grounds, it is recognized that this implies an effort to increase output. There are also the beginnings of systematic research on consumer demand.

In setting agricultural procurement prices, there is increasing recognition of a rising supply curve of effort in response to higher incomes. It is recognized also that the *structure* of farm prices affects the allocation of effort among alternative products. Prices of meat, milk, and other particularly scarce products have been raised sharply on occasion to shift agricultural capacity toward these products.

What is still lacking in the more conservative countries, including the USSR, is: (1) Any acceptance of spontaneous price-output results in an unguided market as being socially desirable. On the contrary, to say that an economic development is "spontaneous" is a way of condemning it. (2) Any conception of a Walrasian system in which all prices and quantities are interrelated, and which might be given a welfare interpretation. (3) Any willingness to admit supply-demand concepts to the core of the production apparatus, that is, the realm of industrial raw materials, capital goods, and intermediate products.

Hungary and Yugoslavia, on the other hand, recognize the advantages of, and the requirements for, market coordination and flexible pricing. To the extent that the socialist economies rely increasingly on market relations among enterprises rather than on administrative supervision as a control device, market economics will become increasingly relevant for their purposes. They will also encounter such familiar Western problems as possible abuse of monopoly power. Both Yugoslavia and Hungary already have legislation intended to combat this tendency.

There is danger here of misunderstanding. East European reformers are quick to point out that steps toward relaxation of central controls and increased use of market signals are in no sense a "return to capitalism." There is no question of abandoning public ownership. Greater use of markets is advocated as a means of strengthening economic planning rather than weakening it. The market is a tool, not an autonomous entity. Market equilibrium remains a managed equilibrium. Prices, even flexible prices, remain policy instruments. Profit does not appear spontaneously and belong as of right to the enterprise which earns it. Its size and allocation are tailored to incentive needs and investment requirements.[16]

Even should decentralization proceed further, then, "their markets" will not be exactly like "our markets." The market mechanism will continue to be a regulated mechanism. The art of managing this kind of "mixed economy," of combining decentralized decision making with central controls, is still in its infancy. The problems involved are being debated in a quite pragmatic way by East European economists and planners. Out of this continuing discussion and experimentation will come many lessons in applied economics, which in turn should suggest new formulations of microeconomic theory.

16. A good statement of this view appears in the study by Friss, *Economic Mechanism in Hungary*.

"This function of the plan is combined with the function of the socialist market. This combination makes it possible to obtain a truer picture about the partial processes going on in the economy, about the perpetually changing needs of society and, especially, of the individual consumers, than we were able to obtain in the past. This market will not be simply the theatre of an unlimited assertion of spontaneous processes; it will be affected by economic and administrative regulators serving to realize the major objectives laid down in the national economic plan." (p. 12).

And again: "Evidently, in the framework of this organic unity of economic control the functions of the market itself are determined by conditions and rules laid down in central decisions coordinated within the national economic plan. Thus, in our concept the market is a regulator which, in its turn, is centrally regulated and thereby made suitable to help the realization of the national economic plan. On the other hand, the processes unfolding on this market, resulting from decentralized economic decisions, will have a feedback effect on the national economic plan: they serve as its check-up and may even lead to its modification" (p. 41).

Less Developed Economies

Market economics has come under heavy fire in the LDCs on grounds of both *realism* and *relevance*. This reflects a view, already criticized above, that Western price theory is concerned essentially with optimal resource allocation. This orientation strikes many LDC observers as a major defect. The key policy problem, it is argued, is to *increase* resource supplies and resource productivity. This may require, not the marginal adjustments of micro theory, but major structural changes—a "big push." For such changes, it is said, market economics provides little guidance.

Further, it is argued that markets in the LDCs are so disjointed and imperfect that concepts of price-quantity equilibrium in a market, and of the mutual adjustment of interrelated markets throughout the economy, have little descriptive value. Prices do not reflect opportunity costs and so are not useful as policy guidelines. Western market economics, in addition to asking the wrong questions, yields wrong predictions and wrong policy suggestions. From this it is natural to conclude that the market mechanism cannot be relied on as an instrument of growth policy. It must be largely superseded, and major decisions made directly by government.

There is some truth in each of these lines of argument, but there is also a tendency to push them too far. So it may be useful to advance some countervailing points, intended to set the issues in better perspective. The problem of securing additional resources from domestic or foreign sources is certainly important; but it is far from the sole concern of growth policy. The resources already available are often not fully utilized, and those in use are often poorly deployed. Not infrequently this arises from inefficient government intervention in the private economy, in ways which familiarity with the working of markets might have warned against. If, by fuller utilization and better allocation of resources, current output can be raised by 25 per cent this is surely not irrelevant to growth.[17] It enlarges the country's capacity to save, invest, and export as well as the level of consumption.

The problem of allocating increased resources is also not simple. Models which assume that an additional $3 million of foreign capital is transmuted magically into an additional $1 million of domestic output do a disservice to policy makers. It is notorious that actual incremental capital output ratios vary widely, by economic sectors, by countries, by time periods. Nothing is easier than to waste resources. The problem of spreading additional resources efficiently over a wide variety of uses is a microeconomic problem. All the procedures of project evaluation and cost-benefit analysis depend on micro concepts. True, micro theory by itself does not provide an overall growth strategy. But to say that microeconomics cannot do everything is quite different from concluding that it can do nothing.

Turning to criticisms of unrealism, it is true that Western theorists often start from assumptions of pure and perfect competition. But they are quite accustomed to grappling with imperfect markets. The fact that barriers to free occupational choice produce wage differentials larger than could persist under free competition has been familiar for a century. Since the 1930s there has been much attention to the effects of monopoly, oligopoly, product differentiation, uncertainty, and speculation in commodity markets. The primitive market structures of the LDCs typically produce an abnormally wide dispersion of prices for comparable goods and services—wide wage and salary differentials, large variations in interest rates, variation in sellers' prices for the same commodity, and wide manufacturing and distributive mar-

17. The only estimate of this kind which I have seen is by Arnold Harberger. He concluded that for economies at the level of Chile, Brazil, and Argentina, reallocating resources with existing production functions" would raise national welfare by no more than 15 percent" (Arnold C. Harberger, "Using the Resources at Hand More Effectively," *American Economic Review*, May 1959). For countries at a lower level of development, however, the potential improvement might be greater.

gins. An economist approaching one of these economies with
open eyes can trace the sources and consequences of market
imperfections, and proceed to consider how markets might
be redesigned to advantage.[18] A background of market
theory is decidedly helpful in this undertaking. And the
undertaking itself is worthwhile *unless* one entirely rejects
markets and prices as instruments of economic policy.

The question of how far markets can be relied on for
economic control, and at what points they need to be supplemented or superseded, is in any economy a complex issue on
which easy formulations are not helpful. The need in the
LDCs for an active government policy to take account of externalities, interdependencies, and market distortions is surely not in question. But one must remember also that these
are mixed economies, with a relatively small public sector,
and limited capacity for public administration. Administrative competence, indeed, is one of their scarcest resources,
and needs to be carefully conserved and allocated. This being
so, government must rely to a considerable extent on indirect
guidance of the economy through price cues and monetary
incentives. It needs, therefore, to have an accurate picture of
the economic mechanism which government is trying to
manipulate. But this is precisely the task of microeconomic
research, guided by micro theory.

To argue that microeconomic theory is useful, however, is

18. Myint, after noting that perfect competition is never found in
any real world economy, developed or underdeveloped, comments as
follows: "What is more interesting is to find out how far these two types
of country suffer from the same types of market imperfection and how
far the existing theories of imperfect competition arising out of the
problems of the mature industrial economies are relevant to the underdeveloped countries at a much earlier stage of development in market
institutions. Further . . . it would be interesting to find out how far the
different types of underdeveloped country suffer from different types of
market imperfection. But many critics have been distracted by the easy
target offered by the perfect-competition model from making a "realistic" exploration of how the market mechanism actually works or fails
to work in the different types of underdeveloped economy" ("Economic
Theory and the Underdeveloped Countries," *Journal of Political Economy*, Oct. 1965).

not to say that everything taught in Western graduate schools is equally useful. Some of contemporary microeconomics is doubtless quite exotic and far from any explanatory or policy usefulness. In eonomics, as in manufacturing, the LDCs may be better off with a somewhat antiquated technology—more of Marshall and less of Debreu.

INTERINDUSTRY ANALYSIS; OPTIMIZING MODELS

Interindustry Analysis

This technique is macroeconomic in the sense of covering (in principle) the entire economy, but microeconomic in the sense of revealing intersectoral flows. A 200 by 200 table is *quite* micro, while a 12 by 12 table is much more aggregative. A common procedure, particularly in the LDCs is to do considerable disaggregation for the sector in which one is especially interested—say, modern manufacturing industry—while covering the rest of the economy in a few broad categories. This amounts to exploring a "corner" of the economy, in which data are relatively reliable and which is considered strategic for policy.

There is by now a voluminous input-output literature, and the advantages and limitations of the technique are well known. The limitations arise largely from the fact that physical input-output relations (including *capital* as well as *current* coefficients) and also the structure of relative prices are taken as constant. But in fact these data are constantly changing, and this is true especially of economies which are undergoing rapid structural shifts. Thus tables prepared for a particular year rapidly become outdated, and frequent re-estimation is necessary. The great advantage of the technique is its clear distinction between *total output* and *output for final use,* which makes it possible to calculate how a change in the pattern of final output will alter the corresponding composition of total output. This is especially important in a complex economy with a large volume of intermediate output.

A familiar cliché states that, while interindustry analysis has been developed mainly in the West, it really comes into its own under conditions of socialist central planning. Neither half of this statement is entirely true. Looking first at Western uses, it is a misconception to regard interindustry analysis as applicable *only* to problems of comprehensive planning. It is useful wherever one wishes to trace the indirect consequences of a shift in final demand. Suppose, for example, that the United States and the other Western countries suddenly established a free-trade regime. Output of some goods in the United States would decline because of import competition, while output of others would rise because of greater export possibilities. What would be the eventual effect on output and employment in each industry and region of the country? Or suppose that peace should break out, and that military procurement were to drop by $25 billion, this being offset by an equal increase in private consumption expenditure. What would be the resulting shift in resource allocation, by industries and regions? Such questions are obviously important, and even the rough predictions provided by interindustry analysis are useful.[19]

Granted all this, the potential usefulness of the technique still appears greater in the socialist countries. In principle, it has important advantages over the traditional method of material balances in formulating output plans. The inverted matrix permits quick computation of the implications for total output of any change in the menu of final output. Just to emphasize the distinction between total and final output, which in the past has been blurred by planners' concentration on total output only, is a contribution to planning methodology. The internal consistency of a proposed production plan is readily checked, and it is feasible to draft several consistent plans among which policy makers may choose.

19. Both these problems have been the subject of actual research studies. On the impact of reduced military expenditures, see Wassily Leontief and others, "The Economic Impact of an Arms Cut," *Review of Economics and Statistics*, Aug. 1965, pp. 217–41.

There has accordingly been extensive research on input-output methods in the socialist economies. A recent survey lists nine input-output tables prepared for the USSR, and twenty for other East European countries, during the years 1957–63.[20] The number must now be substantially larger. The great majority of these were ex-post tables rather than planning models, and most of them were in value terms rather than physical units. In addition to the national tables, there had been by this time more than 20 regional tables for different republics of the USSR.

Despite this research activity, the indications are that the new techniques have thus far had little influence on planning practice. As regards the USSR, Treml reports that "After eight or nine years of experimentation . . . input-output techniques have neither replaced the planning apparatus nor been integrated with it. . . . a prominent [Soviet] input-output specialist, summarizing Soviet input-output studies, regretfully notes that so far the new methods have not found concrete applications in planning."[21] This may change with time; but the gap between research workers in the Academy of Sciences and the practical planners in Gosplan remains wide.

The reasons go deeper than mere bureaucratic resistance to change. The information flow has serious deficiencies, and was organized for control purposes rather than for economic analysis. Thus it follows administrative line rather than the commodity lines needed for input-output work. Tables constructed in physical terms are cumbersome, and can encompass only part of the economy; but working in value terms lands one in the deficiencies of the Soviet price system. The necessity of considerable aggregation, even in the most de-

20. V. G. Treml, "Input-Output Analysis," in the previously cited Hardt, *Mathematics and Computers.* For a subsequent analysis of the 1966 Soviet table, see L. Volodarskii and M. Eidel'Man, "Basic Results of the Interbranch Balance of the USSR for 1966," *Voprosy Ekonomiki,* Sept. 1969, no. 4, reported in *Problems of Economics,* Sept. 1969, pp. 29–51.

21. Hardt, *Mathematics and Computers,* p. 102.

tailed (about 400 by 400) tables prepared to date, blurs the meaning of input coefficients; and changes in future coefficients relative to the past are a major item of bargaining between Soviet enterprises and higher administrative levels. Finally, none of the Soviet tables to date has incorporated primary resource constraints, though such constraints obviously exist. So planning officials who question the present applicability of the new techniques are not merely obscurantist.

In Hungary and some of the other East European countries, where quantitative economics is well developed and planning attitudes are relatively experimental, practical application of interindustry analysis may have gone further. This would have to be explored country by country. In any event, there appears to be an important potential for future development in this direction.

When we turn to the less developed economies, data limitations are of primary importance. Interindustry analysis depends on reasonably precise input and output measurements. In the LDCs these are available at best for "modern," factory-style industry. Since this may constitute 10 percent or less of national output, the technique is less feasible than in developed countries where industry may form 30 to 50 percent of output. Moreover, structural changes are often more pronounced in the LDCs, so that input coefficients are particularly unstable.

The structure of the input-output tables which have been prepared in the LDCs is heavily influenced by data availability. Industry is typically subdivided to the two-digit level, yielding 12 to 20 industrial sectors. The remainder of output, however, is treated in very aggregative terms. All agricultural forms a single sector, and so do all service activities. Even the industrial sectors are still quite aggregative, which blurs the meaning of output measurements and reduces the stability of input-output coefficients.

Within the industrial "corner" of the economy, however, interindustry analysis is useful in several ways. First, it reveals data inadequacies and stimulates efforts at data improvement. Second, many LDCs now prepare projections of hoped-for output increases for five or ten years ahead, with a certain amount of industry detail. While these projections lack the control power which they might have in a socialist economy, the exercise is instructive and useful. Interindustry analysis can be used to check the internal consistency of the projections, including the implied levels of imports and exports.

Third, the "backward linkages" and "forward linkages" revealed by interindustry analysis are helpful in selecting industries for preferred treatment, and in revealing the full implications of an industrialization program. It would not be obvious intuitively that the first impact of an import substitution program is normally to *increase* import requirements rather than reduce them, because of larger imports of building materials, machinery, fuels, and raw or semifabricated materials. Interindustry analysis can clarify the size and duration of this "import bulge," and the consequent implications for financing the trade deficit.

Optimizing Models

While input-output analysis can test the consistency of a proposed production program, it says nothing about the optimality of such a program. Efforts have been made, however, mainly by Western economists, to use the input-output framework as a basis for dynamic optimizing models.

The usual structure of these models is as follows: the value of each output is given, usually at existing market prices. Capital and current input coefficients are given and constant. There are no returns to scale, no choice of technology, no technical progress. The problem then is, in the simplest models, to maximize consumption in some future year subject to resource supply constraints, a terminal capital stock constraint to provide for years beyond the planning period, and a constraint on consumption over the intervening years —say, a provision that per capita consumption may at no time fall below its level in the base year.[22] Solution of the model yields not only the menu of outputs but a shadow price for each factor, which will be zero for any factor (such as, possibly, unskilled labor) which is in excess supply.

The results of such exercises have not yet been put to any practical use. With respect to the socialist economies, where their potential usefulness might seem greatest, Montias comments:[23]

> If it is true, as one Soviet expert on input-output recently claimed that "despite a massive expansion of research . . . the method of interindustry balancing has not been introduced into the practical work of planning . . . ", then what should one say of the gap between dynamic optimizing models and their practical applications? In no field of mathematical economics is the discrepancy between the thought and its execution more flagrant. While the models constructed in the Soviet Union are by no means devoid of interest, they are so remote from planning practice that there is little to distinguish them from comparable Western work.

The fact that governments have not yet used the results of such models, of course, does not prove that they are useless. There do seem, however, to be basic and, for the time being, insuperable difficulties in the way of their practical application. Even in a semiindustrialized country, the output menu runs to many thousands of products. To group these into broad categories, as is commonly done, blurs the precision of the estimates. But to take account of each separately would seem to present insuperable information-gathering and computational problems.

22. There are numerous more complex variants of this problem, all of which require the same basic information and involve the same general mehodology. Thus one can maximize consumption over the planning period rather than in the terminal year; or one can maximize for several future planning periods; or one can work with a moving horizon always, say, five years in the future, so that the program is recomputed each year.

23. Hardt, *Mathematics and Computers,* p. 201.

Additional difficulties include: defects of the valuation system on which the results depend; biases in the information flow, arising partly from enterprise self-interest; and unrealism of the assumptions about technology. Of critical importance is the fact that even good computers are not going to be run by angelic administrators. As Lindbeck comments, "every *realistic* theory about the usefulness of planning must include realistic assumptions not only about the behavior of households and firms but also about the behavior of the *planners* themselves, i.e., the politicians."[24] Even in a socialist economy, there is no supreme optimizer, capable of translating the computer printout into binding orders. Decisions are reached rather by struggle and compromise among proponents of different growth strategies, different economic sectors, different regions of the country.

All this is even more true under LDC conditions. In addition to the difficulties already noted, one faces such facts as lack of precise information on the "nonmodern" portion of the economy; unusually distorted price structures; importance of problems of technological choice and technical progress; difficulties of industrial management, which are bypassed by the assumption that all activities can be replicated indefinitely; presence of a government budget constraint, which is usually not included in the model; and the weakness of political leadership and public administration noted in chapter 4.

Optimizing for an economy, then, would seem to be a mathematician's dream which can make little contribution to economic practice. The contribution of programming techniques lies in handling problems of more limited scope, within particular sectors or branches of industry, along the lines noted on pp. 230–32.[25]

24. Assar Lindbeck, "On the Efficiency of Competition and Planning" (Paper presented to International Economic Association Conference on Market Relations and Planning, Czechoslovakia, May 1970).

25. In addition to the earlier references to Soviet applications, we may note that in the LDCs interesting results have been achieved for choice of crops in agriculture and assignment of crops to particular producing

GENERAL EQUILIBRIUM; WELFARE ECONOMICS

This heading might be regarded, in a sense, as including and summarizing all of the foregoing. In its modern development, however, general equilibrium theory has become a special sort of creature. It visualizes a special kind of economy; and it asks certain questions about the operation of such an economy.

While the standard assumptions are well known, it may be well to emphasize their highly restrictive nature. They include: (1) The subject of study is a static economy, in which all variables pertain to the same point in time. Alternatively, the system may be viewed as changing over time, but with the key features remaining constant—a "stationary" economy. (2) The economy is a no-government economy, consisting exclusively of producers and consumers. (3) The number of such units remains unchanged over time, and the number and quality of products also remains unchanged. (4) There is no time lag between production, sale, and consumption of a product, or between these real processes and their effect on the price system. (5) There is no uncertainty—selling and purchasing intentions are always realized. (6) The only information-flows between units in the system consist of price information. (7) There are no indivisible products or productive resources, no increasing returns to scale, no externalities. Isoquants are continuous and concave upward. (8) Each consumer has a definite preference ordering. (9) Consumers

regions. There has also been experimental work on programming a national educational system. On agriculture see the numerous sources cited in Earl O. Heady, Narindar S. Raudhawa, and Melvin D. Skold, "Programming Models for the Planning of the Agricultural Sector," in Irma Adelman and Erik Thorbecke, eds., *The Theory and Design of Development* (Baltimore: Johns Hopkins Press, 1966). On education see Samuel Bowles, *Planning Educational Systems for Economic Growth* (Cambridge: Harvard University Press, 1969); and Irma Adelman, "A Linear Programming Model of Educational Planning: A Case Study of Argentina," in Adelman and Thorbecke, *Design of Development*.

maximize utility, while producing units maximize total profit.[26]

These assumptions clearly add up to a very special case. While mathematical economists have devoted much effort to relaxing one or another of them, these efforts have not changed the basic character of the theory; and textbook statements usually present it in the stark form outlined above.

Given this framework, what is the theory about? What questions does it attempt to answer? The first question concerns the existence and stability of equilibrium. What are the conditions necessary for an equilibrium to exist? If such an equilibrium comes about, will it be stable? One may well doubt whether these are the most significant questions about the operation of actual economies; and these doubts are apparently shared by at least some distinguished theorists. In a recent presidential address to the Econometric Society, Frank Hahn commented: "The study of equilibria alone is of no help in positive economic analysis. Yet it is no exaggeration to say that the technically best work in the last twenty years has been precisely that."[27]

A second and more interesting question is whether such a purely competitive market economy will produce optimal economic results. This application of the model stems from the work of Pareto, who defined an optimum of exchange and production. Such an optimum *assumes* an initial distribution of real income. The optimum does not depend, however, on any assumption of cardinal or measurable utility. It is sufficient that each consumer and factor supplier have a definite preference ordering ("ordinal utility").

The concepts of Pareto optimality and ordinal utility were domesticated in British economics by Robbins, Hicks, and others, and tended gradually to replace the less formal, more value-laden welfare economics of Pigou. The attractiveness of

26. For a more detailed statement, see Kornai, *Anti-Equilibrium*, chap. 3.
27. F. H. Hahn, "Some Adjustment Problems," *Econometrica*, Jan. 1970, pp. 11–12.

the new doctrine is obvious. It appears to be value free, and
in particular to be free of interpersonal utility comparisons
and judgments about income distribution. It can readily be
adapted to idealization of private enterprise, this requiring
only an identification of actual capitalist economies with
the hypothetical general equilibrium system. More generally,
it seems to provide a measuring rod by which one can judge
the performance of any national economy. Compare the
economy's structure and performance with each of the Paretian criteria, and one can tell how far it departs from ideal
efficiency. A good illustration of this approach is Abram
Bergson's critique of Soviet economic efficiency in an earlier
volume of this series.[28]

Almost before its full flowering, however, Paretian welfare
economics came under a variety of attacks, which have substantially reduced its operational significance. Some of these,
involving the formation and validity of consumer preferences, have already been mentioned. Others involve the existence of collective goods, external effects, indivisibilities, and
other aspects of "market failure." It has been pointed out that
efficiency of static resource allocation is not the whole of economic efficiency. Further, the Pareto optimum is a myopic
concept, which shows only that the optimal position is superior to others in the immediate vicinity. The economy is on
an output summit, from which the terrain slopes downward
on all sides. But, as Bergson and others have shown, there
may well be a higher summit several valleys away, and a
massive dislocation of the economy might increase welfare.
It is clear also from trade theory that movement toward the
optimum for a *national economy* will not necessarily increase
global welfare.

There is a further difficulty. Suppose that, in an actual
situation, several of the marginal conditions are not satisfied. Action is proposed to ensure satisfaction of one of these
conditions. Will this increase welfare? Not necessarily. Pareto
optimality turns out to be an all-or-nothing concept. If one

28. Bergson, *Soviet Planning.*

or more of the necessary conditions fail to be realized, satisfaction of the others is not necessarily optimal. Nor does
there appear to be any general rule for working out a "second-
best" solution in such cases.[29] Each case must be worked
through on an ad hoc basis.

The most serious difficulties, however, are those associated
with income distribution. A change in the structure of production, intended to move the system toward a Pareto optimum, will normally change the distribution of income. If
economists are debarred from interpersonal comparisons of
utility, and hence from any evaluation of differing income
distribution, how can we say that the second situation is
"better" than the first? Does this not reduce welfare economics to a dead end of complete futility?

An early effort to get around this dilemma was the "compensation principle." If those who gain from an economic
change can afford to compensate those who lose, and still
feel better off than before, we can speak unambiguously of
an increase in welfare. While the logic of this principle is still
being debated, and restatements of it have become more and
more qualified, its spirit has been invoked in several instances,
usually involving international trade. The United States
Trade Expansion Act of 1962 provided for "adjustment assistance" to companies and workers adversely affected by
tariff reductions. The European Coal and Steel Community,
and the subsequent European Economic Community, involve
a variety of provisions designed to compensate "losers" in
some countries at the expense of "gainers" in others. British
agricultural policy, which operates through subsidy payments rather than price supports, in effect pays farmers to
maintain otherwise unprofitable capacity in the interest of
national security.

29. The basic paper is by R. E. Lipsey and Kevin Lancaster, "The
General Theory of the Second Best," *Review of Economic Studies, 1956–
57*, pp. 11–32, which led to a series of subsequent papers. Some of these
are reprinted in K. Arrow and T. Scitovsky, *eds., Readings in Welfare
Economics* (Homewood, Ill.. Richard D. Irwin, for the American Economic Association, 1969).

Another approach is simply to posit a "social welfare function," involving a political consensus on the desirable distribution of income. Given this, we are once more on firm
ground. Or are we? Can such a concept have an operational
meaning? As Harold Laski is said to have remarked, "When
you meet the general will walking down the street, how will
you recognize it?"

There are also some dissenters who are willing to grasp the
nettle and to assert that economists can make distributional
judgments. Lerner has argued that, if one assumes that
capacity to enjoy income is randomly distributed among
people at various income levels, the intuitive feeling that
greater equality is preferable to lesser equality turns out to
be right.[30] Friedman, while pointing out loopholes in Lerner's case, also argued that a preference for equality can be
justified without invoking interpersonal utility comparisons.
Others imply that possession of fuller information entitles
or even obligates the economist to make judgments about
distribution. Such judgments are going to be made in any
event. Why leave them entirely to the less informed? If one
wants to say, ritualistically, that the economist is not passing
judgment "as economist" but simply as "informed citizen,"
all well and good. The main thing is that he should not be
completely inert. This appears to be the outlook of Tinbergen. It is also the view of Maurice Dobb, and perhaps
of most socialist economists. Such views are currently heterodox, however, and we leave further discussion of them to
chapter 11.

Socialist Economies and Less Developed Economies

We have dwelt at some length on the nature of general
equilibrium theory, because its possible transferability to
other economies is linked with its usefulness on its home
ground; and about this one must have serious reservations.
The arguments over stability of equilibrium appear, from

30. A. P. Lerner, *The Economics of Control* (New York: Macmillan,
1944).

an economic as against a mathematical viewpoint, supremely uninteresting. On the other hand, the Paretian marginal equalities retain a strong intuitive appeal despite "second-best" and other logical objections. One suspects that free allocation of household budgets by consumers, free choice of inputs by producers, equating of a factor's marginal product in alternative uses, and so on does make for static efficiency.

There is little indication from the literature that socialist economists are much interested in the pure theory of general equilibrium. If pressed for an opinion, they might well reply that it is a completely empty system. It is also a system without public goods and central planning, a system in which the abhorrent "spontaneity of the market" reaches its highest point. Nor are socialist economists much interested in equilibrium positions. An equilibrium economy would be a dead economy. The interesting problem is always how to induce change in desired directions. They would also be unimpressed by arguments against interpersonal comparisons of utility. They make distributional judgments every day, and feel quite competent to do so.

The Paretian marginal equalities are another matter, and these are creeping into socialist usage by two routes. On one side the drive for "economic reform," including greater enterprise autonomy, is motivated by a belief that this will permit more efficient combination of inputs, closer correspondence between factor prices and opportunity costs, closer adjustment of production patterns to consumer requirements. On the other hand, those who advocate improvement of central planning are drawing, implicitly or explicitly, on the same body of doctrine. Kantorovich is thoroughly Paretain in urging that factor prices should be "objectively determined valuations" or shadow prices, derived from an economy-wide calculation; that the marginal productivity of a factor in all uses should be equal, and equal to its objectively determined value; and that product prices should correspond to total factor costs. These arguments in favor of "rational" pricing and costing, which appear frequently in the economic journals, seem gradually to be having an impact on practice.

Little need be added as regards the less developed economies. Structurally, these economies are very far from the conditions assumed in general equilibrium theory, so that its descriptive significance is minimal. Again, however, some familiarity with the Paretian criteria may have indirect value precisely because in the LDCs these criteria are often so flagrantly violated. Static efficiency may not be the most important objective in these economies, but neither should it be ignored.

9 THE USEFULNESS OF WESTERN ECONOMICS. II

TRADE THEORY

It is not feasible here to review the present state of trade theory, a task which has recently been undertaken by several authorities.[1] It is pertinent, however, to note the strong revival of work in this area during the past twenty years. For a very long time trade theory stopped at a Ricardian level. More recently, it remained for a generation at a Heckscher-Ohlin level, which seemed intuitively more "realistic" than the Ricardian world. But failure of this model to provide a satisfactory explanation of actual trade flows stimulated a new burst of activity, which has already proven highly productive.

Recent work has taken several directions. First, it has been suggested that, in addition to labor and capital, natural resources should be admitted as a factor; and that technology should either be counted as a factor or handled in some other way. Second, it has been argued that to identify capital with physical equipment is a serious misspecification. Capital formation should be defined to include all expenditures aimed at raising productive capacity, including expenditures

<hr>

1. For an overview, see J. Bhagwati, "The Pure Theory of International Trade: a Survey," in *Surveys of Economic Theory*, 2: 156–239.

on human capital and on research and development.[2] Such a redefinition of capital, plus admission of natural resources, may go far toward explaining the "Leontief paradox."

Third, the development and diffusion of technology have emerged as central issues. Some countries devote more resources to innovation than do others. Product innovations appearing in one country will be oriented in the first instance toward domestic use. Exporting develops as a spillover from satisfactory performance (and learning) in the home market, and the innovating country for the time being enjoys a comparative advantage. As the new technology is diffused to other countries, however, this advantage diminishes and eventually disappears, completing the "product cycle." This diffusion may proceed in several ways, including Schumpeterian imitation by home producers, which are themselves interesting subjects for study.

Fourth, it has been recognized more clearly that trade barriers may distort actual trade flows away from the pattern which would exist under free trade conditions. Measurement of "effective protection," and efforts to estimate its impact, are prominent in recent trade studies.

Much of the recent work has been an effort to dynamize trade theory, to explore the possible contribution of trade to domestic economic growth, and the effects of continuing growth in a group of trading nations on trade patterns and trade terms. This has brought trade theory into close relation with the study of economic development. Indeed, many economists now working in development did their initial work in international economics. There has been considerable work on "foreign aid models," designed to explore the foreign exchange constraint on economic growth, the productivity of foreign capital, and possible time-paths of diminishing dependence on foreign borrowing.

The appearance of the European Economic Community,

2. This view is elaborated in Harry G. Johnson, *Comparative Cost and Commercial Policy Theory for a Developing World Economy* (Stockholm: Almquist and Wiksell, 1968).

and the discussion of other possible free trade areas, has lent renewed interest to the effects of economic integration. Earlier discussions of trade creation and trade diversion have been renewed, and new aspects of the problem have emerged. In the EEC case, for example, one of the most significant effects seems to have been intensified competition in product markets, tending to disrupt price-fixing and cartel arrangements, and to put increased pressure for efficiency on firms throughout the Community. These are effects which might have been predicted from micro theory, but which are rather outside the traditional orbit of trade theory.

In considering the transfer of trade theory to other types of economy, then, we are not talking simply about static comparative cost theory, but about a more varied set of ideas with a strong dynamic orientation.

Socialist Economies

Much of Western trade theory has at least indirect relevance to the socialist countries. There is substantial interchange of products, though little movement of factors, among these economies. Variations in the determinants of comparative advantage—economic size of nations, relative factors endowments, per capita income, level of technology—are as wide as those among the capitalist countries. Moreover, as the socialist economies continue to grow, comparative advantage must be shifting in ways which dynamic trade theory might help to explain. All of them, to be sure, are aiming at across-the-board industrialization. But this does not necessarily reduce the opportunities for profitable trade, as witness the large interchange of manufactures among the industrialized capitalist countries.

Official attitudes toward trade, however, are probably less favorable. The vagaries of foreign demand reintroduce the "anarchy of the market" into national economic plans, and this may create some antitrade bias. While economic nationalism prevents any major steps toward planned bloc integration, the planning system also inhibits movement toward

Western-style free trade. In Myint's term, these are "inward-looking economies." Even with recent economic reforms, bilateral negotiation remains the key feature of the trading system. While enterprises may be encouraged to take greater initiative in locating customers and suppliers across national boundaries, they will scarcely be given a free hand on quantities and prices.

To the extent that planners are interested in comparative advantage, however, the economic reforms make it easier to estimate. Prices within the socialist countries are moving closer to factor costs, and some countries are trying to calculate realistic exchange rates. Thus it is becoming easier to distinguish between profitable and unprofitable trade.

While Western trade theory appears pertinent, it requires considerable reworking to take account of the differing institutional structure. There is already a substantial Eastern literature on pricing problems, convertibility problems, and other aspects of foreign trade. In the West, Peter Wiles has made a major effort[3] to rework international economics in the socialist context.

Less Developed Economies

Trade theory and trade policy for the LDCs has been an area of active controversy, and one must begin by a little sorting out of issues. Critics in the LDCs tend to complain more or less simultaneously about (1) the conceptual structure of trade theory; (2) the size of key parameters, such as the income elasticity of demand for primary products; (3) the trade and aid policies of the more developed countries; and (4) the advice which those countries give the LDCs concerning *their* trade policies. Now while these issues are to some extent related, they are clearly not identical; and it is only with the first issue that we are concerned here.

Perhaps the commonest objection to trade theory is its traditionally static character. It has usually aimed at defining comparative advantage at a point in time, with an implica-

3. Wiles, *Communist International Economics.*

tion that nations should discover and adapt to comparative advantage in this sense. To the LDCs, this means that they should remain locked in to a pattern of primary production which they feel has many disadvantages, while leaving their markets open to imports of manufactures from the industrially developed countries. Their objection to this policy advice tends to be transmuted into criticism of an intellectual structure on which the advice seems to depend.

This line of criticism was more convincing a generation ago than it is today. Much of the recent work in trade theory has concentrated on how comparative advantage *changes,* and on how it *can be changed* by government policies aimed at capital accumulation and technical progress.

Next, trade theory tends to reason about commodities A, B, and C, without specifying beyond this. It is argued, however, that commodities are not actually free and equal. The concept of an inherent superiority of manufacturing goes far back in economic thought. In crudest form, it points out merely that value added per worker in industry is typically above that in agriculture, so that transferring labor to industry raises per capita output. In more sophisticated form, industry is regarded as more "progressive," that is, as contributing to technical progress, capital accumulation, development of a more skilled labor force, development of modern urban communities. There is obviously something to this contention, but it is not clear that such truth as it may contain is incompatible with existing economic theory.

A related argument is that exchange between primary producing and industrial nations works out unfairly because of differences in market structure. Primary products are sold in competitive markets, so that cost reductions are reflected quickly in a lower price. The manufactured goods of the industrial countries, however, are sold in monopolistic or oligopolistic markets at controlled prices. Thus the gains from technical progress tend to be appropriated by organized labor in higher wages, or by owners in higher profit margins, without any price reduction. Terms of trade, then, are bound

to turn increasingly against the primary producer. This resembles the argument that, in domestic trade, the farmer is
consistently exploited by the manufacturer who is able to sell
at "administered prices." This view was urged in the United
States during the 1920s and 1930s, and formed part of the
rationalization for farm price support programs. Evidence
on long-term price behavior, however, lends little support to
this line of argument on either the domestic or the international level.

Myrdal has advanced the concept of "cumulative circular
causation." When the equilibrium of a social system is dis-
turbed by some event, the system may embark on a cumulative upward or downward movement. Quite possibly "the
rich get richer and the poor get poorer." The argument was
developed initially for relations among regions of a country.
If one region gets a head start in economic development, the
very fact that it has a head start will make it progressively
more attractive. Capital and high-quality manpower will
tend to drain toward it from more backward regions, and this
"backwash effect" will make the latter less and less attractive
for economic development. Thus, instead of the equalizing
tendency often assumed to result from trade, one gets a cumulative disequalizing tendency.[4]

The *possibility* of this kind of development within a country must certainly be admitted. Something like this may have
happened in the American South between 1870 and 1930;
and it is often argued that the Northeast of Brazil suffers from
a similar disability. But Myrdal moved rather too quickly in
transferring the concept to the international sphere, ignoring
the absence of the free factor mobility which is important to
his internal argument. The international case is less fully
and satisfactorily developed than the internal case, and must
be considered a suggestive analogy rather than a demonstration.

4. This view is developed in G. Myrdal, *Economic Theory and Underdeveloped Regions* (London: Gerald Duckworth, 1957). See also his
Development and Underdevelopment (Cairo: National Bank of Egypt,
1956).

Finally, we may note the "unavoidable trade gap" line of argument. For an LDC exporting mainly primary products, a combination of supply inelasticity within the country and low rate of demand growth in the developed world may set a definite export ceiling. At the same time, the growth rate permitted by domestic resource supplies may call for imports of capital goods, industrial materials, and intermediate products which (even if consumer goods are completely excluded) add up to more than the export ceiling. Burenstam Linder has argued[5] that such a structural gap is not readily closed by conventional measures, such as exchange rate adjustments or shifts in domestic expenditure, and that a forced reduction in the growth rate may be the only alternative. Even if this view were accepted, however, it would seem to constitute a "state of the world" objection rather than a theoretical objection, since the argument is developed with familiar concepts.

While one must sympathize with the difficult problems which the LDCs face in their foreign economic relations, and while many of their complaints against the trade and aid policies of the MDCs may be justified, there seems no warrant for concluding that modern trade theory is incapable of analyzing these problems or that it somehow contains an anti-LDC bias. LDC experience suggests new applications of trade theory, and perhaps some need for theoretical revisions; but the innovative work of the past two decades goes a good distance toward meeting these needs.

SHORT-RUN MACROECONOMICS: MONETARY THEORY

From about 1930 to 1960 this was the fastest-growing branch of Western economics, and attracted much of the best talent in the profession. The "Keynesian revolution" was not a one-shot affair. It initiated a sequence of theoretical development which has continued to the present time.

Keynesian *macro-statics* led quite early to *macro-dynamics*,

5. Staffan Burenstam Linder, *Trade and Trade Policy for Development* (New York: Praeger, 1967).

that is, to models in which the behavioral equations include variables of differing dates. This led naturally to efforts at *statistical implementation* of macro-dynamic models. A further step was development of macroeconomic *policy models* which, as Tinbergen points out, can be regarded as the inverse of the descriptive models. Tax rates, government expenditure, money supply, and the exchange rate are treated, not as givens, but as *instrument variables* which may be altered by policy. We then set out to discover what values of the instrument variables are consistent with the desired values of such *target variables* as employment, the price level, and the balance of payments.

There are trade-offs among targets—more of one means less of others. Policy design thus requires a preference function which may rest simply on the economist's own hunches, or which may be thought to embody the preferences of governmental "policy makers." This suggests problems to which we shall return in chapter 11: is there any point in trying to look behind policy makers' preferences to citizens' preferences? Do the policy makers themselves know what they want? Can economists discover the policy makers' preferences by direct inquiry, or by inferences from their behavior?

Once the preference function has been specified, the selection of instrument variables becomes mainly a technical problem. Mainly, but not entirely. Certain instruments may have side effects which are considered costly per se, as witness the common statement that "direct price controls are harmful." Moreover, as Tinbergen has emphasized, policy design may extend to various "depth levels."[6] He distinguishes (1) *quantitative* policy within a fixed structural framework: for example, a change in income tax rates, or in public expenditure, or in the exchange rate; (2) *qualitative* policy, which involves structural alterations of a nonbasic character, such as introduction of a new type of tax; and (3) *reform*, involving more far-reaching institutional changes such as introduction of a

6. See in particular Tinbergen, *Economic Policy: Principles and Design.*

social security system, or nationalization of certain industries. This again raises questions. Some economists would consider institutional redesign as beyond their sphere, as "not economics." Is this a correct view? Is it an equally correct view in *all* types of economy at *all* stages of development?

Monetary theory, at one time virtually the whole of macroeconomics, has now been subsumed into a larger system. Demand and supply equations for money enter as an important component of macro models. Monetary control, widely regarded as ineffectual in the 1930s and subordinated to the necessities of war finance in the 1940s, has reemerged as a major policy tool. Over the past twenty years there have been major controversies over the definition of money, the nature of the demand function for money, the channels through which (and the lags with which) money supply changes affect household and business expenditures, and the question whether formula control of money supply à la Friedman would work better than discretionary control. Analytically, the participants in these debates have never been as far apart as popularly supposed, and have tended to draw closer together over the course of time. As Johnson points out, "The approach to monetary economics that has been emerging in the past few years, from both 'Keynesian' and 'quantity' theorists, is an outgrowth of the formulation of monetary theory as part of a general theory of asset holding. The essence of the new approach, elements of which are to be found in recent works of such diverse writers as Cagan, Tobin, Friedman, and Brunner, is to view a monetary disturbance as altering the terms on which assets will be held (by altering either preferences among assets or the relative quantities of them available), and so inducing behavior designed to adjust the available stocks of assets to the changed amounts desired."[7] To the extent that one can speak of a "new quantity theory," it is a much more complicated creature than the earlier constructs of Fisher or Marshall.

7. Harry G. Johnson, "Monetary Theory and Policy," in *Surveys of Economic Theory*, 1: 27.

During the past twenty years the "macro boom" has tended to be superseded by the "economic development boom," the "growth theory boom," and (most recently) the "public sector boom." The very successes of macro theory and policy have perhaps made this area seem less intriguing. It would be premature, however, to conclude that we know all the answers. As bits of evidence one may cite: continued lack of agreement on the determinants of business investment; controversy over the way in which financial intermediaries alter the impact of monetary policy; the fact that some forecasting models still do not perform significantly better than naive models; the stubborn persistence of inflation in the United States during 1969–70 despite severe monetary restraint and rising unemployment. Such things suggest the areas of ignorance which still remain after decades of theoretical and statistical work.

Socialist Economies

It is conventional to say that macroeconomics can have little application in a socialist setting. Macroeconomic balances are planned along with physical production, and "business cycles" cannot occur by definition. (Actually, the pre-1940 type of business cycle is no longer prevalent in capitalist economies either; but this is commonly taken as indicating the *importance* of macro theory rather than the contrary!)

In chapter 3, however, we noted that the socialist countries do have economic fluctuations, in the form of marked year-to-year variations in the growth rate. This seems to arise partly from overtaut output and investment plans, which lead to bottlenecks in the supply of both domestic and imported materials, which eventually force a downward revision of output schedules. Under the socialist trading system, with its very limited credit facilities, imports cannot be increased beyond the limit of export availabilities. Thus the smaller East European economies, in particular, face a balance-of-payments constraint, leading to the "stop-go economy" familiar in some of the Western countries.

Another familiar Western problem—an unduly rapid advance of money wages under conditions of high employment —also exists in the socialist countries. As we noted in chapter 6, no one has a strong vested interest in repressing the advance of wages, and interenterprise competition for labor produces a substantial "wage drift." The excess of money demand is countered mainly by direct price controls, creating the chronic state of suppressed inflation which Galbraith (with reference to the wartime American economy) termed "the disequilibrium system." This is a workable but not very comfortable system, and efforts to develop an "incomes policy" which would cut at the roots of demand pressure will undoubtedly continue, along lines somewhat resembling the Western efforts.

The economic reforms in the socialist countries seem likely to increase the importance of macroeconomic diagnosis and policy. To the extent that investment planning and financing are decentralized, investment fluctuations may become more pronounced. To the extent that prices are made more flexible, repressed inflation may tend to pass over into open inflation. At the same time, Western instruments of monetary and fiscal control will also become more relevant. These are already the main instruments of macro policy in Yugoslavia; and their significance is growing in Hungary and elsewhere. Thus the extent to which Western macroeconomics will become more relevant in the future depends partly on the pace of the decentralization movement. On the other hand, the pace of decentralization may be retarded by reluctance to face greater macroeconomic instability.

While *some* theory of short-term fluctuations thus appears relevant to socialist economies, it is equally clear that this cannot be a carbon copy of Western macro theory. Because of the differences in foreign trade arrangements, investment planning, price setting, and monetary-fiscal institutions, a substantial amount of theoretical adaptation will be necessary.

Less Developed Economies

The need for, and feasibility of, a theory of short-term fluctuations depends on the stage which a particular country has reached in the evolution from subsistence production to a highly monetized, market economy. In an economy of self-contained agricultural producers, such a theory would not be very interesting. But as industrialization and monetization proceed, price and output fluctuations become more important and deserving of analysis. At the same time, transfer of Western theory without careful reworking can be quite misleading.

Western macro theory emphasizes changes in private investment as the main source of income fluctuations. In the LDCs other variables are relatively more important. A major source of instability is fluctuations in export proceeds. Moreover, the channels through which fluctuations in export receipts react on domestic income depend partly on the *products* in question, and cannot be understood without microanalysis of the main exporting industries. Further, in predominantly agricultural countries, a bad harvest can cause a recession; and "harvest theories" of the business cycle, which in the West are merely an episode in the history of economic thought, retain greater relevance in the LDCs. In some countries, too, habits of fiscal discipline are not well established, and budget defcits are a major source of monetary expansion and inflationary pressure.

Another difficulty is that any kind of aggregative analysis is on tenuous ground in economies which are quite fragmented. Western macro models assume sufficient homogeneity of behavior, interconnectedness of markets, and similarity in price movements to make aggregation a plausible procedure. The fact that aggregation is less plausible in the LDCs underlies the objections of Rao, Seers, and others to uncritical application of the multiplier concept. Depending on *who gets* an increment of income, and on the relation of this group to the rest of the economy, secondary income effects may range from several fold to zero. The assumption of a stable multiplier over time is unwarranted. Useful efforts at prediction lead back to microanalysis.

Western monetary theory, increasingly complex and rarefied, also involves rather specific assumptions: a world of portfolio selectors, individual and corporate, with stable preference systems; an interconnected and flexible system of interest rates; a network of commercial banks and financial intermediaries through which the monetary authorities can operate to achieve desired results. This body of thought has limited relevance to economies in which the supply of financial assets is very limited, habits of holding money and securities are poorly developed, and the network of financial institutions is fragmentary.

The controversy over inflation in some of the Latin American countries is a case in point. While theories of "structural inflation" may be partly an excuse for fiscal indiscipline, they are not wholly that. Because of limited monetization of the economy, limited interaction among sectors, and low supply elasticities in some sectors (notably agriculture), monetary expansion tends to run directly into inflation with little effect on output. And the efforts of major groups to protect themselves against inflation, perfected by decades of experience, provide an unusually effective spiraling mechanism. A specialized model is required to explain price behavior in these countries.

The limitations of Western monetary theory are accompanied by limited applicability of the standard policy instruments. In very open economies, with year-to-year fluctuations in the trade balance, government's ability to control the money supply is limited. Open market operations are in general not feasible because of the thin market for government securities. Discount rate changes are sometimes used in the financially most developed LDCs, but their impact is not very strong. Reserve requirements are effective for local banks but not for the foreign banks which are prominent in many countries. So the LDCs have had to develop a variety of "unorthodox" instruments for cushioning the impact of trade fluctuations on the domestic economy: special controls over foreign banks, marketing board arrangements, multiple exchange rate systems, special deposit requirements against prospective imports.

Overall, then, Western macroeconomic theory requires much adaptation to make it useful for prediction and policy purposes in the less developed countries.

LONG-RUN MACROECONOMICS: GROWTH THEORY

This long-neglected branch of economics has undergone rapid development in the last two decades. The models which have been developed are highly aggregative. They usually include only two inputs, labor and capital, and one or at most two outputs, a consumer good and a homogeneous capital good. They usually assume perfect competition in product and factor markets, and factor prices equal to marginal products. Beyond this, there are two major variants: (1) fixed coefficient, or Harrod-Domar, models in which there is no factor substitution; and (2) flexible coefficient, or neoclassical, models in which factor substitution is permitted. In the latter case the aggregate production function is usually, though not necessarily, assumed to be of a Cobb-Douglas type.[8]

Within this framework, growth theory asks two main questions: (1) Given certain rates of increase in labor and capital inputs, plus (in more complex models) a certain rate and direction of technical progress, what will be the "steady state" growth rate of output? How will this growth rate be affected by changes in one or more of the parameters? This *comparative dynamics* is logically similar to the comparative statics used in other branches of economics. (2) If the economy is not initially on a steady state growth path, will it converge to-

---

8. A Cobb-Douglas production function is one which can be written:
$$Q = A K^{\alpha} L^{\beta}$$
where A, α, and β are positive parameters. If $\alpha + \beta = 1$ then there are constant returns to scale. $\alpha + \beta < 1$ implies decreasing returns and $\alpha + \beta > 1$ implies increasing returns.

ward such a path or move farther away from it? This is a problem in the stability of equilibrium.

This kind of theorizing is highly abstract. How far the results can be given a plausible economic interpretation is not clear. But whatever the direct usefulness of growth theory, it has had important side effects. First, it has stimulated efforts at estimation of national production functions from time-series data. There will no doubt be differing views of the usefulness of this procedure. Strictly, a production function describes input-output relations for a single homogeneous product. What sense can one give to the concept of an aggregate production function for a complex economy with hundreds of thousands of products? What does "total output" really mean in this case? Can we assume that the price relations on which the value total depends reflect accurately the marginal social valuation of various products? The same question arises with respect to factor prices. Beyond this lie well-known index number problems, to which there is no agreed solution.

The narrower the product group, the more sensible is the effort at fitting production functions. It makes more sense for American agricultural output than for total output, and still more sense for hybrid corn production. A great deal of such detailed work has been undertaken in recent years, with interesting results.

Most intriguing is the finding that increases in conventionally measured inputs often account for only a minor part of the increase in output. This has led to efforts to explain or eliminate the residual. One approach is to incorporate changes in factor *quality* into the production function by developing measures of "vintage capital" and "enriched labor." Most of what we label as "technical change" may be embodied in improved factor inputs. Recent work on the economics of research and development stems largely from the revival of growth theory.

Growth theory and growth measurement have also provided a new framework for economic history. In the United

States at least, the role of economic history in the economics curriculum has been quite unclear. It has sometimes appeared as an assortment of descriptive materials unrelated to the mainstream of economic thought. It is now being viewed increasingly as the quantitative analysis of long-term growth, which both relates it to a core of theory and brings it closer to other branches of economic study. Scholars such as Kuznets, Abramovitz, and Rosovsky represent this newer emphasis.

Thus far we have been considering positive economic models, aimed at *explaining* observed growth rates. But there is also a normative variant, which is concerned with defining optimal growth paths. This line of inquiry was stimulated by a 1935 paper by John Von Neumann, published in English translation in 1945. Subsequent work has been carried on mainly by mathematicians, and by economists with strong mathematical interests. The problem is usually to maximize the discounted value of consumption over an infinite time period, or alternatively to maximize discounted consumption over a finite period subject to the requirement of a terminal capital stock. The models are even more aggregative than the positive models described earlier. The Von Neumann model involved one "Shmoo-type" good, which could either be eaten or used as a tool. Capital is usually the sole source of output increases. Indeed, these models are perhaps best regarded as models of optimal capital accumulation over time; and their special kind of unreality is reminiscent of other work in capital theory. Consumption is often taken as freely adjustable, though some models (more realistically) treat some minimum consumption level as a constraint.

The structure of normative growth models seems to have been shaped largely by mathematical convenience, and it is not yet clear that they can be given any useful economic interpretation.

Socialist Economies

The positive growth models developed in the West are market-economy models; but this does not necessarily make them inapplicable to socialist conditions. True, rates of increase in factor supplies are strongly influenced by government decisions. But one could imagine that factors are continuously reallocated among branches of the economy in an optimal manner, and that correct "shadow prices" are attached to them. On these assumptions, Western models would be as applicable—or inapplicable—as on their home ground.

The questions posed by the Western models, however, may not be very interesting in the socialist setting. In the West, the notion of a single output growing at a stable rate can be interpreted as a variety of outputs growing at mutually consistent rates, determined by differing income elasticities of demand and differing rates of technical progress. But growth in the socialist economies has not been of this "balanced" character. Rather, it has been Hirschmanesque growth, in which certain sectors are deliberately pushed ahead of others, leading to bottlenecks which then force attention to lagging sectors. This zigzag path may eventually converge toward a balanced economy, but over a long run which is so long as perhaps not to be very interesting.

The difficulties in the way of statistical implementation of growth models also appear more serious than in the West. Both capital stock figures and appropriate rates of return on capital are unusually difficult to estimate; and biases in product pricing will affect the behavior of total output.

Despite these difficulties, there has been much estimation of production functions for the socialist economies by Western scholars, and studies of this type are beginning to appear also in the socialist countries.[9] These studies suggest a marked increase of incremental capital-output ratios for most socialist countries during the 1960s, and a lower rate of increase in total factor productivity during this same period. This has a

9. See Abram Bergson, *The Real National Income of Soviet Russia Since 1928* (Cambridge: Harvard University Press, 1961); Abram Bergson and Simon Kuznets, eds., *Economic Trends in the Soviet Union* (Cambridge: Harvard University Press, 1963); Denton, F. G., "A Recent Study of Soviet Economic Growth, 1951–63," *Soviet Studies,* April 1968, pp. 501–09; and Miklos, A. and Zhukova, I., "Experiences in Economic Growth in Certain CMEA Countries," *Acta Oeconomica, 1968, 3.*

certain diagnostic value, though it does not really explain
what has occurred.

The question to which normative growth models address
themselves—the optimal rate of capital accumulation over
time—is certainly of practical interest, since policy makers
can control the accumulation rate with reasonable precision.
So economists in some socialist countries have taken an active
interest in these models, though there is little reference to
them in the Soviet literature. It is not clear, however, that
they do more than confirm the intuitive feeling of socialist
planners that maximal growth requires a high, sustained rate
of capital formation. Nor are they helpful in allocating capital among sectors and products, which is the most important
kind of planning decision.

Less Developed Economies

Both the Harrod-Domar and neoclassical types of
growth model are developed country models, of little use in
the less developed economies. One reason is their assumption
that the growth process is already underway "before the cur-
tain rises." They do not face the crucial question of *how
economic growth begins.* Further, they suffer from over-
aggregation. This is not so serious in the more integrated
Western economies, where smooth resource reallocation
among sectors, and synchronized advance of the economy
over time are not completely implausible assumptions. But
the essence of underdevelopment is a sharp cleavage between
"modern" and "traditional" production. Nor can one get
around this by applying standard growth theory only to the
modern sector, treating the larger traditional sector as a
residual. The behavior of the traditional sector as factor supplier and product demander, including its gradual transformation and annexation to the modern sector, is an integral
part of early economic growth.

In large measure, then, a growth theory adopted to LDC
conditions has to be constructed from the ground up. Much
has already been done in this direction, mostly by economists

working in the Western countries. The models are normally two-sector models, though the dividing line between sectors is drawn somewhat differently by different authors. They are usually oriented toward heavily populated countries and assume the existence of "surplus labor" which again is defined somewhat differently by different writers. Modern industrial activities constitute the dynamic sector, which draws labor, foodstuffs, and (in some models) finance from the traditional sector. A certain rate of output increase is required in the traditional sector, however, if the demands of the modern sector are to be met without disturbing the internal terms of trade. The "success criterion" in these models is basically an employment criterion. Given some exogenous rate of population increase, labor must be absorbed into employment rapidly enough to reduce and eventually eliminate the initial labor surplus.

This line of theorizing is still in its early stages; but one can visualize several possibilities for its future development. First, in existing models the internal operation of the traditional sector is often left rather shadowy. In other cases, it depends on specific assumptions about agricultural organization. There is need for a variety of models of low-income agriculture, adapted to differing tenure situations, which can be used in examining the response of agriculture to changes in population, techniques, trade relations with the modern sector, and export possibilities. Under conditions of rapid population growth, in which the rural labor force is normally rising despite rural-urban migration, the possibility of absorbing more labor time in agriculture without depressing marginal productivity is a key issue.

Second, there is need for further disaggregation. Traditional urban production, which is a large employer of labor in most LDCs, differs significantly from traditional agriculture. Government employment differs significantly from employment in private industry. Further, any realistic model should contain a foreign sector, since trade and capital movements are usually substantial. The common objection is that one cannot derive a general solution for a model with four or five sectors. But a good deal can apparently be done by simulation techniques, and experiments of this sort are already underway.

Third, the world of LDCs is very heterogeneous, in terms of relative factor endowments, of size and trade involvement, of degree of industrialization and monetization. It is unreasonable to expect that a single growth model can handle these varying situations. Rather, we should look forward to a variety of models relevant to important subcategories of economy, but which will still have a certain "family resemblance."

The normative wing of modern growth theory has little relevance to LDC conditions. These models are usually completely aggregative. Their results can scarcely be applied to economies in which sectoral cleavages and interaction are the essence of the growth problem.

The LDCs also lack either a market mechanism or a political mechanism capable of indicating the "social rate of time preference" which is crucial in optimizing models. Even if this rate were known, LDC governments lack power to decree a national rate of saving and capital formation. In virtually every LDC the domestic savings rate is below what would be desirable. To raise the gross savings rate from, say, 10 to 15 percent, is a difficult and important problem. But it is doubtful that a finance minister who had studied the turnpike theorem[10] would be any farther ahead in meeting this problem.

WESTERN ECONOMICS: A SUMMING UP

We suggested at the outset that it is no longer useful to regard economic theory as a unified body of thought, and

10. The simplest turnpike theorem shows that in a many sector economy with linear production relations the most efficient growth path is one which moves as quickly as possible to optimal relative sector sizes and then follows a balanced growth path. The optimal path or "turnpike" is independent of where the economy starts out and will be followed for a time to reach any long-run objectives in the least time.

that different tools require separate evaluation. We suggested
further that, when one attempts to apply a particular Western tool to a different kind of economy, it will rarely be found
either fully applicable or completely useless. It will normally
be of some use *with proper adaptation;* and the interesting
question is what degree of reworking is required in each case.

TABLE 9.1

Degree of Adaptation Needed

Branch of "Western" economic theory	For socialist economies	For less developed economies
1. Microeconomics proper	Large	Large
2. Normative microeconomics	Small	Small
3. Market economics	Large	Moderate
4. Interindustry analysis	Small	Small
4a. Overall programming models	Small	n.a.
5. General equilibrium	Large	n.a.
5.a Welfare economics	Moderate	Small
6. Trade theory	Moderate	Moderate
7. Short-run macroeconomics; monetary theory	Moderate	Moderate
8. Growth theory: positive	Moderate	Large
8a. Growth theory: normative	Small	n.a.

Note: The letters n.a. indicate a degree of relevance so low that the question
of adaptability does not arise.

Our observations on this point in the last two chapters are
summarized in table 9.1. A notation of "large" adaptation
means that the branch of theory in question would need to
be rethought from the ground up.. "Moderate" adaptation
means substantial revision of orientation and assumptions,
leading to models with some family resemblance to Western
models, but specialized in different directions. "Small" adaptation means that, with minor revisions, the tool would function about as well—or as badly—in other economies as on its
home ground.

The table illustrates the complexity of any serious effort
at evaluation. It is not meaningful to say that "Western
theory" in general works well or badly in another type of
economy. Some tools work well with little change, others do

not. The picture is mixed, and requires careful discrimination.

It is interesting that, for about half the items, the degree of adaptation needed *differs* as between the socialist and the less developed economies. Given the large structural difference analyzed in Part One, this should not be surprising. Another interesting feature is that the tools which are transferable with only slight adaptation are the *normative tools with a mathematical base*—normative microeconomics, interindustry analysis, overall programming models, and models of optimal growth. The tools of positive analysis, on the other hand, usually require either moderate or large adaptations in being transferred to a different setting. Mathematics is much the same everywhere. Economics is not.

A tool may work well in a technical sense and still not be very useful. If it is a positive tool, its predictions may lie in an area of low policy importance. If it is a normative tool, the optimizing problem which it solves may bear no reasonable resemblance to any real-world problem. Our evaluations on this front are summarized in table 9.2. The ratings assume that the Western tool in question has been successfully reworked and adapted to its new setting. We then ask whether the effort was worthwhile, by rating the *adapted* tool as having "high," "moderate," or "low" relevance for the kind of economy in question.

The relevance of a Western tool in its home setting cannot be taken for granted. Thus table 9.2 contains three columns, corresponding to our three-way classification. The items on our list, on the average, do *not* get a higher rating for relevance in the capitalist economies than they do (on the assumption of adequate adaptation) in the other two groups. The older branches of positive economics on the whole fare better than the newer optimizing tools. The only normative tool set which gets a consistently high rating is normative microeconomics as applied to problems of limited size. For such problems, the values of all economic variables can be taken as given by markets or administrative decisions; and

TABLE 9.2

Degree of Relevance (After Necessary Adaptation)

Branch of "Western" economic theory	Capitalist economies	Socialist economies	Less developed economies
1. Microeconomics proper	High	High	High
2. Normative microeconomics	High	High	High
3. Market economics	High	Moderate	High
4. Interindustry analysis	Moderate	High	Moderate
4a. Overall programming models	Low	Moderate	Low
5. General equilibrium	Moderate	Low	Low
5a. Welfare economics	Moderate	Moderate	Moderate
6. Trade theory	High	High	High
7. Short-run macroeconomics; monetary theory	High	Moderate	High
8. Growth theory: positive	Moderate	Moderate	High
8a. Growth theory: normative	Low	Moderate	Low

there is an optimizer capable of utilizing the results. For economy-wide models these conditions usually do not hold, and the results are mainly of intellectual rather than practical interest.

THE THREE-WAY INTERCHANGE OF IDEAS

Why should we assume that useful analytical concepts originate only in the West? Is this not a kind of intellectual imperialism? Should we not expect a substantial feedback of new theorizing from the socialist and the less developed countries?

In the less developed countries there is little evidence as yet of theoretical innovation. Most of the theoretical and descriptive work on these economies has been done by outsiders, mainly from the capitalist countries. Economists in the LDCs are as able as anywhere else, but their numbers are small, and the pull of practical activity in governmental organizations is strong. In addition to the inherent interest of such work, it carries superior income and status. Academic work is usually poorly paid, and oriented toward teaching rather than research. In all of the less developed world there are perhaps a dozen facilities of economics with adequate staff and facilities to produce a good research output.

This situation, while understandable, is deplorable. It is even less desirable over the long run for a country to import its economics than to import its food or textiles.

The situation in the socialist countries is quite different. University systems are better developed, economics is one of the most popular subjects, and the number of practicing economists is large. While most of these are in government service, there are many opportunities also in university teaching and in research institutes attached to the academies of science. The number of such permanent "think tanks" is substantially larger than in the capitalist countries; and the title of "academician" carries prestige as well as material perquisites.

The research output in economics is difficult to appraise without knowledge of the relevant languages. The flow of translated materials from the Soviet Union, however, suggests that old-style "political economy" no longer dominates the scene. A decade ago *Voprosy Ekonomiki* was a rather dreary journal, with a high proportion of articles devoted to ideological disputation. Today, economic writing in this and other Soviet journals is much more operationally oriented. A list of the commonest article topics in recent years would include: the use of mathematical techniques in economic planning; planning methodology in general; pricing methods; appraisal of investment effectiveness; labor supply and labor force utilization; pricing arrangement in intrasocialist trade; agricultural pricing and procurement; and the Soviet economic reforms of the mid-1960s. The discussion of difficulties and errors in economic management seems considerably franker than it was in earlier times.

While these studies involve interesting conceptual problems, their main orientation is toward development of operational rules for economic management. There is little pure theory in our sense. Indeed, the word "theory" appearing in the title of an article indicates usually that the author is about to wrestle with some point of Marxist doctrine. Nor is there much positive economics, in the sense of presentation of empirical results with no immediate policy purpose.

The main thing which is going on in the socialist countries is a great deal of "learning by doing." The areas which loom large in policy making have been suggested in earlier chapters: applying a distinctive strategy of long-term growth; developing a "regulated market mechanism"; managing an economy under continuous excess demand; trying to increase the efficiency of collectivized agriculture; developing techniques of educational-occupational planning; designing a route toward eventual consumer affluence.

It is these problems which fill the literature. If we look for an abstract picture of how socialist economies operate, comparable to the idealized pictures of Western market economies, we shall not find it. But this is not really surprising. Western economics reflects more than two centuries of inter- action between theoretical discussion and economic observa- tion. The socialist economies, with the exception of the USSR, have had only about a generation of experience. So it is natural that scholarly discussion should still be in a formative stage.

Moreover, since economics in these countries is largely an operational tool, one can scarcely separate "pure" from ap- plied economics. Much of the thinking has been done by people directly engaged in, or at least very close to, economic management. Their conclusions are embodied mainly in procedures and rules-of-thumb, which have not yet been elevated to general principles and synthesized in textbooks. While there is a growing body of oral tradition, much of this has not been written down; and much of what has been written is not yet available in English. But if one takes a modest view of what is meant by an "economic concept," many such concepts are floating around in the socialist coun- tries. One can reasonably predict that a generation from now there will be a more coherent body of "socialist economics."

In the Western countries this evolving socialist economics may be mainly of intellectual interest; but it may have more practical interest for the less developed countries. The development problems of these countries have some ana- logues in socialist experience. They are "have not" countries, starting from a low level of income and institutional devel- opment. Like the socialist countries, they have a strong urge toward purposeful management of the economy, rapid growth rates, across-the-board industrialization, and large structural changes.

Some less developed countries, such as China and Cuba, have chosen the path of comprehensive socialization under Communist party leadership. One can at present only specu- late on whether this offers a faster route to economic devel- opment than the "mixed economy" route. The evidence is not yet in. But even a LDC which chooses the mixed economy route can learn from observation of socialist experience. First, socialist writers correctly emphasize the importance of political and social institutions. In a country where the dominant groups have an interest in blocking economic change, it is likely that change will be blocked. Second, the socialist concentration on rapid development of a heavy industrial base is relevant to a dozen or so of the larger LDCs—countries like India, Pakistan, Indonesia, the Philippines, Brazil, Mexico. The merit of this prescription is not beyond dispute —indeed, it is disputed by some Western economists—but it clearly deserves consideration.

Third, socialist experience (along with nineteenth-century capitalist experience) suggests that growth requires forced austerity in consumption while the investment rate is being raised. A "soft state" which is unable to do this cannot expect to achieve rapid growth. To say that it cannot be done, that under modern political conditions the public will demand a welfare state before the economic base for such a state has been laid, is simply to deny the possibility of development. Fourth, the LDCs can probably learn more about educational-occupational planning from the socialist countries than from the West. Western systems are relatively luxurious, with a high consumption element, marked inequality of opportunity, and inadequate linkages between the school world and the world of employment. A poor country needs a more austere and productivity-oriented system; and here the socialist countries have the greatest body of relevant experience.

Finally, the experiments in Hungary and elsewhere with a complex control system combining administrative and market regulation may yield useful lessons. LDC politicians with a socialist orientation sometimes speak as though one must be antimarket at all points, as though administrative regulation were inherently superior. This "orthodox Stalinism" is now passing out of favor in the USSR and Eastern Europe, while more flexible and pragmatic control systems are developing. Some LDCs may be willing to accept a "regulated market system," even though they would not accept an uncontrolled market system.

One should expect, then, that Western economic ideas will face lively competition from the socialist countries in the export markets of the third world. In the end, the LDCs themselves will have to decide what to accept, what to reject, what to invent.

PART FOUR
PERSPECTIVES

10 ON COMPARATIVE
ECONOMIC STUDIES

We say "studies" rather than "systems" because of the ambiguities attaching to the latter term. Any economy constitutes a system in the sense that it works, it does not fly apart; but it does *not* constitute a system in the sense of conforming to any one principle of organization. To imply that it does obliterates the question of the *proportions* in which different control principles are mingled in any concrete case.

Suppose one thinks, as does the writer, that economics is in some sense a global subject. Suppose one believes that economic theory and practice can benefit by drawing on the experience of economies in all parts of the world. What are the implications for the organization of our teaching and research? What meanings might be given to "comparative economics," beyond the connotations which it has carried in the past?

The aim of this chapter is to set out a menu of possibilities. We shall not worry about how these fit logically together, or how they might actually be fitted together in course organization. Our purpose is not to describe a certain kind of *course,* but rather a certain kind of *approach,* which could in principle pervade the entire curriculum.

ANALYSIS OF IDEAL TYPES

This is not a new suggestion. Economists have been defining and analyzing types of economy for a long time. Even so, the possibilities have not been fully explored. There is, in fact, a serious scarcity of well-developed ideal types.

Most familiar is the *perfectly competitive market economy*, with private factor ownership and (usually) without government. It has been developed, in both positive and normative variants, over a century of economic thought. It can be regarded as the primordial type because of its long lineage and because other models usually assume a working knowledge of it as a point of departure.

Closely related is the model of *market socialism*, developed independently by Lange and Lerner in the 1930s. By a kind of sleight of hand, the competitive market model is adapted to demonstrate that its central propositions about pricing and resource allocation are logically independent of property ownership. It is socialist only in the sense that aggregate investment is centrally determined, that prices are centrally announced rather than cried out by participants in the market, and that the profit which managers maximize does not belong to private owners. But prices are still expected to balance supply and demand, they still emerge by a process of *tatônnement*, they are in fact just the old, familiar, competitive market prices. Resource allocation is also identical with that in the competitive model.

It is not necessary to demonstrate that this model bears little relation to real-world socialist economies. In particular, it is misleading to identify it with the economy of Yugoslavia. The most distinctive Yugoslav institution, worker ownership, is syndicalist rather than market socialist in origin.

Considering the richness of our knowledge of capitalist economies, the scarcity of capitalist-type models is rather surprising. There is, of course, the Marxian model of *monopoly capitalism*, to which students might well be exposed as an offset to the competitive market model. But in addition it should be possible to construct a *big-business-plus-welfare-state* model, which would be closer to contemporary reality than either of these. Many relevant ideas are lying about in the literature: in Joan Robinson's famous chapter on "a world of monopolies"; in Schumpeter's demonstration that monopolies may in a dynamic sense be highly competitive; in Myrdal's analysis of the evolution of the welfare state.[1] Among recent writers, Galbraith has doubtless come closest to producing a workable model of modern capitalism: largely self-financed, technologically self-propelled, dynamically though not statically competitive, managed by a technocratic elite, deeply involved with government, exercising a substantial degree of "producer sovereignty" over the consumer. Galbraith's picture may be regarded as overdrawn, but this is a necessary characteristic of ideal types. The fact that it is not generally recognized in the profession as a workable alternative to the competitive model may be due partly to its being formulated in terms comprehensible to the general public rather than in more exotic language. But this may reflect as much on the state of the profession as on the model itself.

There are several possible socialist-type models, not all of which have been fully developed in the literature. First, there is what Montias has termed a *mobilization system*, often found in the early years of a newly socialized economy. Party leaders set ambitious output targets, but the path to these targets remains unclear. Plans do not embody ex ante consistency and, indeed, may deliberately reject it in favor of a "storming" approach. As imbalances develop, they are resolved on an ad hoc basis by application of priorities. There is heavy reliance on party loyalty and on moral as against material incentives. This model corresponds somewhat to experience in the Soviet Union during the First Five-Year Plan, in Eastern Europe up to 1953, in China during the "Great Leap Forward," and in Cuba during the 1960s.

Second, there is the model of what Wiles terms *state socialism*, a centrally administered economy "open at both ends." There are consumer goods markets at one end of the production chain and labor markets at the other, but the intervening production apparatus is controlled by administrative

1. Myrdal, *Beyond the Welfare State.*

direction. As against the mobilization system, this type shows greater effort at ex ante consistency in planning, smaller variance among sectors in plan fulfilment, heavy emphasis on material incentives. This is the "traditional Soviet" or "command economy" model.

Third, one could formulate a model of *computopia*, of a fully rationalized command economy. The institutional structure of such an economy would resemble the state socialist model. (Not even the most ambitious central planners visualize allocation of workers to jobs or rationing of all consumer goods among households.) The valuation of end products would be determined "from outside"—possibly, though not necessarily, on the basis of revealed consumer preferences. Given such valuations, plus technical possibilities and resource constraints, programming methods can be used to deduce an allocation of resources which will maximize national output. The exercise also yields correct valuations (shadow prices) for each factor of production. Such a programming model, as explained in chapter 6, has pedagogical value in explaining what is meant by rational resource use.

Fourth, one could try to model a *decentralized socialist economy*, combining elements of central direction with enterprise freedom to respond to market signals. Work in this direction would probably lead to a set of related models rather than to a single model. The reason is that there are varying *degrees* and numerous *dimensions* of decentralization. The dimensions include production, pricing, material flows, finance, research and development, and information. There is no single-dimensional scale, by application of which one can say that economy A is "more decentralized" than economy B. There might nevertheless be certain configurations of these variables which occur in practice more frequently than others, and which might lend themselves to schematization.

All of the above are *exclusive* types, that is, they are designed specifically to differ from other possible models of economic organization. A different kind of effort is to develop an *inclusive* model, that is, a schema of sufficient generality that, by further specification, it can be made to fit any concrete economy. General equilibrium theory has sometimes been regarded as having this character, but this is clearly incorrect. Not merely is this a market model, but it is a very specialized kind of market model.

An interesting attempt to develop a truly general schema has been made by Janós Kornai,[2] The Kornai system include *real units,* which use inputs to produce outputs; and *control units* which issue directions to these units. There are horizontal ("market") relations among real units and vertical (administrative or "planning") relations among control units and between them and the real units. Each unit has state variables, inputs, and outputs. The inputs and outputs include information as well as goods—indeed, as regards control units, information flows are of major importance. Each unit also has a response function, indicating the response to any input change, but this function is stochastic rather than deterministic.

Firms in this system do not optimize. Rather, decisions result from a clash of specialized interests within the firm. The same clash occurs within higher-level control units, leading to compromise policies. The market behavior of buyers and sellers (including search activity, salesmanship, product quality variations, and new product development) is strongly influenced by the general state of "pressure" or "suction" existing in the market. Along these lines, Kornai believes, a genuine synthesis of macro- and microeconomics might be accomplished. He demonstrates that, by specific assumptions about information flows, decision rules, response functions, and so on, the Walrasian general equilibrium can be derived as a special case of his own system.

COMPARISON OF CONCRETE ECONOMIES

A second possibility is to compare the structure and performance of concrete national economies. This kind of

2. In his previously cited study, *Anti-Equilibrium.*

study should be differentiated clearly from analysis of ideal types. It should preferably involve quantitative analysis, and it should include as wide a range of economies as possible.

Such studies require no assumption that "economic system," however defined, will turn out to be a significant independent variable. Level of development, as indicated crudely by per capita income, is usually important and sometimes predominant. Still other variables, such as political independence or degree of population pressure, may be found important. Whether there is also a "systems effect" is something which should emerge from the analysis instead of being prejudged at the outset.

There is already much research of this character; but because of conventional stereotypes, it is often not recognized as "comparative economics." Simon Kuznets has analyzed long-term movements in population, national output, capital formation rates, sector composition of output, income distribution, and other key variables for some twenty countries. These are mainly the Western industrial countries, because few others have the long time series required for this kind of work. As other countries develop better data and a longer period of "modern economic growth," it should be possible to extend the range of such comparisons.

Frederic Pryor has also been active in this kind of work. In chapter 3 we noted his comparative study of public goods output in a number of capitalist and socialist countries. A "systems effect" was observable for some kinds of output, but for others per capita income seemed to be the main determinant. In another (presently unpublished) study, he has compared establishment sizes in different branches of manufacturing in selected capitalist and socialist countries. Here the most important determinant appears to be the size of the domestic market—large economies tend to have relatively large plants. A comparative analysis by Joe Bain of plant size, firm size, and concentration ratios, limited mainly to the industrialized capitalist countries, appeared as an earlier volume in this series.

To give a few more examples: Chenery and others have compared interindustry relations in a number of countries. These are similar in the sense that, in every economy, certain industries have stronger "linkage effects" than do others. Chenery has also analyzed the composition of manufacturing output in a substantial number of countries, of different size and at different levels of per capita income. Houthakker has made a cross-section study of personal saving, business saving, and government saving in a large number of countries, including many of the LDCs. He has also made international comparisons of income elasticities and other characteristics of consumer demand. Balassa has compared the growth strategies of semiindustrialized countries, including socialist economies as well as LDCs, with particular attention to trade participation and trade policies. There is a growing number of Western economists with sufficient knowledge of *both* the socialist economies and the LDCs to embark on comparisons of global scope.

Work on comparative analysis of factor productivity has been carried on by two rather distinct groups. Students of international economics have tried to explain how marked productivity differences, which seem to conflict with the common assumption that all countries have access to the same technology, can arise and persist. Students of socialist economies have also tried to estimate relative factor productivities, most commonly between the American and Soviet economies, but in some cases between the East European and West European countries.

This leads to a word on comparative evaluation of economic performance. This is, of course, a strictly academic exercise. No country ever has or ever will change its economic system because another system has scored higher on some economist's rating chart. But the exercise has much intellectual interest and some pedagogical uses.

The analysis can be conducted at various levels. One can compare the (hypothetical) advantages and disadvantages of ideal types of economy. This is an exercise in pure theory. Alternatively, one can compare the performance of the "mixed economies" in which we actually live, perhaps selecting countries in which the mix is substantially different. In either case, the first problem is to agree on *performance criteria*. A number of criteria would probably be widely accepted: *full mobilization and use of resources; static technical efficiency* (operation on the production frontier); *static allocative efficiency*, defined in the usual way; *dynamic technical efficiency* (rapid development of new products and production techniques); *dynamic allocative efficiency* (capital accumulation at an optimal rate, defined by some combination of individual preference and national priorities). To this some would add *income distribution*, in the sense that performance on this front should be measured, even though judgments of desirable distribution may differ. *Speed of adaptation* to exogenous change might also be included.[3]

The next step is to analyze the performance of each economy on each of these counts. This is still a venture in positive economic research. Data difficulties will lead to some imprecision in the estimates, and each observer may interpret the evidence somewhat differently. But these are differences of *fact*, which do not raise any problem of value judgments.

The difficulty is that, as between any two economies A and B, A will usually outrank B on some counts but not on others. This raises a weighting problem: how *important* is each criterion in making an overall evaluation of performance? There seems no objective way of resolving this question, and

3. Interesting lists of such criteria will be found in the previously-cited studies by Janos Kornai and Assor Lindbeck. The Kornai list includes: growth rate of output, investment, and consumption; rate of technical progress; adaptive properties of the system; level of employment; income distribution; cultural and social development; and the distribution of property and power. The Lindbeck list includes: full mobilization and use of resources; static allocative efficiency and optimality; static technical efficiency of production units; dynamic allocative efficiency and optimality; dynamic technological efficiency (a high rate of new product and new process development); and efficiency in information and coordination.

differences of judgment about it may produce insoluble differences on the overall ranking. When each evaluator is obliged to state his weighting system explicitly, however, the basis of disagreement has at least been clarified.

THEMES FOR COMPARATIVE ANALYSIS

Still another approach to the study and teaching of comparative economics is to focus on significant themes which require the use of analytical models plus institutional and historical knowledge. Our suggestions on this front are merely illustrations drawn from a wider range of possibilities.

The "Mix" of Control Systems

It is a truism that every economy includes elements of both market organization and administrative direction. Kornai goes further in distinguishing *three* basic kinds of control mechanism: (1) a Walrasian market mechanism, or "price system"; (2) a hierarchial planning system, in which orders are transmitted from superiors to subordinates; and (3) a vegetative mechanism, involving routinized responses to observed changes—for example, production schedules are increased when orders from customers increase, or when inventories fall below some conventional level. This resembles the autonomous nervous system of the individual, in which stimuli produce responses without involving the higher brain centers.

Since some mixture of control principles occurs in any concrete economy, such an approach opens up wide possibilities of comparative study, in which the LDCs appear as natural members of the scene rather than as intruders into a capitalist-socialist comparison. This should lead also to a clarification of central concepts, which remain fuzzy after decades of debate. What do we actually mean by a "market mechanism"? Is it the bare creature of general equilibrium theory, in which economic signals are exclusively price signals, and there really are no market relations among firms? Or should this picture be enriched by adding such facts of life as industrial concentration, buyer-seller negotiation, product as well as price

variation, and technological change? Could a Walrasian price
mechanism actually function without the support of Kornai's
"vegetative system"?

Similar difficulties arise in the concept of "planning." The
concrete activities which pass under this heading differ widely
as between capitalist, socialist, and less developed economies.
Is it feasible or useful to attempt any general definition of
"planning"? Or should one merely distinguish subspecies?

This kind of study leads also into basic issues of economic
policy. The question "What are markets good for?" arises in
every economy on earth. Every country faces problems of what
decisions can be made efficiently through markets, how existing markets might be redesigned and improved, the areas in
which the market must be superseded by collective decision
making, the most effective way of blending administrative direction with market controls. Experience on these matters in
one kind of economy may have considerable transfer value to
others.

Optimal Organization of Interdependent Activities

This is not a different area from that just discussed, but
rather a different way of viewing the same complex of problems. One can imagine an economy consisting of small and
specialized production units, whose activities were coordinated entirely through markets. But in actual capitalist economies, large corporations usually carry on a wide range of
interrelated activities. Many transactions occur in "internal"
rather than external markets. The firm's activities are coordinated through a hierarchical system of management. External markets are expected to coordinate the activities of
different hierarchical systems, but are not entirely successful.
For example, one system may inflict damages on another for
which it is not charged, or receive benefits for which it does
not pay.

In the Soviet economy, industries of national importance
constitute in effect a single "firm," supervised by a hierarchy
involving many layers of control. Even assuming that the

managers constitute a self-contained hierarchy, independent of the party hierarchy, the system involves problems familiar to any student of large organizations. The ultimate supervisor is very remote from the individual production unit. Perfect coordination would imply that the ultimate supervisor knows everything his subordinates know; but this is not possible. Messages traveling up the chain are subject to information loss and to optimistic distortion, while orders transmitted down the chain are similarly distorted. One result is that enterprises located many tiers below the top, which are not in direct communication with each other, find it in their own interest to engage in duplicating or even mutually frustrating activities. The system falls short of efficient specialization.[4]

Such problems of administrative coordination provide much of the impetus for "reform" experiments in the socialist countries. But the point is that they are endemic in large organizations, and there has been experimentation in the West as well as the East. The General Motors Corporation, whose annual budget is larger than that of many of the smaller countries, is often presented as a model of efficient decentralization, in which subordinates are given substantial autonomy accompanied by effective measures of performance. It seems clearly useful to undertake comparative study of organization across conventional "system" lines.

Socialization in the Western Economies

It is often said that some of the Western countries are significantly more "socialist" than others. It is also often hypothesized that all these countries are moving in a socialist direction—if not Schumpeter's "march into socialism," at least a gradual creeping movement.

"Socialist" in this connection presumably does not mean "Eastern," which would mean a sharp break with past political traditions. So what does it mean? Enlargement of govern-

4. This problem among others is explored in an interesting paper by Tjalling Koopmans and John M. Montias, "On the Description and Comparison of Economic Systems," mimeographed (1969; to be published in a forthcoming conference volume).

ment's share of property ownership? Growing importance of
public goods relative to private goods? More extensive government intervention in the private economy? More extensive redistribution of income through nonmarket channels?
Some combination of these things?

Assuming that one could develop a satisfactory index of socialization, it might be interesting to apply this to the major
Western economies. One can predict that the United States
would *not* emerge as nearest to "pure capitalism," but it is not
certain which country would occupy this position. Possibly
Japan among the major countries, perhaps Switzerland
among smaller countries. One could also examine time trends.
Are the socializing tendencies of a type which can be projected
linearly into the future, or are they moving asymptotically
toward some equilibrium level?

A Convergence of Economic Systems?

Are the capitalist and socialist economies becoming, in
some significant sense, more nearly similar, and is this tendency (if it exists) likely to continue in the future?

Interest in this question is partly political. Economists,
along with others, hope for a reduction of the national rivalries which have plagued the twentieth century. One would
like to believe that, if the *economic* systems of different countries were to become more similar, this would contribute to
peaceful relations among them. Unfortunately, there is no
solid reason to think that such a result would follow. But policies apart, the convergence question has substantial scientific
interest.

The discussion is clouded also by ideological preconceptions. Intellectual and political leaders in both camps tend to
assert doctrines of one-directional convergence: "Of course,
we are not changing; but the other group is moving in our
direction." In Marxist theory, the orthodox view is that capitalist countries *must* move eventually toward socialism. Any
extension in the Western economies of public ownership, of
welfare measures, of indicative planning, of measures to con-

trol aggregate demand, is interpreted as evidence of such a movement. Socialist economies, it is argued, are growing up within the outer shell of capitalism, just as capitalist economies developed within the feudal framework at an earlier stage. So, there is convergence, but it is "convergence toward us." Similarly, Western observers tend to interpret any movement in the East toward opportunity-cost calculations, enterprise autonomy, and reliance on profit indicators as a "return to capitalism."

When one tries to overcome such preconceptions and approach the issue in a scientific spirit, the first question is "Convergence of *what?*" Does one mean convergence in *per capita income,* or in the *sector composition of output,* or in the *management of productive resources,* or in the broader *politico-social system?* These are different things, and convergence in one sense would not necessarily imply convergence in others.

Economists would tend to emphasize methods of resource management, that is, the institutional organization of the economy. Tinbergen argues rather convincingly that in this respect there has been a modest degree of convergence.[5] This is partly because some economic problems are common to socialist and capitalist countries, some methods of handling these problems work better than others, and governments in all countries have some capacity for learning from past mistakes. Thus even without deliberate imitation, they will often be led in a similar direction.

For example, the socialist economies have: accepted substantial wage-salary differentials as necessary on incentive grounds; accepted the scarcity of land and capital, and begun to make appropriate changes in cost calculations; taken modest steps toward decentralized decision making on investment,

5. Jan Tinbergen, "Do Communist and Free Economies Show a Converging Pattern?" *Soviet Studies,* April 1961, pp. 333–41. Galbraith takes a somewhat similar position; but Wiles and some other Western scholars have expressed a contrary view. For a Soviet critique of Western convergence theories, with particular reference to Galbraith, see I. Dvorkin, "The Scientific-Technical Revolution and Bourgeois Economic Theories of Socia'ism," *Problems of Economics,* Jan. 1970, pp. 59–90.

outputs, and production techniques; and begun to liberate
some prices from direct administrative control. The capitalist
countries on their side have: taken steps to control economic
fluctuations; continued to increase the relative size of the
public sector; achieved a considerable degree of income redistribution through nonmarket channels; and imposed a
wide variety of controls on private-sector operations.

As a consequence, the two groups have become more similar
on such points as: sustained growth at generally comparable
rates; the share of GNP directed toward investment purposes;
output of public goods as a proportion of national output;
development of a minimum standard of living for all citizens;
equal opportunity for education, training, and employment;
and even, possibly, the influence of consumer preferences on
production decisions. This has come about through a two-
sided, rather than a one-sided, movement. In some respects the
socialist economies have shifted toward Western institutions
and practices, while in other respects the capitalist economies
have moved closer to the socialist pattern.

Having said this, one must immediately add that the two
groups of economies remain different in other major respects.
Nor does it seem likely that the dividing line between them
will be eroded simply by passage of additional time. Recent
structural changes in the Western economies have been
mainly of two kinds. Some are once-for-all changes, which cannot be repeated by definition. Having devised techniques for
regulating aggregate demand, one does not have to do it
again. Equal opportunity for admission to higher education
can be established only once. Other developments seem inherently self-limiting. Output of public goods is limited by
income elasticities of demand for such goods, as expressed
through political channels. Social security systems and income
redistribution plans reach a level beyond which political and
economic pressures bar further extensions. Nationalization
seems unlikely to expand much beyond its present boundaries.

It seems likely, then, that "socialist" tendencies in the capitalist economies will not grow indefinitely along a linear path, as is sometimes contended by both proponents and critics of "creeping socialism." Rather, they will tend toward an equilibrium level beyond which Western politico-economic structures will remain rather stable. Along the same line, one can argue that market tendencies in the socialist economies will not go beyond a certain point, though perhaps for politico-bureaucratic reasons rather than "intrinsically economic" reasons (whatever that might mean).

Thus major differences in politico-economic structure seem likely to continue for the foreseeable future. It should be repeated, however, that there is a wide range of opinion on this matter. This is why it remains an intriguing theme for research and teaching.

COMPARISON WITHIN SECTORAL SPECIALTIES

Most economists do not deal with total economies, but operate rather on a sectoral basis. We are first and foremost agricultural economists, or labor economists, or public finance men. Courses in such areas usually begin by setting forth the appropriate analytical tools, and then apply them to American economic performance and related policy issues.

But there is no real reason why a public finance man should confine his attention to the American fiscal system. He can equally well work on fiscal problems in Japan, Mexico, or Morocco. Courses can be developed in which American experience is supplemented by material from a wide range of other economies. In this sense, anyone can be a "comparative economist."

This seems both a feasible and a desirable direction of movement for our profession. There is the normal scientific consideration that hypothesis building and hypothesis testing should rest on as wide a range of observations as possible. If forty or fifty countries have data on a certain problem, this gives us the possibility of forty or fifty independent experiments. Unless we take advantage of these other laboratories, we can never be sure how far conclusions drawn from American experience are generally valid.

Further, more is known about the American economy than about most others, and so the prospective returns from economic research are higher abroad than at home. As we multiply research projects and doctoral dissertations on the American economy, as we push harder on the intensive margin of scientific cultivation, we find ourselves dealing increasingly with trivia. But abroad, and particularly in the less developed countries, there are economies about which there is little systematic knowledge. We do not understand the anatomy and physiology of these economies. The basic research which could lead to such understanding has scarcely begun. On this extensive margin of research, yields are higher than at home; and economists above all people should understand the advantage of reallocating resources toward high-yield areas.

The advantages of a comparative approach may be illustrated briefly from three areas—agricultural economics, labor economics, and industrial economics. Consider first agriculture, the world's oldest and largest industry, and one which is in some sense a problem in almost every country. The issues on which comparative experience can be brought to bear include: the characteristics of production functions for various agricultural products; the extent to which farmers optimize in production and investment decisions; related to this, farmer's responsiveness to changes in relative product prices and profitability; the optimum size of production unit, and the effect of different land tenure arrangements on farm productivity. The list could readily be lengthened. It is significant that over the past decade there has been a marked increase in the proportion of pages in the *Journal of Agricultural Economics* given to research on foreign agricultural systems.

In every economy, too, labor is quantitatively the most important factor of production; and much of the nation's capital stock is embodied in human form. Thus labor economics is a subject of universal interest. Some of the issues which arise in any economy are: the determinants of labor force participation rates and other dimensions of labor supply; the degree of underemployment or underutilization of the labor force; the mechanisms by which people are recruited into and trained for expanding industries and occupations; the importance of wage differentials as a recruitment device, and the reverse influence of supply-demand shifts on the wage structure; the role of education in limiting access to the higher occupations, and the proper planning of educational investment; and the distribution of real income between wage earners and other groups in the economy. These questions are thoroughly *economic*, and amenable to theoretical and quantitative techniques; and on most of them data are available from a large number of countries.

The manufacturing sector poses a variety of interesting issues: (1) Only in the vast American market is atomistic competition feasible for any considerable number of industries. Throughout most of the world, monopoly and oligopoly are practiced and even approved. There are numerous hypotheses about how this might affect current production efficiency, technical progressiveness, and price-output policies. How do these hypotheses fare when tested against cross-national experience? (2) Choice of production techniques is usually assumed to depend on relative factor prices. To what extent can this be verified by observation of countries with different factor price ratios? (3) Factor productivity in the same kind of industry varies substantially from country to country. This might be explained by a variety of hypotheses: that factors assumed to be identical are not in fact identical; that production functions are different; that managers do not succeed in achieving the lowest technically feasible production costs, and that the degree of managerial underperformance varies among countries. Which of these (or other) possibilities is most important in practice?

The present series was intended mainly as an experiment in sectoral comparison. It was hoped that the volumes in various specialized areas might demonstrate the advantages of a comparative approach and might encourage more economists to reorient their research and teaching in this direction. While no such venture works out precisely as planned, the experiment has achieved a good measure of success. Some of the studies have been confined largely to the Western economies, mainly because of data difficulties. But a number of others— notably the Phelps Brown, Kindleberger, and Musgrave volumes—are comparative in a broader sense, containing ideas and information on economies in each of our three categories. Overall, the series has perhaps served to illustrate both the usefulness and the serious difficulties of comparative analysis at this stage of data development.

11 ON THE SCOPE OF ECONOMICS

Robbins's vision of economics made its impact because of its clarity and internal consistency. It visualized a market economy in which aggregate fluctuations were not serious, in which long-run growth was a subject for the economic historian rather than the theorist, in which the economist functioned mainly as analyst and observer of autonomous processes. The economy and the economist were *defined* in such a way that the preeminence of resource allocation problems could be asserted as a logical consequence. The Robbins view had the further comfortable feature of simplifying the economist's problems. Freed from old-fashioned classical concerns with political objectives, and from semisociological inquiries into resource supplies and technology, he could function as precise scientist within a limited and manageable terrain.

Much theoretical work and much historical experience has flowed under the bridge since Robbins wrote. How should economics be conceived forty years later? Let us review the complex of interrelated issues outlined in chapter 1: the usefulness of Western economic tools in differing types of economy; the question whether economics viewed on a world scale is one subject or several; the relation of economic theory to economic research and policy making; the boundaries which demarcate economics from other fields of study. In reviewing these issues we shall both summarize what we have learned in previous chapters and lay a basis for a revised definition of economics.

ONE ECONOMICS OR SEVERAL?

The conflict in the literature on this point, and more particularly the differing view of Western and Eastern economists, was noted in chapter 1. What is the argument about, and what judgment can one form concerning it?

Western economists have usually asserted, or simply assumed, that there is a single structure of economic theory. Robbins was quite clear on this point. His definition of economics was universalistic, divorced from empirical observation or policy concerns, entirely independent of time and space.[1] Nor could there be any disagreement among reasonable men about how the subject can best be pursued.[2] What this really meant was that, for Western market economies as of 1930, a single definition was considered feasible; and other economies were considered either unanalyzable or not very interesting. It is pertinent to observe that Oskar Lange, in his "Western" period, expressed somewhat similar views. His methodological writings imply that there is a single economics, and its growth is identified with the emergence of market economies.[3]

1. A portion of the citation in chap. 1 is worth repeating: "No one will really question the universal applicability of such assumptions as the existence of scales of relative valuation, or of different factors of production, or of different degrees of uncertainty regarding the future. . . . It is only failure to realize this, and a too exclusive preoccupation with subsidiary assumptions, which can lend any countenance to the view that the laws of Economics are limited to certain conditions of time and space." Robbins, *Essay*, p. 80.

2. "This essay . . . seeks to arrive at precise notions concerning the subject matter of Economic Science and the nature of the generalisations of which Economic Science consists. . . . as a result of the theoretical developments of the last sixty years, there is no longer any ground for serious differences of opinion on these matters, once the issues are clearly stated" (Robbins, *Essay*, p. xiv.)

3. "The development of economics as a science is closely connected with the growing preponderance of the market in modern times. The coordinating operation of the market and, at times, the failure of the

The Marxian tradition is quite different. "Bourgeois economics" is regarded as a system of apologetics for capitalism. At best, it has some limited explanatory value under capitalism, but is irrelevant to a socialist economy. This view was strongly stated a half century ago by Bukharin,[4] and more recently was elaborated by Lange in his "Polish government official" period. In his major work on political economy he explains that there are several species of economics, each appropriate to a certain stage in the development of property relations and economic organization, to a particular "social formation."[5] To be sure, certain laws may be common to two or more systems which have common features of production organization and exchange relations. Lange apparently believed this to be true of "the laws of the market (the law of supply and demand, laws of price formation)" and of "a number of general laws of money circulation." These exceptions cover a considerable amount of territory.

---

market to achieve coordination of decisions have posed the intellectual problems which have led to the emergence and growth of economic science" (Oskar Lange, "Scope and Method," pp. 19–32).

4. "Political economy is a science . . . of the unorganized national economy. Only in a society where production has an anarchistic character, do laws of social life appear as 'natural,' 'spontaneous' laws, independent of the will of individuals and groups, laws acting with the blind necessity of the law of gravity. Indeed, as soon as we deal with an organized national economy . . . the economy is regulated not by the blind forces of the market and competition, but by the consciously carried out *plan*. . . . The end of capitalist and commodity society signifies the end of political economy" (cited in Alec Nove, *The Soviet Economy:* An Introduction [New York: Praeger, 1961] p. 266).

5. "Political economy, as Engels observed, 'deals with material which is historical, that is, constantly changing. . . .' The economic laws are not universally valid covering all stages of social development but are historical laws dealing with definite stages. . . . Thus, there is 'the political economy of the primitive community . . . the political economy of feudalism, the political economy of capitalism, and the political economy of socialism. Each of these "political economies" deals with the economic laws specific to its social formation, the mode of operation of that formation, and its "economic laws of movement," thereby providing an explanation of the process of emergence, development and decay of each social formation concerned' " (Lange, *Political Economy*, 63, 94).

But there are also laws which are specific to a particular "social formation." The distinctive feature of the socialist epoch, for example, is the appearance of deliberate economic control. Under capitalism, economics seeks to explain the spontaneous interplay of private actions, producing results which no one intended and no one is in a position to control. The resulting laws are thus interpreted as superhuman, natural, or eternal. But "economic laws operate differently under socialism. Socialist relations of production mean that it is possible to control economic laws; conditions are created in which the operation of those laws conforms more and more closely to the intentions of man."[6]

The outlook of socialist economists, however, is by no means homogeneous. The orthodox or two-worlds view is asserted most strongly by those who teach and write on "political economy." But economists engaged in enterprise management, in higher-level economic planning, or in research institutes closely allied to planning activities, while they would subscribe to the established doctrine in principle, show less concern with it in their day to day operations. In addition to their use of such "neutral" devices as interindustry economics, operations research, and programming, there is active discussion of wage setting, opportunity costs, price-cost relations, and market disequilibria in terms which are not too different from those used in the West. How far this represents borrowing from the Western literature, and how far it represents reinvention of similar concepts under the stress of necessity, we may leave to the historian of economic thought.

One may well question the assertion that under capitalism, economics simply *predicts* spontaneous development, while under socialism, economics serves to *control* the course of events. Under capitalism, there is collective decision making within the public sector. There are also important elements of public control in the private sector, guided in part by economic analysis. While central controls are doubtless stronger

6. Oskar Lange, *Political Economy*, p. 79.

in the socialist economies, they are not all-encompassing. Spontaneous reactions of consumers, workers, and managers play a considerable role, and positive economics is not without value.

The question whether there can be a single structure of economics turns largely on what one conceives economics to be. If it is a coherent ideological system with political as well as economic components, such as classical liberalism or classical Marxism, the two-worlds view follows automatically. Marx set out to explore historical change in politico-economic institutions, and the inevitable (as he thought) transformation of one system into another. He analyzed the operation of capitalism, not as an end in itself, but in order to predict the future of capitalism. Most contemporary Western economists would say, "This does not impress me as an interesting question. If it can be a fruitful problem, which is doubtful, it is somebody else's problem rather than mine." But to this a socialist economist might well reply, "It is nevertheless a basic issue, and more important than the things on which you are working." Nor would he be without Western sympathizers with this position.[7]

When one argues for a one-world view, as most Western economists would do, one is adopting a narrower and more technical view of economics. One is saying that economies can be analyzed without adherence to a particular theory of politics or history.

There are several versions of the one-world approach, some of which are more persuasive than others. We are all familiar with the textbook assertions that every economy must "solve"

7. See, for example, Joan Robinson's comment: "The orthodox economists have been much preoccupied with elegant elaborations of minor problems, which distract the attention of their pupils from the uncongenial realities of the modern world, and the development of abstract argument has run far ahead of any possibility of empirical verification. Marx's intellectual tools are far cruder, but his sense of reality is far stronger, and his argument towers above their intricate constructions in rough and gloomy grandeur" (*An Essay on Marxian Economics* [London: Macmillan, 1957], p. 2.)

four (or five, or six) "basic economic problems." This is a truism, but perhaps a rather trivial one. It glosses over the more important truth that the decision-making mechanism differs among countries, and may yield decidedly different results.

A second, more interesting approach is through efforts to develop a descriptive schema of sufficient generality that, by further specification, it can be made to fit any concrete economy. Such a schema, which Kornai terms an "economic systems theory," would then become the framework for a unified economic science. The difficulty inherent in any such effort is that, as the system gains in generality, it necessarily loses in concreteness. The test of its usefulness is whether, by detailed specification, one can actually redescend to structures which somewhat resemble the economies we know.

Third, there is a considerable sense of identity among those economists, East and West, who work on normative rules for decision making, at levels ranging from the enterprise to the economy. Here the emphasis is on mathematical techniques, which appear value free and are readily communicable across national lines. This creates an impression of a common economic science which may be rather misleading. For it is only the mathematics which is common, while national economic structures remain diverse. We argued in chapter 8 that techniques for overall programming of an economy can have little application in either the capitalist or less developed economies; and that even in the socialist economies, where they might seem potentially applicable, they have been used only for problems of limited scope.

Fourth, and perhaps most useful, is the tool-kit view of economics used in earlier chapters. Most of our present tools have been developed by Western economists; but adaptation and new tool construction by non-Western economists is a rapidly growing industry. The socialist and the less developed economies are deeply involved at present in economic engineering but, with some lag, new theoretical developments may be expected to follow from this practical experience. New concepts from these sources may well be increasingly important in the world tool-kit.

We have emphasized also that, while there are some concepts of universal applicability, most theoretical tools are of a more specialized character. Present tools have been specialized with an eye to the operating characteristics of Western capitalist economies, and require considerable reshaping to fit other kinds of economy. Further, the relative usefulness of different branches of theory varies with the policy priorities of the economy in question. In this sense, "socialist economics" or "LDC economics" has a different flavor from Western economics. Thus we return, in a qualified way, to a two-worlds or, more properly, a three-worlds view of our subject.

THE USEFULNESS OF ECONOMIC THEORY

While there continue to be antitheorists in our profession, their number and influence has undergone a secular decline, as both the functions and limitations of theory have become more clearly understood. But "theory" covers a vast terrain, including very diverse kinds of activity. There is macro theory and micro theory, positive economics and normative economics, tool-oriented theory and problem-oriented theory. It may be indiscreet for someone who is mainly a tool user to express opinions on the contribution of these various types of study. On the other hand, consumer preference may play a useful role in economics as well as in the economy.

The past fifty years have seen wide swings in the balance between micro- and macroeconomic work. Before 1930 economics was essentially microeconomics. Money was a veil, and monetary theory was peripheral. The "value and distribution" textbooks of the 1920s, which now have such a dated look, represent this emphasis.

The Great Depression and the innovative work of Keynes, Robertson, and the Stockholm school produced a major shift toward macro theory, which for a time almost swamped interest in micro economics. But this trend was also overdone; and beginning around 1950 there was a strong revival of micro economics which is still continuing. This was apparent, first, in the effort to analyze the grand aggregates of the Keynesian system. As soon as we look beneath such aggregates as the consumption function, the investment function, the demand function for money, we find ourselves building models which rest on micro reasoning. More recently the rise of growth theory, initially completely aggregative, has stimulated microeconomic work on the "quality" of labor and capital, and on the process of technical change.

Most of the policy issues which have emerged during the past generation—poverty and income distribution, deterioration of urban areas, equality of educational and occupational opportunity, overpopulation, environmental control, removing the blemishes of the market economy—are micro problems. Analysis of collective decision making also requires micro reasoning, whether of a normative character (cost-benefit analysis), or an explanatory character (models of citizens and legislators). Those who still insist that macroeconomics should receive major weight all the way from the principles course through graduate school are practicing a conventional wisdom just as obsolete as that of their predecessors in the 1920s, who failed to recognize the rise of new problems and new modes of thought.

If this is true in the Western countries, it is even more true on a world scale. A glance back to our rating tables in chapter 9 indicates that Western micro tools are both more relevant and require less reconstruction in being transferred to socialist and less developed economies than is true either of short run macroeconomics or of growth theory. This wide applicability of microanalysis stems from the ubiquitousness of individual economic "actors"—consumers, workers, farmers, industrial managers. In all economies such actors have some latitude for decision, and their preferences are transmitted in some measure through market linkages. Moreover, in both the socialist and less developed economies, markets are likely to become better rather than worse over time, and their deliberate use by economic officials is likely to increase.

So Robbins was correct in identifying micro theory as the core of economic analysis. He was wrong only in failing to make the most of this insight: in casting doubt on the possibility of *any* structure of macroeconomics, in denying the feasibility of analyzing collective decision making, in writing off by inference the study of non-Western economies, in stressing static resource allocation to the exclusion of dynamic problems. He would have been on sounder ground in recognizing all these as feasible extensions of economic analysis, but feasible *only* on the foundation of micro theory whose necessity he so rightly asserted.

Positive economics there is no need to define; but *normative* economics can be used in a variety of ways. It can mean the inversion of a predictive model to yield a policy model á la Tinbergen. It can mean any effort to combine welfare criteria with positive economic knowledge to yield policy conclusions. We have used it here in a more limited sense to denote formal optimizing models aimed at solving a decision problem.

In such models, all the *economic* parameters are given at the outset. Deriving a solution then becomes a strictly mathematical operation. Whether the solution is of any economic interest depends on whether there is an actual decision problem corresponding somewhat to the hypothetical one, and recognized as such by someone with authority to act. There must be *an optimizer*.

Optimizing tools were developed initially for micro problems at the level of the plant or firm; but they have since been extended to considerably larger problems. They clearly can be extended whenever the basic conditions are met: objectively given input values, output values, time preferences, technological relations, and decision rules; and the presence of an optimizer capable of applying the results. Thus a Soviet official charged with planning the expansion of the cement industry, or with minimizing the cost of transporting coal from mines to users, can readily apply programming methods.

We argued in chapter 8, however, that they cannot sensibly be stretched to embrace an entire economy. The informational and technical problems are simply too great. While these can be "solved" by drastic simplification of the model, one then has a pseudo-problem which no longer resembles any real-world situation. Further, no one official or group is in a position to optimize for an economy. This is true even in the USSR, and clearly much more true in Brazil or Thailand.

Failure to appreciate this has caused confusion, especially in development economics. Considerable effort has been spent on developing pseudo-optimizing models for various LDCs, though data difficulties alone make such efforts abortive. This has diverted talent from the basic need to improve our positive economic knowledge of these economies, which is still very limited.

In positive economics, some theorists are highly tool oriented while others have a strong empirical orientation. What is the relative contribution of these differing theoretical "styles"? How far is it desirable that theorists should also be engaged in research, and how far must theory "live a life of its own"? How far is a theoretical contribution to be judged by the technical skill displayed as against the substantive importance of the problem?

The main tradition of economics, we believe, regards theory as a tool for investigating reality. Development of hypotheses with explanatory power may indeed require long and elaborate chains of deductive reasoning. But the theorist is deeply concerned with the empirical reference and the testability of his propositions, as well as with their logical consistency. The facts of economic life are in center stage. The model is not there to be admired. It is there to be used.

In this spirit, economics has progressed through an informal but effective collaboration between research workers and empirically oriented theorists, often combined in the same person. Major theoretical contributions have typically come from men with strong empirical and policy interests. Historical examples are Marshall, Pigou, Ohlin, Robertson,

Schumpeter, Keynes. Among contemporaries, without meaning to slight other notable scholars, one can point to Kaldor,
Hicks, Meade, Tinbergen, Friedman, Samuelson, Solow,
Tobin, and Stigler. Some of these theorists are also accomplished mathematicians, but they have not allowed technique
to dominate their choice of problems.

The strongly tool-oriented theorist faces a number of dangers. When "theory leads a life of its own," interest in the
actual economic world may tend to diminish. Choice of problems may be biased in the direction of technical feasibility
rather than intrinsic importance. There is a temptation to
display skill in minor variations on existing models rather
than breaking ground in new directions. [8] The tool-oriented
theorist can readily slip over into what one may call "pseudo-
theorizing," that is, the framing of highly artificial problems
which have no real-world counterpart and no explanatory
usefulness.

It is dangerous, of course, to dismiss any conceptual scheme
as useless. A highly unrealistic model today may be a first step
toward more realistic models tomorrow. But the structure of
the problem sometimes precludes any approach toward reality; and in any event, the second step is rarely taken. Tool-
oriented theorists sometimes come close to asserting that
economics *is* essentially a logical edifice—a mere spinning out
of all possible implications of economizing behavior. In an
empirical science such as economics, this is a methodological
heresy.

---

8. As Hahn and Matthews commented at the end of their review of
modern growth theory, "While not disparaging the insights that have
been gained, we feel that in these areas the point of diminishing returns
may have been reached. Nothing is easier than to ring the changes on
more and more complicated models, without bringing in any really new
ideas and without bringing the theory any nearer to casting light on the
causes of the wealth of nations. The problems posed may well have intellectual fascination. But it is essentially a frivolous occupation to take
a chain with links of very uneven strength and devote one's energies to
strengthening and polishing the links that are already strong" (F. Hahn
and R. C. O. Matthews, "The Theory of Economic Growth," *Surveys of
Economic Theory*, 2:112).

The question of tool-oriented versus empirically oriented theory bears no intrinsic relation to the issue of verbal versus symbolic language: but in practice there is no doubt some connection. The temptation to engage in pseudo-theorizing seems especially strong among people trained as mathematicians, engineers, or natural scientists, who sometimes shift into economics without learning much about any actual economy. Being long on technique and short on substantive knowledge, they understandably exploit their comparative advantage in symbol manipulation, at the same time insisting that what they find easy to do really *is* economics after all. People whose training and interests are genuinely economic have often been too timid, or even too gullible, to point out that the king has no clothes.

The advantages of mathematical method in forcing clear definition of problems and checking errors of reasoning are well known. At the same time the power and abstractness of these tools is conducive to their misuse, a danger which the best theorists have recognized.[9] The persistent refusal of

9. Baumol comments: "No doubt the fault lies not with the instrument but with its user; yet it must be recognized that here is a tool which readily lends itself to such abuse. One . . . difficulty is the construction and manipulation of mathematical models for their own sake, where the ultimate criterion of success is the degree of entertainment provided to the model builder. Elaborate superstructures are erected to show off spectacular applications of esoteric theorems with little regard for relevance or illumination. The writer indulges himself in what has been described by a great economist as illicit intercourse with beautiful models.

"A second, and not unrelated, shortcoming of the mathematical tools arises out of the ease with which obscurity can be mistaken for profundity. . . . The fact of the matter is that mathematics is devoid of empirical content. Mathematics can impart neither substance nor truth to a model in which these qualities are not present to begin with" (William J. Baumol, "Economic Models and Mathematics," in Krupp, *Structure of Economic Science*, pp. 93–94).

A much earlier comment by Alfred Marshall is still worth quoting:

"In my view every economic fact whether or not it is of such a nature as to be expressed in numbers, stands in relation as cause and effect to many other facts: and since it never happens that all of them can be expressed in numbers, the application of exact mathematical methods to those which can is nearly always a waste of time, while in the large majority of cases it is positively misleading; and the world would have

some mathematical theorists to explain their results in generally comprehensible language is, as Stigler has noted, profoundly unscientific and produces a natural suspicion that the results are of little consequence.[10]

POSITIVE ECONOMICS AND POLICY

Classical and neoclassical economists in the British tradition were infused with reforming zeal. Economics was pursued as a tool of economic betterment, and was believed to lead to definite conclusions about welfare.[11] Hence the attention to the gains from international trade, the possibilities of increasing returns and technical progress, the use of market prices as indicators of social cost and benefit, the possibility of increasing total utility through income transfers. This was part of nineteenth-century optimism and liberalism, with its devotion to individual freedom and betterment, and its be-

---

been farther on its way forward if the work had never been done at all. It is chiefly when the mathematical method is used not for direct construction, but to train sound instinctive habits (like the practicing of scales on the piano), that it seems to me generally helpful" (Letter to A. L. Bowley, 1901, reported in A. C. Pigou, *ed., Memorials of Alfred Marshall* [London: Macmillan 1925], p. 422).

10. After arguing that mathematical economists have a duty to provide translations of their work, Stigler concludes: "The failure to provide these translations is a renunciation of the canons of scholarship. The failure may be justly, if harshly, attributed to one of three causes. Laziness. Or snobbishness. Or a sense of shame at the abstractness of the analysis—accompanied by an illegitimate desire to talk of the real world before one has taken into account its central features. These are not good excuses, but I can find no other. The queen of the sciences should not be made a puppet of a scientific oligarchy" (George J. Stigler, *Five Lectures on Economic Problems* [New York: Macmillan, 1950], pp. 43–45).

11. "Most important contributions of the social sciences are due to passion for social justice and betterment. The discoveries of classical economics were thus ideologically motivated by passion for freedom and justice as well as by the interests of the industrial middle class. . . . 'Conservative' motivations . . . tend to disfavor, while 'progressive' motivations . . . tend to favor the attainment of scientifically valid results in the domain of the social sciences. For it is the desire for change and betterment, whether conscious or subconscious, which creates the inquisitiveness of mind resulting in scientific investigations of human society" (Lange, "Scope and Method," p. 24).

lief in the perfectibility both of man and his social institutions. It is reflected in the label "political economy," which was standard terminology until at least 1914.

The shift in emphasis from the 1920s onward may be viewed partly as an intrusion into Anglo-Saxon economics of the continental tradition, which was more abstract and less humanitarian. Particularly influential was the Paretian distinction between propositions about exchange or production and propositions about income distribution, and his insistence that economics cannot establish one distribution as superior to another. This view, accepted and expounded by Robbins, Hicks, and others shaped the subsequent development of welfare economics.

It came to be generally (though not universally) accepted that interpersonal comparisons of utility are unfeasible, and that in consequence, economics can say nothing about the desirability of income transfers.[12] Since almost any conceivable policy action does involve some redistribution of income, this means that we can say little about policy in general. Subsequent efforts to escape from this conclusion via the "compensation principle," the "social welfare function," and other devices have not been very successful and have served mainly to increase the vacuousness of welfare economics.[13]

The view that economics must be value free in this sense is itself not entirely free of value judgments. It implies a preference for the status quo, since a change in the status quo can hardly ever be demonstrated to be desirable. For this reason, the proposition has appealed more to opponents than to proponents of change.

12. See, for example, Abba Lerner's ingenious effort to salvage conclusions about the welfare effect of income transfers by applying a probability calculus (*The Economics of Control* [New York: Macmillan, 1944]). See also the more recent dissenting opinion in Dobb, *Welfare Economics.*

13. "The attention of the best theoretical minds has thus been shifted from . . . the essentially *practical* problem of the allocation of scarce resources to that of identifying an unambiguous increase in the welfare of all persons. . . . This kind of question, I submit, is scholastic and without practical application in economics or politics" (Wiles, *Political Economy of Communism*, p. 91).

The result has been to drive an intellectual wedge between the economist and the policy maker. The task of the (positive) economist is to develop explanatory statements about the operation of the economy, from which he can predict the probable consequences of various policy actions. But at this point he must stop. He dare not say "Do this rather than that," since this implies precisely the distributional judgments which he is forbidden to make. Someone else must decide. (Who this "other" may be is usually not clearly specified. A legislator, or body of legislators? An administrative official? At any rate, a wise man, whose range of vision includes all the political and social considerations beyond the economist's ken.) This restricted role of the economist has been indicated by relabeling the subject "economics," or even "economic science" (an apparent effort to identify with the objectivity and "hardness" of the natural sciences).

We do not mean to caricature this view. It has merit in emphasizing that research problems must be approached in an objective spirit, without one result being preferred to another. It has the further merit of emphasizing that almost any economic change does have distributional effects, whose direction and size need to be estimated. It flashes a signal light to remind the economist that if, after making such estimates, he still says "I prefer Plan A to Plan B," he is making a distributional judgment.

But to say that economists *do not*—or if they do, that they *should not*—make distributional judgments is to go too far. And fortunately, economists do not really practice what some of them preach. This appears, first, in their choice of subjects, as shown by successive waves of fashion in economic studies: the interest in trade unionism and minimum wages during the 1910s and 1920s; in aggregate fluctuations and stabilization policies during the thirties and forties; in the economic development of poor nations aided by income transfers from richer nations during the fifties and sixties; and presently in a complex of domestic issues ranging from racial discrimination through environmental control to the pathology of metropolitan areas. Each of these waves of interest stemmed from a belief that change involving, among other things, some redistribution of income might be preferable to the *status quo*. Economists not only analyze consequences but at times declare their own policy preferences. Their contributions to the policy debates of the past thirty years do not seem less useful than those of public officials and other groups. If it makes anyone happier to have the economist cross himself before each policy pronouncement and say, "Lord, I mean it only as a citizen," all well and good. This does not change the operational effect.

Economists are also turning increasingly to an analysis of how the decisions of those "others," whose wisdom is supposedly superior to their own, are actually reached. They are turning, that is, to analysis of nonmarket devices for collective decision making. We have already suggested that this can be a fruitful sphere of activity.

The writer's view of this thorny area can be summarized as follows: First, one should distinguish between value judgments which are stated explicitly and those which are inserted in a concealed or implicit way. The latter are dangerous, since they lead to an essentially political argument disguised as a scientific argument. Second, one should distinguish between the judgments of importance which are inevitable in selecting research subjects and developing hypotheses, and the preferences among goals which are involved in making policy recommendations. The latter problem can be avoided by the research economist who stops short of policy analysis. But third, it is permissible and useful for an economist who so chooses to enter the policy realm. His preference scheme, of course, should be stated explicitly. But if this is done, the economist's special skill in analyzing alternatives might be considered to give him a comparative advantage in sorting out preferred courses of action.

This activist view of the economist's role appears to be shared by such respected figures as Jan Tinbergen and Gunnar Myrdal.[14] It is a view which would probably be disputed by other Western economists. One should not expect full agreement in this realm, since a preference for the role of analyst as against that of analyst-cum-actor involves value choices which each economist must make for himself.

We should add that self-doubt about the economist's practical role is confined largely to the Western countries. In the socialist and less developed economies, most economists are engaged in making and administering economic policy; and it is doubtful that they draw fine distinctions between their analytical and decision-making functions. Nor are they hesitant about asserting distributional preferences—for example, an egalitarian preference for income distributions in the current period, or a low rate of time preference as regards inter-

14. Tinbergen's view is suggested by the following comment: "The contribution made to our problem by most of present-day economists has been to declare the comparison of different individuals' satisfaction an impossibility. This contribution is not very constructive, since it implies (i) that all feelings about social justice are meaningless, (ii) that the scientist cannot make any contribution, and (iii) that it is left to others, who often lack scientific education, to make such contributions. The first implication is especially important since it implies that the numerous decisions actually made about questions of distribution could just as well have been made differently" (*Economic Policy: Principles and Design*, pp. 22–23).

And Myrdal, in discussing the social scientist's relation to action, remarks: "The scientist—even if his knowledge is conjectural in certain respects—is in a position to assist in achieving a much wiser judgment than the one which is actually allowed to guide public policy. . . . Nor can we argue that 'the facts speak for themselves' and leave it 'to the politician and the citizen to draw the practical conclusions.' We know even better than the politician and the ordinary citizen that the facts are much too complicated to speak an intelligible language by themselves. They must be organized for practical purposes, that is, under relevant value premises. And no one can do this more adequately than ourselves.

"There is a common belief that the type of practical research which involves rational planning—what we have ventured to call 'social engineering'—is likely to be emotional. This is a mistake. If the value premises are sufficiently, fully, and rationally introduced, the planning of induced social change is no more emotional by itself than the planning of a bridge or the taking of a census" (Gunnar Myrdal, *An American Dilemma*, vol. 2 [New York: Harper and Row, Torchbook Edition, 1969], p. 1044).

generational transfers. While we may feel that they go rather far in making such judgments, there is at the same time something attractive about their positive and operational approach to their tasks.

THE BOUNDARIES OF ECONOMICS

We have noted the steady narrowing of the scope of economics over the past century. This tendency, indeed, is evident throughout the social studies. Psychologists have tended to become animal experimenters. Philosophers do less moral philosophy and more symbolic logic. Political scientists are interested, not so much in collaborating with economists, as in becoming more *like* economists by building pure models of political behavior. In this search for "hardness," the social disciplines have drawn farther away from each other, leaving an ever-larger uncultivated area.

In this uncultivated middle ground lie many issues which used to be considered central to economics and which are still highly important, particularly in economies at an early stage of development. Why is it that so many gaps appear in the Western tool-kit when we confront the problems of the less developed countries? Why is it that we seem to have little to say about how economic growth begins, about the relation of agricultural organization to agricultural productivity, about transfer and adaptation of technology, about population growth and methods of population control? It is because such issues have come to be regarded as "not really economics."

Who, then, is to cope? The conventional answer is either to hope that a scholar in some other discipline will pick up the problem (which he may regard, however, as "really economics" and outside his sphere!) or to organize a cross-disciplinary research group. Both kinds of effort—to get people in other disciplines to take an interest in problems which we consider important, and to develop systematic cooperation across disciplinary lines—are clearly worth pursuing. But the fact that mountains of foundation money have been poured into such ventures, with a disappointingly small yield, suggests that the difficulties are serious.

Another possible approach is for economists to stretch the conventional boundaries of their discipline, appropriating usable concepts whenever they can be found, inventing them where they do not exist, trying to achieve integration of knowledge "within one skull." This is a difficult endeavor, since it involves conceptual innovation and may require work in areas where quantitative data are fragmentary. But it is not inherently less rigorous than work on narrowly defined "economic" subjects. Algebra and rigor are not synonymous.

Let us sketch some possible directions of experiment, most of which are already being pursued in some measure:

1. The "givens" of resource allocation theory are variables from a broader standpoint. If one is interested in economic growth, for example, it becomes important to explain *changes* in factor supplies, production techniques, and productivity levels.

Population, long relegated to the demographers, seems in process of being reclaimed as an area of economic study. Here one has a solid quantitative base in census records, vital statistics, family sample surveys, and so on. While the determinants of fertility and mortality are not purely economic, neither are they so obscure as to be beyond the economist's ken. Some of the most sophisticated work on fertility in developed countries has been done by Ruggles, Orcutt, Easterlin, Kuznets, and other economists. On the policy side, too, family planning programs are amenable to cost-benefit techniques which have long been familiar in other areas. The fact that such programs have important noneconomic aspects should not deter the economist from deploying his own tools to best advantage.

There is renewed interest in labor force participation rates and in labor force quality. Participation rates in the United States have been thoroughly investigated, and there is a growing volume of evidence from other economies. For example, women's participation rates are substantially higher in socialist than in capitalist countries. Why is this? Does it represent "exploitation" or "liberation" of women in those countries?

Labor force "quality" tends to become a residual, difficult to measure or explain. In countries at a low income level, nutrition, health, and physical vigor are important dimensions of quality. So is work experience and motivation for work. In countries at a higher income level, quality is more often associated with general education and specific vocational training. Recognition of this is partly responsible for the increasing research on educational investment and the returns to such investment.

Modern interest in technology stemmed originally from Schumpeter's assertion that monopoly is more conducive than competition to technical progress, the subsequent denial of this by other economists, and an acceleration of research on who actually produces usable inventions. It was stimulated further by econometric growth studies, which typically reveal a large "residual" increase in output not accounted for by conventionally measured inputs. Part of this is presumably due to "technical progress" in a strict sense, so there has been intensified effort to define, measure, and account for such progress. The question of what kind of technology can appropriately be transferred from developed to less developed countries, and how actual transfers occur, has become a central issue in development economics.

Capital supply now tends to be visualized, not as quantitative increase in capital of an unchanged type, but in terms of capital as carrier of technical progress ("embodied technical change"), and as employer and trainer of labor. This lends new interest to a branch of economics which until recently had appeared unusually arid.

2. A second group of "givens" in conventional microeconomics is the preference systems of consumers, workers, and business managers. Given these things, the solutions appear by computer printout. There is no longer anything that can be called human behavior. But in actuality there is human behavior: we can make observations of it; we already know something about it. The marked revival of interest in the

theory of the firm, and the development of alternatives to the profit-maximizing model, were noted in chapter 8. There has been considerable investigation of the impact of advertising on consumers, the strength of brand preferences, and related matters. We should in time be able to determine how much there is to the Galbraith hypothesis of "producer sovereignty."

3. Western theory pays little explicit attention to *economic institutions*. We assume, and usually correctly, that the institutional framework facilitates economic progress rather than blocking it. But in other economies, and notably in the LDCs, this is not a safe assumption. Some institutions may impede progress, while others which might facilitate it are missing. This poses an *analytical* problem of tracing the relations between institutional structure and economic performance, and a *policy* problem of institutional redesign.

A leading example is the relation between agricultural organization and agricultural efficiency. The literature abounds with confident assertions on this matter: "collective farming can never be efficient," "landlordism reduces the tenant's incentive," "the owner-operated farm is most likely to approach maximum efficiency." Such statements rest largely on implicit theorizing. It would be better to develop explicit hypotheses which can be tested against production data.

Another problem, familiar since classical times, is the consequences of monopolistic versus competitive organization of industry. This includes not merely pricing but also technical efficiency, product quality, inventiveness, and other dimensions of economic performance. There has been some hypothesis testing in this area, but most of the important issues remain unsettled. On another front, Fuchs has emphasized that our view of long-run economic tendencies is based largely on observation of manufacturing, and that examination of the growing service sector often yields opposite conclusions. The micro efficiency of public management as against private management, and how this differs among countries and industries, is a large unexplored area. One may agree, with Tinbergen, that policy in this respect should be guided by efficiency rather than ideology; but we do not know enough to apply efficiency criteria with any confidence.

We are not suggesting mere description or cataloging of economic institutions. Rather, we are urging careful analysis of structure-performance relations. Such work can be as rigorous as any other kind of economic study.

4. The growing wealth of economic data, and the growing sophistication of statistical techniques, has produced a strong orientation toward quantitative studies. Economists must have numbers. So there is a tendency to concentrate on areas where numbers are most readily available—"under the street lamp where the light is"—rather than on poorly lit areas where the most interesting problems may lie.

This tendency prompts several reflections. First, we need constantly to reexamine the foundations of our measurement systems, to be sure that we are not engaging in pseudo-precision. The apparently operational character of macroeconomic models, for example, rests on the conventions underlying our systems of national accounts. Many of these conventions, such as the definition of capital and capital services, the meaning of final output, and the valuation of government production, are clearly debatable, and a shift to different concepts would make a large difference in the results. This is important, especially for estimates of long-term growth, and accounts for certain doubts among both economists and laymen as to whether welfare is actually rising as rapidly as GNP totals suggest. Further, the aggregation procedure rests on an assumption that market prices of inputs and outputs are "correct" in a Paretian sense. To the extent that this is not true, the significance of the totals is reduced.

Second, we are perhaps too ready to dismiss interesting research problems as unquantifiable. Thus some data-rich areas are investigated beyond the margin of profitability, while others with a higher potential yield lie neglected. Ideally, research priorities should be based on the substantive importance of the problem; and we should not accept an apparent unavailability of data without strenuous effort to overcome it.

Consider, for example, a program of "community development" in a less developed country, in which public works are locally organized and constructed with labor contributed by community members. One can easily do a descriptive, non-analytical study of such a program; and many such have been done. But one can do more. Costs can be calculated with some accuracy, benefits with rather less accuracy. Cost-benefit ratios can be compared for different types of work project—roads, streets, schools, irrigation works, health centers, parks, and playgrounds. The cost of works construction by the community development route can be compared with the costs of the same projects done by the ministry of public works on a contract basis, which may indicate that scarce resources can be "stretched" through organizational innovations. Where the community is free to choose among a variety of possible projects, one can derive the "revealed preference" of the villagers among various types of public good.

Third, the possibility of verification is not the only measure of merit. Economists made much progress in an era when, because of poverty of data, theorizing was necessarily well in advance of verification. We should not be less venturesome than our predecessors in developing hypotheses which cannot presently be subjected to any quantitative test.

5. Western microeconomics has traditionally focused on resource use in the private sector. Economists have tended either to assume away the public sector, as in general equilibrium analysis, or to be quite naive about its operation. They have often seemed to assume that governments are run by philosopher-kings, benevolent and omniscient, who optimize in using resources to meet citizens' preferences. But the optimizing government is an even less plausible creature than the optimizing consumer or business firm; and as the public sector has grown in relative size, collective decision making has emerged as an important frontier of research.

Arrow and others have worked on the nature and aggregability of individual preferences for public goods. Even if such preferences can be aggregated in principle, is there any practicable way of discovering them? Decisions about public goods output are made by voting—either (rarely) a direct referendum by members of a community, or (more commonly) a vote of the citizens' elected representatives. How does this mechanism work? Few political scientists have tackled the problem of how differences in the political mechanism will affect its economic results, perhaps because analysis of economic results lies outside their disciplinary boundaries.[15] But economists have now begun to move into this area. There have been efforts to construct models of decision making by direct vote, say of farmers in a rural community voting on road construction for which they will have to pay.[16] There have also been attempts to model the behavior of elected representatives. An interesting example is Coleman's "log-rolling model," in which each legislator is assumed to maximize his chances of reelection, and in which vote trading between legislators is permitted.[17] Legislator A can then "buy" votes on the issues which matter most to him by "selling" his vote on issues which matter least. If there are many legislators and many issues, this "political market place" may yield results analogous to those of a competitive market for private goods.

While these early efforts may be regarded as crude, they lie in an area of great substantive importance. Here, then, is another frontier on which one may hope that economists will push forward vigorously in the future.

TOWARD A POST-ROBBINS DEFINITION

The allocation of given resources in a regime of competitive markets is a neat, manageable problem to which eco-

15. There is an occasional exception, as for example, Aaron Wildavsky, *The Politics of the Budgetary Process* (Boston: Little Brown, 1964), an analysis of federal budgetary decisions in the United States.

16. Gordon Tullock, "Problems of Majority Voting," *Journal of Political Economy*, 1959, p. 71–79; reprinted in K. Arrow and T. Scitovsky, eds., *Readings in Welfare Economics* (Homewood, Ill.: Richard D. Irwin, for the American Economic Association, 1969). Several other papers in this volume are also relevant to the present subject.

17. James S. Coleman, "The Possibility of a Social Welfare Function," *American Economic Review*, Dec. 1966, pp. 1105–22.

nomic techniques can be applied with maximum advantage. And they have been so applied by generations of economists. Mill may have been wrong in 1848, and Robbins may have been wrong in 1932, in implying that the resource allocation problem is thoroughly understood. But surely in 1970 we can say that this terrain has been relatively well explored; and if economics were only this, intellectual pioneers might well turn to other subjects.

But we hope to have demonstrated that economics is more than this. There are other major types of economic study. There is the non-Western world, with its novel institutions, policy problems, and potential theoretical contributions. There are the border areas which neither economists nor other social scientists have cultivated with much success.

The theory of resource allocation remains central in the sense that other branches of theory interlock with and depend upon it. Without it, we could scarcely claim to have a science of economics. But around this central pillar there has been a proliferation of theoretical tools which could scarcely have been predicted in 1930. At the micro level, there has been progress in the positive economics of the firm, in the development of normative tools for optimizing, and in the application of cost-benefit analysis to public sector activities. At an aggregative level, there is improved understanding of the sources of economic fluctuations and economic growth, at least in the Western economies. Robbins was doubtless right in arguing that such vast aggregates as national product can never have the unambiguous meaning of an individual preference map. But there is now substantial consensus that the advantages of aggregation outweigh its ambiguities and limitations. Thus we have made marked progress both above and below the level of aggregation used in Marshallian market economics.

One's conception of the scope of economics is enlarged also by looking beyond the Western world to the socialist economies and the less developed countries. The difficulties which these countries present to economic analysis, while severe, are not as insuperable as has sometimes been thought. True,

conventional tools do not explain the decisions which emerge
from the administrative hierarchy in a socialist economy. But
to say that these decisions are "arbitrary" is a meaningless
statement, an abandonment of any effort at understanding.
Explanation may involve novel concepts, drawn from such
areas as information theory and organization theory; but
surely economists are sufficiently clever and innovative to
deploy such tools. In the less developed countries, too, transfer of Western theoretical concepts involves much rethinking and adaptation to a different environment. But this is no
more unmanageable than other challenges which economists
have faced and surmounted in the past.

The need to widen the focus of economic analysis has been
underlined by the revival of interest in long-term growth. In
the developed countries, it is clear that most of the increase
in output is attributable to changes in factor quality and factor productivity. This has opened up frontiers for research
on human investment, the sources of invention, the diffusion
of technical progress, and other things previously taken as
"givens." In the less developed countries too, it is clear that
economic growth does not result automatically from "plug-
ging in" larger quantities of capital or other inputs. This
can be done in an equation, but it cannot be done in an
economy. The structure of economic and political institutions is central, and until we know more about how this
structure conditions economic performance, we cannot claim
to have a theory of early economic growth. To dismiss this
range of issues as "noneconomic" is an abandonment of responsibility. To try to shift them to other social scientists is
not feasible. To assume that quantitative analysis of institutional problems is impossible is merely unimaginative.

Economics, then, is more than "the science which studies
human behavior as a relationship between ends and scarce
means which have alternative uses." It is concerned also with
changes over time in resource supplies, technology, and the
organization of production; with short-term fluctuations in
resource use; and with long-term trends in the size and com-

position of national output. It is concerned with the behavior of economic decision makers, in the public as well as the private sector; and with economic organization, in the sense of structure-performance relations. Its scope is not limited to the Western market economies, but extends to the curious variety of national economies throughout the world.

In each of these dimensions, economics is more than Robbins supposed. While we continue to quote him, we no longer follow him. It is time that our definitions were revised to correspond with our practice.

BIBLIOGRAPHY

Because of the broad scope of this essay, it would not be appropriate to attempt a comprehensive bibliography. This is a highly selective listing of books which are judged to be of substantial and continuing importance. Articles and other short pieces of writing are not included. Textbooks, in general, are not included.

CAPITALIST ECONOMIES; WESTERN ECONOMIC THEORY;
GENERAL WORKS

American Economic Association, Readings in Selected Areas of Economics. 12 vols. issued through 1970. Available from Richard D. Irwin, Homewood, Illinois, publishers to the Association.

American Economic Association and Royal Economic Society, Surveys of Economic Theory. Vol. 1: Money, Interest, Welfare; Vol. 2: Growth, Development; Vol. 3: Resource Allocation. London: Macmillan, New York: St. Martin's Press, 1965 and 1966.

Bain, Joe S. International Differences in Industrial Structure. New Haven: Yale University Press, 1966.

Ellis, Howard, ed. A Survey of Contemporary Economics, Vol. 1. Homewood, Illinois: Richard D. Irwin, for the American Economic Association, 1949.

Frei, Rudolf, ed. Economic Systems of the West, 2 vols. Basel: Kyklos-Verlag; Tübingen: J. C. Mohr (Paul Siebeck), 1957 and 1959.

Friedman, Milton. Essays in Positive Economics. Chicago: University of Chicago Press, 1953.

Goldsmith, Raymond. Financial Structure and Development. New Haven: Yale University, 1969.

Haley, Bernhard, ed. A Survey of Contemporary Economics, Vol. II (Published for the American Economic Association. Homewood, Illinois: Richard D. Irwin, 1952.

Hague, Douglas C., ed. *Price Formation in Various Economics.* New York: St. Martin's Press, 1967.

Hutchinson, T. W. *The Significance and Basic Postulates of Economic Theory.* London: Macmillan, 1938.

————. *"Positive" Economics and Policy Objectives.* London: Allen and Unwin, 1964.

Keynes, John Nevile. *The Scope and Method of Political Economy.* London: Macmillan, 1891.

Kindleberger, Charles. *Foreign Trade and the National Economy.* New Haven: Yale University Press, 1962.

Kirschen, E. S.; Benard, J.; Besters, H.; Blackaby, F.; Eckstein, O.; Faaland, J.; Hartog, F.; Tosco, E., and Morissens, L., *Economic Policy in Our Time.* 3 vols. Amsterdam: North-Holland; Chicago: Rand-McNally, 1964.

Koopmans, Tjalling C. *Three Essays on the State of Economic Science.* New York: McGraw-Hill, 1957.

Kornai, Janos. *Anti-Equilibrium.* Amsterdam: North Holland, 1971.

Krupp, Sherman R., ed. *The Structure of Economic Science.* Englewood Cliffs, N.J.: Prentice-Hall, 1966.

Lange, Oscar. *Political Economy.* Vol. 1. London: Pergamon Press, 1963.

Lundberg, Erik. *Fluctuations and Stabilization.* New Haven: Yale University Press, 1968.

Martin, Kurt and Knapp, John, eds. *The Teaching of Development Economics.* Chicago: Aldine, 1967.

Musgrave, Richard A. *Fiscal Systems.* New Haven: Yale University Press, 1969.

Myrdal, Gunnar. *The Political Element in the Development of Economic Theory.* English translation by Paul Streeten. Cambridge: Harvard University Press, 1965.

Phelps Brown, Henry. *The Economics of Labor.* New Haven: Yale University Press, 1962.

Pryor, Frederic L. *Public Expenditures in Communist and Capitalist Nations.*
Homewood, Ill.: Richard D. Irwin, 1968.

Robbins, Lionel. *An Essay on the Nature and Significance of Economic Science.* 2d ed. London: Macmillan, 1935.

Robinson, Joan. *Economic Philosophy.* London: Pelican Books, 1964.

Rosovsky, Henry, ed. *Industrialization in Two Systems.* New York: John Wiley, 1966.

Stigler, George J. *Five Lectures on Economic Problems.* New York: Macmillan, 1950.

Tinbergen, Jan. *Central Planning*. New Haven: Yale University Press, 1964.
Wallich, Henry C. *Comparative Monetary Systems*. New Haven: Yale University Press (forthcoming).

SOCIALIST ECONOMIES

Ames, Edward. *Soviet Economic Processes*. Homewood, Ill.: Richard D. Irwin, 1965.
Balinsky, Alexander; Bergson, Abram; Hazard, John N.; and Wiles, Peter. *Planning and the Market in the U.S.S.R.: the 1960's*. New Brunswick, N.J.: Rutgers University Press, 1967.
Balassa, Bela. *The Hungarian Experience in Economic Planning*. New Haven: Yale University Press, 1959.
Bergson, Abram. *The Economics of Soviet Planning*. New Haven: Yale University Press, 1964.
————. *The Real National Income of Soviet Russia Since 1928*. Cambridge, Mass.: Harvard University Press, 1961.
Bergson, Abram, and Kuznets, Simon, eds. *Economic Trends in the Soviet Union*. Cambridge, Mass.: Harvard University Press, 1963.
Bićanić, Rudolf. *Problems of Planning: East and West*. The Hague: Mouton, 1967.
Bornstein, Morris, and Fusfeld, Daniel. *The Soviet Economy: A Book of Readings,* 3d. ed. Homewood Ill.: Richard D. Irwin, 1970.
Bornstein, Morris, ed. *Comparative Economic Systems: Models and Cases*. Homewood, Ill.: Richard D. Irwin, 1969.
Brown, Alan A., and Neuberger, Egon, eds. *International Trade and Central* Planning. Berkeley and Los Angeles: University of California Press, 1968.
Dobb, Maurice. *Welfare Economics and the Economics of Socialism*. Cambridge: Cambridge University Press, 1969.
————. *Soviet Economic Development Since 1917*. Rev. and enl. ed. London: Routledge and Kegan Paul, 1966.
————. *On Economic Theory and Socialism: Collected Papers*. London: Routledge and Kegan Paul, 1955.
————. *An Essay on Economic Growth and Planning*. London: Routledge and Kegan Paul, 1960.
Dunlop, J. T., and Federenko, N. P., eds. *Planning and Markets,* New York: McGraw-Hill, 1969.
Donnithorne, Audrey. *China's Economic System*. London. Allen and Unwin, 1967.
Eckstein, Alexander; Galenson, Walter; and Liu, T. C., eds. *Economic Trends in Communist China, Chicago:* Aldine, 1968.

Feiwel, George R., ed. *New Currents in Soviet-Type Economies: A Reader.* Scranton, Pa.: International Textbook, 1968.

Feinstein, Charles H., ed. *Socialism, Capitalism, and Economic Growth: Essays Presented to Maurice Dobb.* Cambridge: Cambridge University Press, 1967.

Friss, István, ed. *Reform of the Economic Mechanism in Hungary.* Budapest: Akadémiai Kiádó, 1969.

Hardt, John P.; Hoffenberg, Marvin; Kaplan, Norman; and Levine, Herbert S., eds. *Mathematics and Computers in Soviet Economic Planning.* New Haven: Yale University Press, 1967.

Horvat, Branko. *Towards a Theory of Planned Economy.* Belgrade: Yugoslav Institute of Economic Research, 1964.

Kalecki, Michael. *Introduction to the Theory of Growth in a Socialist Economy.* Oxford: Basil Blackwell, 1970.

Kantorovich, L. V. *The Best Use of Economic Resources.* Cambridge, Mass: Harvard University Press, 1965.

Kaser, Michael C. *Comecon: Integration Problems of the Planned Economies.* London: Oxford University Press, 1965.

Kaser, Michael C., ed. *Economic Development of Eastern Europe.* New York: St. Martin's Press, 1968. London: Macmillan, 1968.

Kornai, Janos. *Mathematical Planning of Structural Decisions.* Amsterdam: North-Holland, 1967.

Lange, Oskar. *The Political Economy of Socialism.* Hague: Van Keulen, 1958.

Montias, John Michael. *Central Planning in Poland.* New Haven: Yale University Press, 1962.

————. *Economic Development in Communist Rumania.* Cambridge: M.I.T. Press, 1967.

Moorsteen, Richard, and Powell, Raymond P. *The Soviet Capital Stock.* Homewood, Ill.: Richard D. Irwin, 1966.

Nemchinov, V. S. *The Uses of Mathematics in Economics.* Cambridge: M.I.T. Press, 1964.

Nove, Alec, *The Soviet Economy: An Introduction.* New York: Praeger, 1961.

Pryor, Frederic L. *The Communist Foreign Trade System.* Cambridge, Mass.: M.I.T. Press, 1963.

Robinson, Joan. *An Essay on Marxian Economics.* London: Macmillan, 1957.

Sik, Ota. *Plan and Market Under Socialism.* Prague: Academia Publishing House, 1967.

Ward, Benjamin. *The Socialist Economy.* New York: Random House, 1967.

Wellisz, S. *The Economies of the Socialist Bloc.* New York: McGraw-Hill, 1964.

Wiles, Peter J. D. *The Political Economy of Communism*. Cambridge: Harvard University Press, 1962.
———. *Communist International Economics*. New York: Praeger, 1969.

LESS DEVELOPED ECONOMIES

Adelman, Irma and Morris, Cynthia T. *Society, Politics, and Economic Development*. Baltimore: Johns Hopkins Press, 1967.
Adelman, Irma and Thorbecke, Erik, eds. *The Theory and Design of Development*. Baltimore: Johns Hopkins Press, 1966.
Baldwin, Robert. *Economic Development and Export Growth: A Study of Northern Rhodesia, 1920–1960*. Berkeley and Los Angeles: University of California Press, 1966.
Baran, Paul A. *The Political Economy of Growth*. New York: Monthly Review, 1957.
Barber, William J. *The Economy of British Central Africa*. Stanford, Calif.: Stanford University Press, 1961.
Bauer, Peter T., and Yamey, Basil S. *The Economics of Underdeveloped Countries*. Chicago: University Press, 1957.
Boserup, Esther. *The Conditions of Agricultural Growth*. Chicago: Aldine Press, 1965.
Bowles, Samuel. *Planning Educational Systems for Economic Growth*. Cambridge: Harvard University Press, 1969.
Coale, Ansley, and Hoover, Edgar M. *Population Growth and Economic Development in Low-Income Countries*. Princeton: Princeton University Press, 1958.
Diaz-Alejandro, Carlos. *Essays on the Economic History of the Argentine Republic*. New Haven: Yale University Press, 1970.
Fei, John C. H., and Ranis, Gustav, *Development of the Labor Surplus Economy: Theory and Policy*. Homewood, Ill.: Richard D. Irwin, 1964.
Furtado, Celso. *Development and Underdevelopment:* Berkeley: University of California Press, 1964.
Gerschenkron, Alexander. *Economic Backwardness in Historical Perspective*. Cambridge: Harvard University Press, 1962.
Hagen, Everett E., ed. *Planning Economic Development*. Homewood, Ill.: Richard D. Irwin, 1963.
Haq, Mahbub ul. *The Strategy of Development Planning: A Case Study of Pakistan*. Karachi: Pakistan Branch, Oxford University Press, 1963.
Helleiner, Gerald. *Peasant Agriculture, Government, and Economic Growth in Nigeria*. Homewood, Ill.: Richard D. Irwin, 1967.

Hirschman, Albert O. *The Strategy of Economic Development.* New Haven: Yale University Press, 1958.

Ishikawa, S. *Economic Development in Asian Perspective.* Tokyo: Kinokuniya Bookstore Co., 1967.

Johnson, Harry G. *Economic Policies Toward Less Developed Countries.* Washington: Brookings Institution, 1967.

———. *Money Trade and Economic Growth.* Cambridge, Mass.: Harvard University Press, 1962.

———. *International Trade and Economic Growth.* London: Allen and Unwin, 1958.

Klein, Lawrence, and Ohkawa, Kazushi, eds. *Economic Growth: the Japanese Experience since the Meiji Era.* Homewood, Ill.: Richard D. Irwin, 1968.

Lewis, Stephen R. *Economic Policy and Industrial Growth in Pakistan.* London: Allen and Unwin, 1969.

Lewis, Sir Arthur. *The Theory of Economic Growth.* Homewood, Ill.: Richard D. Irwin, 1955.

———. *Development Planning.* New York: Harper and Row, 1966.

Linder, Staffan Burenstam. *Trade and Trade Policy for Development.* New York: Praeger, 1967.

Lockwood, William W. *The Economic Development of Japan,* Princeton: Princeton University Press, 1954.

Martin, Kurt and Knapp, John. *The Teaching of Development Economics.* Chicago: Aldine, 1967.

Meier, Gerald M. *The International Economics of Development.* New York: Harper and Row, 1968.

Mellor, John W., et al. *Developing Rural India: Plan and Practice.* Ithaca: Cornell University Press, 1968.

Myint, Hla. *The Economics of the Developing Countries,* London: Hutchinson, 1964.

Myrdal, Gunnar. *Economic Theory and Underdeveloped Regions.* London: Gerald Duckworth, 1957.

———. *Asian Drama.* 3 vols. New York: Pantheon Books, 1968.

Nurkse, Ragnar. *Problems of Capital Formation in Underdeveloped Countries.* Oxford: Basil Blackwell, 1953.

———. *Patterns of Trade and Development.* Stockholm: Almquist and Wiksell, 1959.

———. *Equilibrium and Growth in the World Economy.* Cambridge, Mass.: Harvard University Press, 1962.

Ohlin, Goran. *Population Control and Economic Development.* Paris: OECD, 1967.

Prest, Alan R. *Transport Economics in Developing Countries.* New York: Praeger, 1969.

Reynolds, Clark W. *The Mexican Economy: Twentieth Century Structure and Growth*. New Haven, Yale University Press, 1970.

Robinson, E. A. G., ed. *Problems in Economic Development*. London: Macmillan, 1965.

Rostow, W. W., ed. *The Economics of the Take-off*. London and New York: Macmillan, 1963.

Sandee, Jan. *A Demonstration Planning Model for India*. Calcutta: Indian Statistical Institute, 1960.

Schultz, Theodore W. *Transforming Traditional Agriculture*. New Haven: Yale University Press, 1964.

———. *Economic Growth and Agriculture*. New York: McGraw-Hill, 1968.

Snodgrass, Donald. *Ceylon: An Export Economy in Transition*. Homewood, Ill.: Richard D. Irwin, 1966.

Southworth, Herman M., and Johnston, Bruce F., eds. *Agricultural Development and Economic Growth*. Ithaca: Cornell University Press, 1967.

Stolper, Wolfgang. *Planning Without Facts*. Cambridge: Harvard University Press, 1966.

Supple, Barry, ed. *The Experience of Economic Growth*. New York: Random House, 1963.

Thorbecke, Erik, ed. *The Role of Agriculture in Economic Development*. New York: National Bureau of Economic Research, 1969.

Tinbergen, Jan. *The Design of Development*. Baltimore: Johns Hopkins Press, 1958.

Waterston, Albert. *Development Planning: Lessons of Experience*. Baltimore: Johns Hopkins Press, 1965.

Youngson, A. J. *Possibilities of Economic Progress*. Cambridge: Cambridge University Press, 1957.

INDEX

Agriculture: in socialist economies, 65, 173–77; prices in socialist economies, 90; collective farms, 173–75; increased productivity needed in LDCs, 185–87; LDC growth models, 226; research in foreign systems, 300

Autarky in socialist countries, 87

Borrowing by LDCs, 200

Capital: use of in LDCs, 105–07

Capital formation: in capitalist economies, 37, 38–39, 129–30; in socialist countries, 77–79; in Yugoslavia, 78; in LDCs, 103–04, 194–96, 274; in Soviet Union, 164–65; in Romania, 165; rate of, 272

Capitalist economies: classification of, 31, 34; government expenditure, 36–38; public sectors, 36–39; capital formation, 37, 38–39, 129–30, 143; redistribution of income, 39; extent of socialization in, 39, 55–56, 295–96, 298; coordination through markets, 40–41; competition and monopoly, 40–45, 144–45; labor markets, 44–45, 137–39; changes in production structure, 45–46; urbanization, 46–47; growth, 47–49, 141–44; investment, 48; foreign trade, 49–50, 51–52, 130–33; unemployment, 50, 51–52; business cycle, 50–51; inflation, 51, 129–30; incomes, 52–53; plan-

ning, 54–55; government intervention, 53–55; important policy areas, 127; regulation of aggregate demand, 129–30; public and quasi-public goods, 133–36; housing problem, 136; market economics in, 232–34; macroeconomics in, 261–64; use of growth theory in, 268–70

Capital movements, 121–22; in LDCs, 110

Centralized planning: textbook picture under socialism, 147; defects in, 148–49

"Centrally planned economies," 66–72. *See also* Socialist economies

China: economy, 70–72; agricultural development, 174–75

Committee on Mutual Economic Assistance (COMECON), 89–90, 177–78, 179

Comparative economics: development, 22–23; traditional, 23–25; new content, 26; current research, 290

Computers: use of in Soviet Union, 161–64, 288

"Computopia." *See* Computers

Consumer goods: socialist economies, 73–74, 168–69; comparison of socialist and Western distribution techniques, 170–72

Consumer demand in socialist economic theory, 216–17, 219–20, 221

Consumer preferences, 40–41, 172

339

fulness of, 213–14; adaptation
needed, 274–76, 308–09; relevance, 276–77; in socialist
economies, 280; in LDCs, 320;
since 1830, 327
Trade: Western countries, 49; socialist economies, 49–50, 88–89,
177–80; LDCs, 50; effect of planning on, 84–85; comparison of
role in socialist and capitalist
countries, 85; bilateral negotiation in socialist economies, 85,
89, 258; composition of in LDCs,
109–10; and economic blocs,
119–22; East-West, 120; between LDCs and socialist countries, 120–22; balance-of-payments adjustments, 131–33; in
Hungary, 155; in Poland, 179;
primary exports prices, 198; and
economic development, 256
Trade theory, 255–61; updating
of, 255–56; in socialist economies, 257–58; and LDCs, 258–
61; LDCs and primary pro-

ducers, 259–60; Myrdal concept
of "cumulative circular causation," 260

Underemployment in LDCs, 200–
03
Unionism: effect on markets, 144–
45

Wages and salaries: comparison
between socialist and capitalist
countries, 92–93; in socialist
countries, 92–93, 222, 235, 265;
agricultural, 176–77; rates in
LDCs, 202
Walrasian market mechanism,
293–94
Welfare economics, 94, 212, 249–
52, 315–16
Work, in socialist countries, 221–
22

Yugoslavia: economy, 69–70, 286;
capital accumulation, 78; unemployment, 82; pricing, 236